SPECULATIVE FORMALISM

diaeresis

SPECULATIVE FORMALISM

Literature, Theory, and the Critical Present

Tom Eyers

Northwestern University Press
Evanston, Illinois

Northwestern University Press
www.nupress.northwestern.edu

Printed in the United States of America

10 9 8 7 6 5 4 3 2 1

Library of Congress Cataloging-in-Publication Data

Names: Eyers, Tom, author.
Title: Speculative formalism : literature, theory, and the critical present / Tom Eyers.
Other titles: Diaeresis.
Description: Evanston, Illinois : Northwestern University Press, 2016. | Series: Diaeresis
Identifiers: LCCN 2016045870 | ISBN 9780810134317 (cloth : alk. paper) | ISBN 9780810134300 (pbk. : alk. paper) | ISBN 9780810134324 (e-book)
Subjects: LCSH: Formalism (Literature) | Literature—History and criticism—Theory, etc. | Literature—Philosophy.
Classification: LCC PN98.F6 E96 2016 | DDC 801.95—dc23
LC record available at https://lccn.loc.gov/2016045870

In Memory of Dr. Eric Nuetzel

Contents

Acknowledgments

Readers of my first two expressly "philosophical" books may be surprised by the literary terrain explored here, although those familiar with my *Post-Rationalism* may see strong parallels with the themes addressed there. Crossing disciplinary boundaries, in this case from continental theory and psychoanalysis to a theoretical and comparative literary studies, can be arduous work, but the travel was significantly eased by a group of eminent literary minds who have accepted a stranger in their ranks with grace and generosity. I should mention in this light Eyal Amiran, Jonathan Arac, Guinn Batten, Tim Bewes, Bruno Bosteels, Paul Bové, Jonathan Culler, Dillon Johnston, Anna Kornbluh, Patricia de Man, Tracy McNulty, Mary Mullen, Emilio Sauri, and Daniel Hoffman-Schwartz.

All of the participants in my and Mary Mullen's seminar at the American Comparative Literature Association conference in 2015 on formalism and history offered perspectives crucial to the book as it was intensively revised. I'm indebted to audiences at Duquesne University's Centre for Qualitative and Interpretive Research, at the Society for Phenomenology and Existential Philosophy annual conference in 2013, at the Modern Language Association meeting of 2015, at the department of Comparative Literature at Cornell University, and at the English department at Princeton University, where canny and provocative questions pushed me to clarify and refine key aspects of my argument. At Duquesne, I've benefited from a pluralistic atmosphere, such that my literary research has not only been tolerated but notably encouraged. The chair of the philosophy department, Ron Polansky, deserves particular thanks, as does Dan Selcer, who asked just the right question at just the right time and has been an especially valuable mentor and friend during my time in Pittsburgh. Fred Evans has proven a crucial interlocutor, a generous mentor, and a warm friend, and I have benefited from the work of Jennifer Bates, whose sophisticated parsing of the philosophy/literature border zone set a daunting but valuable example to follow.

Students from both Philosophy and English at Duquesne who participated in my graduate seminar Philosophical and Literary Modernisms in Spring 2015 raised conundrums I could never have posed, and provided answers I could not have anticipated. I should also mention the inspiring graduate student organizers of the Pittsburgh Summer School in Continental Philosophy, who invited me to deliver much of this book as a series of lectures in the summer of 2014, alongside Bruno Bosteels and Paul Livingston, magnificent interlocutors both: Jim Bahoh, Martin Krahn, Jacob Greenstine, and David Mesing deserve especial mention for their organizational acumen as well as their philosophical intelligence, two things that, alas, don't often run together smoothly, for this author at least.

Jonathan Culler provided a meticulous reading of the manuscript that led to significant improvements. His mentorship has been especially crucial to me in the last few years, and I'm as grateful for his kindness as I am for his extraordinary intellect.

I remain substantially indebted to Adrian Johnston. Ever since I met Adrian at a conference in Dundee, Scotland, deep in the thickets of my Ph.D., he has been an uncommonly attentive supporter of my work. The support of Adrian's coeditors at the Diaeresis series at Northwestern University Press, Slavoj Žižek and Todd McGowan, is humbling indeed.

Henry Carrigan has proven an exemplary and supportive editor. Two anonymous readers for Northwestern University Press contributed highly useful suggestions for revision, and this is a better book as a result. Christi Stanforth provided a sensitive and meticulous copyedit.

My parents, John and Judy Eyers, and my sister, Alice Eyers, remain loving and supportive in times good and bad.

Arielle Teer arrived in my life late in this book's composition, but its completion will forever be marked by that effervescent and ongoing encounter.

Finally, the book is dedicated to the memory of Dr. Eric Nuetzel. Eric was an eminent psychoanalyst and psychiatrist based in St. Louis, and an engaged intellectual whose interests ranged across literature and art, theater and opera, politics and philosophy. He served as my faculty mentor during my time as a Mellon postdoctoral fellow at Washington University in St. Louis, and his openness, thoughtful mentorship, kindness, and eager love for the pursuit of knowledge made my first two years in the United States richer than I could ever have hoped for.

Introduction

> Theoreticians of literature who fear they may have deserted or betrayed the world by being too formalistic are worrying about the wrong thing: in the spirit of Kant's third *Critique*, they were not nearly formalistic enough.
>
> —Paul de Man, "Kant's Materialism"

> The poetic work of fictioning is the immanent capacity to produce truths, from the interior of a limit and a constraint that are always those of language.
>
> —Judith Balso, *Affirmation of Poetry*

> It Must Be Abstract.
>
> —Wallace Stevens, "Notes toward a Supreme Fiction"

This book proposes a new theory of literary form and formalization. I will claim that literature works not through any kind of reflection or mimesis, nor through any overrunning of literary forms by their historical contexts or determinants. Rather, I will argue that literary texts, insofar as they are able to at least partially break free from their prior determinants and refigure those determinants anew, embody a formal speculative capacity that prevents their final absorption or neutralization by those prior conditions, even as the result may well be stasis or immobility rather than, say, contestation or critique. This capacity will be shown to enable a transport outward from literature's seemingly sealed bounds, just as form and formalism are more regularly assumed to ignore such a transport, sealing literary language within itself. Speculative formalism, as a theory of literary form in particular, will identify a shared incompletion across both literary language and its various outsides—materiality, history, politics, nature—that, far from preventing literature from interfacing with those outsides, rather makes such a nonmimetic reference possible, in a connective movement that puts impasses to creative use.

Just as it is impossible to fully totalize a formal language, whether "natural" or mathematical, such that it could also be thought of as consistent (think, paradigmatically, of Russell's paradox, of Gödel's incompleteness theorems),[1] so the formalization or attempted totalization of literature's outsides via the resources of literary language results in similar impasses, comparable dehiscences shared across literary form and its worlds. While such gaps tempt and then thwart any *direct* access of literary signifiers to their referents, they nonetheless open the path to a different kind of reference, the experimental permutations of which will be pictured in a variety of ways in all that follows. Critics of literary-critical formalisms have more often assumed that attention to the paradoxes of form inevitably leads to linguistic insularity, to an endless reflexive self-undermining that makes of literary form the "prison-house" diagnosed so eloquently by Fredric Jameson.[2] My contrary claim is that it is this initial self-reference or self-reflexivity that is, in fact, an opening to the only kind of reference available to literature.

It is worth offering at the outset an intuitive version of my argument, the insufficiency of which will, I hope, be progressively mitigated over the course of the book as a whole. Consider that, as Jacques Derrida[3] as much as Bertrand Russell or Gödel has shown, any attempt to push beyond the formal imperatives of varying kinds of language in order to exhaustively account for their possible instantiations must reach a limit, a point at which the structure is undercut by the gaps or lacunae that it otherwise relies on for its self-definition. Jacques Lacan, in his definition of the Real as that which can be inscribed through a necessary "impasse of formalization,"[4] recognized too the inevitability of such blind spots, their arising when any formal structure or system is pursued on its own terms and followed to its ultimate consequences. Equivalent impasses may also be found in the multiple outsides of such formal structures, insofar as they, too, in their unpredictable multiplicity, are lacking in totality, are too diffuse to be held in view at one and the same time.

Think, for example, of any attempt to exhaustively catalogue something like the "earth" or the "planet": the latter are both excessively expansive metacategories and wildly heterogeneous objects and processes in the world. Just as the categories fail to encompass the heterogeneity of their referents, so the material processes that roughly correspond to them (the impacts of changing climates, clashing sociopolitical conditions) are resistant by definition to symmetry, to cohesion, to predictability in advance. The constitutively incomplete languages that would do the totalizing nonetheless remain eager to overrun their particular objects, to encompass the latter in a definitive process of categorization or, as I will come to call it, *formalization.* Immanuel Kant, in his theory of antinomies, understood such impasses to be paralyses of reason.[5] The moral to be drawn from such follies of reason for the philosopher, inevitable as they nonetheless are, is that one should do everything possible to avoid them, to place limits on the extension of reason such that it only applies itself to phenomena it can properly know. By contrast, I hope to show in all that follows that literary forms offer us an especially vivid demonstration of the productive character of antinomies, indeed of the attempt to push oneself beyond such antinomies' limits in the search of pastures new. Such attempts are never entirely generalizable; rather, they are always routed through and transformed by the more particular texts that are put in their service and that may come to resist or deny them in turn.[6]

There are, then, broadly speaking, two kinds of constitutive formal incompletion at issue, the first to be identified in literary language per se, the second in the apparent outsides of literature, its various worlds or fields of reference, its historical and political "contexts"; and, as the reader will notice in much of what follows, the theory of reference advanced in the book will just as often lead us to question the very pertinence of any symmetrical opposition of text to context, of literary form to any absolute "outside." Nonetheless, an initial reading could well be content to insist on the primacy of such impossibilities only insofar as they defeat mimetic ambitions, in their demonstration of the inanity of the mimetic fallacy, such impasses then becoming, as in Kant, the proper end points of any truly critical process of analysis. Such an outlook would celebrate the impasse as the final defeat of prior referential illusions, of what Paul de Man referred to as the "ideology" proper to any realist theory of literary communication,[7] although, as the fourth chapter will demonstrate, de Man's writing, and deconstruction more generally, contains resources that push beyond this more simplistic affirmation of the nihilistic dis-figuration of all literary figures.

But the second approach would suggest that, far from marking the end of the process, such impasses—in literary form and its apparent referents both—are in fact to be understood only as the beginning, as the initial point at which literature begins to register its nonmimetic, tropic sympathy with the shared decompletions and disengagements proper to those various supposed "outsides," whether natural, historical, political, or material. Both domains—literary language and its apparent outsides—should be said to share inherent and formative limits to their possible totalization, the latter commonality then to be taken as itself a kind of speculative link or reference between the two, one irreducible to mimetic or historicist accounts of literature's successes. "Speculative formalism," that is to say, would refuse a familiar critical dichotomy or forced choice between, on the one hand, an account of literature that would emphasize its reflective or reproductive capacities (such reflective capacities most often said to be in the service of accessing historical contexts or scenes of various kinds), or, on the other, one that would foreground literature's fictive internal self-reference and self-foundation.

I should at this juncture explain what may well seem an eccentric choice of term. For an account of literary reference that would seek to avoid idealist, or more generally metaphysical, crutches, the foregrounding of "speculation," as especially bound up as it is with the Hegelian legacy in philosophy, may well seem quixotic. But my hope is that my appropriation of the term here, used in a fashion inassimilable either to German idealism or recent "speculative realisms," may polemically claim for a formalism especially influenced by Marxism and materialism more generally a stake in the explanation of literary productivity. To write of a "speculative" formalism is simply to acknowledge that literature, far from being only a mimetic vehicle or a site of endless interiority, is a peculiar site of *production* in its own right, one whose peculiarities are what allow it an awkward connection to its various others. While it is not my intention to propose any absolute homology between the account of speculative literary production adduced in what follows and the Marxist insistence on production and reproduction as central to the social, the extent to which my account is indebted to Marxist, and especially Althusserian, accounts of formal complexity will become especially clear in chapter 1, chapter 5, and the conclusion.

This more abstract account has, at the same time, much to tell us about the various literary-critical stories frequently told of the transformative ambitions of various literary schools. The different romanticisms are a useful case study for understanding such ambitions, as are the seemingly skeptical experiments of multifarious modernisms, to say nothing of the evacuation of the referential function to be found, one is so often told, in those cultural forms tagged as "postmodern." All of these familiar cultural narratives and categories will be placed under pressure in the close readings that make up the core of this book.

My perspective will also take in the ways in which literary form may illumine the formal characteristics of other scholarly domains, most notably philosophy. There is a commitment throughout to "theory," understood in its fullest and most transdisciplinary sense, a commitment that will, I hope, place in less-than-sympathetic relief some of the most influential attacks on critical theory that have been issued since theory's heyday in the 1970s and 1980s.[8] If the pursuit of an ambitious theory of literary form defined some of the most expansive work in the critical humanities both prior to the Second World War and during the heady decades of "high theory" after it, such questions have, of late, faded into the background. In their place one finds a renewed commitment to historical methodologies, and a no doubt salutary attempt to open up the ossified Western "canon" to those literatures that have been otherwise invisible to the tradition.

The rise of cultural studies has periodically been condemned by adherents to "high" theory, especially in their deconstructive guise, as a fuzzy capitulation in the face of the difficulties and paradoxes that issue from the philosophical ambitions of theory proper.[9] Nonetheless, I think it important to recognize the real political and intellectual gains that accompanied the expansion of what could count as cultural and canonical. Such advances come from the insistence made by culturalists that sexuality, gender, and race have as much place in the theoretical conversation as genre, narrative, or meter. That said, impoverished notions of cultural content and context have often accompanied the cultural turn. This has frequently brought with it a silence on the question of what I will be tempted more than once to call the "formativeness of form"—the ways literary, philosophical, or even scientific forms enter into conversation with, and retrospectively reconfigure, the formally elastic domains within which, and *against* which, they arise.[10]

Any understanding of the specificity of literary form, that is to say, would need to explain how it comes to slip partially loose of its determining histories and, further, how it may help to reproduce those histories anew. This is another way of saying that, when in denial of form's formativeness, one no longer knows what literature may *do* beyond playing host to the already existing historical pressures of its time. History, on such an account, plays the active parent to literature's passive child, a binary that reproduces at one and the same time the idea of content (now the stand-in for history) as mutable and fecund, and form (here disguised as literature) as static and servile, a seemingly immortal dichotomy traceable back at least as far as Aristotle's *Poetics*. Jacques Derrida and Paul de Man, as figures especially associated with "high theory" in the literary humanities, were very much concerned with the specific truths—the trace structure of meaning, the necessity of aporia—that literary form both acknowledges and conceals, a sensitivity that eluded those partisans of the "culture wars" for whom deconstruction was nothing but a puckish assault on the values of the Enlightenment.[11]

Such truths as deconstruction alighted upon depart, nonetheless, from any notion of verification via correspondence, where an active subject would easily perceive the qualities of a passive object (that binary once again). But truths they are nonetheless, and surely one of the benefits of the work of Derrida and de Man was to show how literature, more than other sources, may finally convince us of the necessary *paradoxicality* of truths, and thus the responsibility for thought more generally (philosophy included) to leave behind the reassuring but false notion that any departure from a subject/object model of cultural legibility is inevitably to land squarely in the quagmire of nihilism or relativism. Even if any explicitly correlational or correspondence-based imagining of literary reference is rare to find indeed, a broadly reflective, even mimetic account of cultural forms as they interact with history and politics is commonplace in the literary humanities, as "history" itself has assumed the role of governing master-signifier in the wake of the eclipse of high theory. To recognize, at any rate, the impurity or ambiguities nested in a discourse—to acknowledge the productive opacities of cultural objects and their "contexts"—is not necessarily to read within them the end of truth or the possibility of judgment per se. In transcending such nagging but artificial oppositions, "theory" in its older acceptation was signally unwilling to let go of the idea of truth itself, even as a positive term and not just something to be borne with stoicism while better, more slippery concepts or categories were invented in turn.[12] That such insights were often produced by way of a hefty labor of critical analysis, rather than with the comforting snap of commonsensical recognition, may usefully come to embarrass us in our contemporary moment of sound-bite politics and academic positivism.

One of the aims of the book, then, is to reimagine such an older species of literary theory, one that may fold crucial historical, political, and contextual questions back into a more fundamental inquiry into the formal logics that are the unstable but constitutive grounds of literary texts. It will be necessary, too, to insist on those features of the "speculative formalism" that is my concern here that, while no doubt informed by deconstruction as summarized above, nonetheless suggest a new, perhaps more positive path for critical-theoretical study, one as concerned with *construction* as it is with the inevitable dissolution of a text's foundations. Form, as it will be understood in what follows, becomes the conflicted, multiply distributed, and plastic site where truths specific to literature are rendered contingent but also given their only opening to the world, and from which other formal logics in other domains may be better understood. In other words, the truths that literature imparts should be more, not less, visible when its formal features are more comprehensively mapped.

Rethinking Form

There are, consequently, many different ways one might go about rethinking form in literature, not least because there are numerous distinct ways that "form" itself might be defined. Even though it is a general category, and one with a long and storied philosophical history, "form" in literary studies most often names particular devices: meter, allegory, metaphor, metonymy, voice, diction, and so on. This nominalism results, despite itself, in the production of the most general of general categories, namely "literature" itself, for despite the reigning historicisms of the last few decades, it is still the relative density of a text's tropic texture that allows us to distinguish it as literary or nonliterary in the first place, and this despite the numerous indeterminate cases that one may invoke. Of course, to propose any definition of form is to inevitably produce an account of content, and the resulting dichotomy threatens, in its inflexibility, to obscure as much as it enlightens. As Wellek and Warren had it, way back in the 1940s, "'Content' and 'form' are terms used in too widely different senses for them to be, merely juxtaposed, helpful; indeed, even after careful definition, they too simply dichotomize the work of art. A modern analysis of the work of art has to begin with more complex questions: its mode of existence, its system of strata."[13]

It is questionable whether the problem is solved by the mere replacement of one set of ambiguous terms—form, content—with another—"system," "strata." And the problems multiply when one seeks a positive, rather than simply negative, purpose for the reiteration of formalist dilemmas. The negative motives are easy enough to list: most importantly, history, instead of being a question to be answered, has threatened to become a catch-all *explanans* to be passively assumed, bringing with it an obfuscation of what makes literature, literature. But what of positive motives? What is to be gained by foregrounding form once again, if indeed we can agree on a definition of what "form" is? An avenue to be staunchly avoided, I think, is what could be characterized as a "retreat" into form. Such an impulse, while masquerading as positive—"Form is where the literary in literature is to be found, and thus it should be the focus of our attention"—is in fact just one more jerk of the knee, in this instance in response to the supposed politicization of the critical humanities in the last few decades.

Such a politicization, itself concomitant with the rise of the various historicisms, is to the contrary to be celebrated, not least for giving us a much more capacious sense of the varieties of literatures, and the uneven contexts of their production and reception. In some of the New Formalist literature,[14] it is argued that Marxist criticism in particular has been deaf to form. Yet anyone who were to seriously study the formalist-Marxist debates in Russia, or to conduct even a cursory reading of the back and forth between Brecht, Lukács, Benjamin, and Adorno, or to immerse themselves in the brief efflorescence of Althusserian criticism, or to read just one of Fredric Jameson's rapidly proliferating books: such a reader would find extraordinarily subtle dialectical articulations of form and history, form and politics, form understood to be always already embedded in multiple precincts of influence, the social awkwardly intercalated with the literary, the historical itself, in its Althusserian reformulation, an already formal arrangement of overdetermined and contingent boundaries and limits. There are significant drawbacks to all of these approaches, for sure, but a convenient forgetting of their fecundity should hardly serve us well.

But it is true that Marxist critics have not always been as attentive to the line as they have been to the geopolitical arena within which literature travels. At this juncture, it may be useful to define just what is meant by form at the level of the line, and how the "speculative formalism" worked out across this book might help us rethink how form works. At one level, this is a relatively simple question to answer. In much of what follows, "form" will be used to designate those aspects of literary texts that, in themselves, are indifferent to theme, character, or what is conventionally known as "content." More positively, I'll be especially attentive to moments of repetition,[15] the consonances and dissonances of rhythm, the ways in which certain images, metaphors, or metonymies come into conflict, and how all of these help produce a nonmimetic kind of reference. Yet these particular instances of form are also to be understood as expressive of a more general logic of form, or *formalization*; this logic, already alluded to above, concerns the creative capacity of impasses. Literature stages better than most phenomena the manner in which, far from shutting down the possibility of meaning, the impossibility of any final, formal integration of a structure and its component parts is the very condition of possibility of that structure.

On this reading, then, form can be understood as both a particular and general category. Particular, in that it is only ever fully manifest in devices, whether classical—meter, genre, and so on—or experimental, less categorizable. But subtending these particular instances of form is a general logic, albeit one whose generality may well be dialectically disrupted and rerouted by the particular means by which it is expressed. The general "logic" of form that I'm concerned with here allows what follows to expand what usually counts as form in literary studies, without thereby losing a critical specificity. At times, I will identify features that, while not "content" in any conventional sense, are nonetheless not reducible to standard accounts of form. Thus, for instance, the heightened rhetoricity of a phrase or stanza may count as an instance of form, provided that it is noticeably distant from whatever "content" may be in question, and insofar as it participates in the nonmimetic but broadly referential process that, I will argue, literary form affords. Just as frequently, I will be concerned to trace the way that poets, Francis Ponge and Wallace Stevens in particular, have constructed their own metapoetic commentaries on their formal innovations, commentaries that are themselves embedded in poems, ambiguously situated between or outside our usual expectations of what properly should count as form and what should be taken as content. This self-reference, then, often serves to destabilize the very distinction between form and content, insofar as this apparently "meta" aspect of the poem's content is also that which allows us to identify its peculiar formal pressures.

A potential problem, nonetheless, should be confronted here. One of the recurrent criticisms of earlier formalist approaches to literature has been the flattening and imprecise language of "form," its tendency to conflate distinct and incommensurable textual strategies. As Daniel Tiffany writes, advocating for a renewed attention to the specificity of poetic diction, "The long modernist preoccupation with *form* has produced an equally lengthy and persistent incomprehension of the problematic of diction."[16] The specific danger of the eclipse of diction may be enlarged and then directed as an accusation to my methodology; after all, wouldn't my proposed enlargement of those literary features that may count as "formal" not risk blurring the particularity of those features, thus all too predictably subsuming literature's specificity under an indifferent and tractionless philosophical framework?—and doesn't my construction of a general logic of literary form risk the same, subordinating the particular to the universal in a philosophical gesture long discredited as an indulgence of abstract aestheticism? I hope to have avoided such a fate by insistently dialecticizing the always unpredictable relationship between the general logic of form just discussed, always pregnantly absent as it is, and the only means of that logic's manifestation, namely the particular devices and inflections that make of literature a specific process in the world. The general logic of form's referential, nonmimetic force that this book tracks, in other words, is, in a sense, nonexistent, always absent, and yet, rather like Lacan's infamous concept of the "Real," it insists, albeit via textual features that are as likely to transform or frustrate it as they are to passively wave it through.

At any rate, my starting point is to resist any over-hasty taking on trust the parity of literary form with its referents; indeed, central to my argument will be the claim that form resists meaning as much as it enables it. Jonathan Culler has recently articulated this position well: "Rhythm, repetition, sound patterning [are] independent elements that need not be subordinated to meaning and whose significance may even lie in a resistance to semantic recuperation."[17] But on my reading, it is this very resistance to semantic recuperation that, paradoxically enough, lies at the root of literature's capacity to refer, even to transfigure, annul, boost, or remain strikingly indifferent to, its historical and political conditions. And so where earlier formalisms tended to set historical and political questions aside, the formalism developed here will rethink history and the social as themselves formal if contradictory logics, logics that may well turn out to be as unexpected, conflictive, and amenable to the new as we have frequently imagined literature to be. Put otherwise, history is not to be conceived of as "context" per se, as an externality ranged dynamically against the passive content that it molds; rather, literary history and politics are especially vivid folds in literary form as such, envelopes that both determine and are determined by the textual or conceptual-scientific structures that too often are assumed to be their mere passive products. But again, this is not to assume, as allegorical readings of literary-form-as-history so often do, that history is always an *interruption* of the text, that history as it is instantiated in form must stand out as an instance of difference or symptomatic intrusion. Rather, as Anne-Lise François has eloquently put it apropos of the indifference of historical time in the romantic lyric, "'history'—temporal change—can thus take place as a passing out of existence, a trailing off or lapse, rather than as a concretization or production of significance."[18] Such will be the distinctive formal invocation of historical-political forgetting characteristic of Ron Silliman's verse, explored in chapter 5, but also threaded unevenly through the book as a whole.

One minor variation on the major theme that the reader is invited to trace in what follows concerns modernism and its critical fates. As well as proposing distinct readings of a number of canonical literary modernists, I will contest the notion that modernist literature, in all its variety, busied itself with the mere staging of the failure of prior mimetic ambitions, the better to enclose literature in a kind of solipsistic aesthetic hall of mirrors. A version of this argument has recently been outlined by Fredric Jameson, a critic with whose insights I will more often find myself in substantial agreement: "[Modernism's] commitment to mimesis must not be misunderstood as a belief that the representation can somehow fully reproduce the original. Rather, the point is to demonstrate its failure, its structural incapacity to represent reality, to designate its grandiose project of doing so as 'mere' art and artifice, in an autoreferentiality of the aesthetic as such and its overweening autonomy."[19]

Reproduced in the view of modernism outlined by Jameson here is something of the view of deconstruction expressed above that, along the way, I'll also need to contest—and deconstruction is, if nothing else, surely the quintessence of a *modernist* critical practice, contrary to its careless conscription in numerous textbook-like accounts to the cause of "postmodernism." The latter term, when allied with "deconstruction," is assumed, via its refusal of a correspondence theory of truth, to inevitably result only in a celebration of the endless play of the signifier. But as the readings of modernist literature that follow will demonstrate, modernist strategies only evoke with an especial power a tendency definitive of literary form more generally. This emerges where the failure of a sign or image to passively mirror its object, the very stopping up of that play of the signifier, is, far from the end point of the process, only the beginning: for what follows is the overcoming of the gap between word and world that, previously, has been assumed to be possible only in a smoother, less agonistic transport of sense. And thus is implied something of a challenge to the very modernism/postmodernism doublet itself, insofar as the latter term is too often assumed—most famously by Jameson himself, of course[20]—to encapsulate the "linguistic turn" in continental philosophy, of which Derrida is the most celebrated and reviled example. By contrast, I read modernism as fully in accordance with the priorities of deconstruction and "theory" more generally. The latter, at its best, was equally concerned to trace the truths proper to the paradoxes of literary form, rather than merely to transcribe their ever-igniting impossibilities, the surrounding heat-haze of which has too often been indeterminately tagged with the term "culture."

Skepticism about Skepticism, or Surfaces and Depths

For all that form has been on the critical back burner, the years since the turn of the millennium have seen a number of calls for a moratorium on the primacy of historical and empirical methods, and for a return to the question of what makes literature, literature. It is possible that this is one consequence of a resurgent positivism in literary studies typified by the so-called "digital humanities," a trend that I examine in some detail in the first chapter to follow.[21] Even if this were so, it is hard to know whether the resulting turn to form is a positive consequence of digital techniques, of their ability to give us access to otherwise hidden formal terrains, or whether such calls reflect a growing frustration with such methods, with the tendency of Franco Moretti and others to argue for technology as a replacement for older, less obviously "objective" kinds of analysis, close reading being Moretti's favored target. If the latter explanation holds true, the New Formalism (to be distinguished, soon, from my own "speculative formalism") may well be dismissed as a mere reaction formation in the Freudian sense, serving to protect against the truths unleashed by precisely such boldly quantitative methods. (This, however, is very far from the conclusion I draw in my reading of the digital humanities in chapter 1.)

Whatever the priorities that fed its emergence, the so-called New Formalism has, thus far, produced little more than manifestos, as suggestive as many of them are; I'll discuss one of the best in the final section of this introduction. For now, it is worth noting that the critical terms of art employed by those seeking a return to form have largely been borrowed, with the occasional tweak, from previous literary-critical formalisms, such that the theoretical ground covered remains restricted to meter, voice, genre, and so on. While crucial to the "speculative formalist" account that follows, and as I've already outlined, such categories mark only the epiphenomena of more general formal processes that literature both announces and defers. But there's another recent "turn" in critical theory that should be addressed here, one gathered under the rubric of "surface reading." Insofar as it is an imperative of literary language, even at its most modernistic and self-conscious, to cover the tracks of its maneuvers, literary theory that holds to an ambition to understand the vicissitudes of form makes little progress if it adopts the skepticism about skepticism that is the signal feature of this latest post-theoretical tendency. Such a turn against critique, broadly understood, would need to be added to the growing list of recent analytical trends that a renewed concern for form may come to contest, a list that has thus far included a thorough rejection of the insights of deconstruction, and an immersion in historical context at the expense of literary specificity.

According to this new addition, older, modernist, and especially Marxist approaches in literary theory (often lumped together as the "hermeneutics of suspicion") were too quick to assume that the surface claims of a text and its historical moment were necessarily misleading. Such suspicious methods apparently compel a skeptical dive beneath that surface in search of a glinting but elusive ideological cause or buried citadel of truth. By contrast, the critic liberated from skepticism is encouraged to revel in the imperfections and ambivalences that make up the most observable aspects of a text in its interaction with its historical surrounds and in its relations with other textual sources; no such deep, hidden cause is required in order to account for such an attractively disharmonious polyphony.

To preview a little of my argument in what follows, the point is not to *reject* this attention to the surface of texts, but rather to insist that literature is quite capable of hiding its tricks, its absent ideological causes, *in plain view*, much like the titular object in Poe's "The Purloined Letter." To recognize this is already to question the very viability of the metaphor of surface and depth, a familiar binary that is linked to others—theory and practice, text and context, activity and passivity—that the "surface readers" are happy to maintain; my principal example, to be introduced presently, is Sharon Best and Stephen Marcus's introduction to a special edition of *Representations* on the theme of surface reading, published in 2009.[22] Such polarities are only ramified by those recent critical approaches, not least the assault on skeptical reading just discussed, that have abandoned with no little pride the philosophical underpinnings of literary analysis. In their place one finds all-too-underdetermined conceptions of history, context, culture, the better, one assumes, to attend to "actuality" rather than mere theory in its supposedly gray and static abstractions. Actuality in its opposition to theory is, of course, another variant of the practice/theory dichotomy already discussed, both dining out on the more than contestable notion that the concepts of "practice" and "actuality" are not already theoretical abstractions, perhaps exemplary ones. I'll take up the theoretical underdetermination of recent empirical and digital approaches to literature in chapter 1.

In consequence, what the reader will encounter over the next five chapters is, despite my precipitous defense of it here, rather far from the "hermeneutics of suspicion" as that now rather hollow notion has been most frequently deployed.[23] Most critiques of ideology begin and end with the content of the text at hand, but this book will not only seek to orient suspicious gazes away from content to form—it will equally serve to trouble the very distinction between form and content as it has traditionally and more recently been received. If form has too often been framed as the immovable and static encasement of a kinetic literary content, the former sluggish in its response to history, the latter obliging in its subservience to whatever context is invoked to explain it, here form will be understood to be as fervid and as fecund as the content that is too often implicitly assumed to do all the work. The fact that this will also require us to place in question the very distinction between content and form, albeit only then, in a broadly dialectical fashion, to construct a theory of *formalization* as bearing synthetically within it the characteristics usually associated with form and content both, will need to be fully explained and justified in all that follows.

Nonetheless, I intend also to follow the lead of that arch antidialectician Louis Althusser, whose striking propositions for a materialist philosophy of art have been underappreciated, despite the heroic efforts of Michael Sprinker and Warren Montag, among others.[24] I will explore an Althusserian reading of critical epistemology at some length in the first chapter. The general thrust of Althusser's theory of "symptomatic reading" closely follows Spinoza's materialist reading of scripture, whereby it is the very materiality of a text, the caesuras and interruptions that define and scar its surface, that should be the focus of any critical analytic gaze.[25] On such a reading, there are no hidden hermeneutic depths to be plumbed. The inconvenient bumps and scratches that bleed out like bruises and that interrupt the process of reading are not to be explained away as symptoms of a deeper thematic conflict or hidden historical wound.

Rather, a text's formal composition is to be taken at face value; as will be seen, its instances of de-formation, of stress and pressure, are always in collaboration with its marks of formation, of security and even of foundation (a term that deconstruction has made us unnecessarily wary of). Those processes, in turn, are always in plain view, distributed on a text's extended surface, and detectable too in the material, historically contingent world that otherwise threatens to appear as the inaccessible "outside" to literature's closed, writerly domains. Skepticism must emerge at those points in the analysis of a text's formal structure that apparently only announce its unqualified success, its mimetic contact with the world. But one should be equally wary of any unqualified celebration of the interior disintegration of a text, its apparently irrevocable solipsisms; deconstructive criticism has too often, I think, fallen into this trap. A clear example of this is to be found in J. Hillis Miller's description of the task of the deconstructive critic, who "seeks to find . . . the element in the system studied which is alogical, the thread in the text in question that will unravel it all, or the loose stone which will pull down the whole building."[26] Rather, the resonance of world and word is to be found in the *non*-mimetic, *non*-correlational but nonetheless *shared* moments of incompletion that define text and materiality, literature and history, such moments, to adopt Derridean parlance, being conditions of possibility as much as of impossibility, and being as likely to register as indifference as they are to impinge in a radical or disruptive register.

At any rate, the avowed rejection in Althusser and others of the surface/depth metaphor alerts us in advance to the first and fatal error that dogs Stephen Best and Sharon Marcus's manifesto "Surface Reading," published in 2009 as the introduction to a special edition of the journal *Representations* that has had a considerable impact. The essay and the special edition it introduces sought to mark a decisive break with the "symptomatic reading" that, for the authors, defined literary-critical practice from the 1970s on. When, belatedly, Best and Marcus acknowledge the source of the phrase "symptomatic reading" in the work of Althusser, they describe it as "assum[ing] that texts are shaped by questions they do not themselves pose and contain symptoms that help interpreters articulate those questions, which lie outside texts as their absent causes."[27] To this, one may simply counterpose the conclusion of Pierre Macherey,

Althusser's most inventive reader and a thinker of great power in his own right who, to the present, has done the most to develop a sophisticated theory of symptomatic reading, one that takes care to elude the metaphors of depth and absence that Best and Marcus kick against: "It is indeed easy to find it [the text] *deep*, like an enigma or mask behind which lurks some haunting presence; this is but one more way of representing the text as a smooth and decorative surface."[28]

On the contrary, and with impeccable fidelity to Spinoza's insistence that a cause only ever inheres in its effects, "this idea of a hidden truth or meaning remains unproductive and misleading: in the proposed exchange between depth and surface there is ultimately just an abstract inversion which disturbs the terms of the problem while leaving the problem unchanged."[29] It is hard, then, to recognize the foe that Best and Marcus set out to oppose, as when they characterize symptomatic reading as taking "meaning to be hidden, repressed, deep, and in need of detection and disclosure by an interpreter."[30] As Macherey's comments imply, symptomatic reading in its structural Marxist acceptation is *anything but* a depth hermeneutics. That post-Freudian psychoanalytic approaches are similarly cautious to avoid a metaphorics of depth—think only of Lacan's fastidious disavowal of any idea of the unconscious as some kind of immeasurably deep cauldron of roiling fantasies[31]—also seems to have bypassed Best and Marcus, for whom psychoanalytic approaches are equally only the bearers of a now-untenable suspicious gaze.

A psychoanalytic suspicion of suspicion, or analysis's unwillingness to collapse the specifically Freudian theory of the unconscious into the older, occult models that Freud defined his own intervention against, is clear enough to discern in *The Interpretation of Dreams*. There Freud's focus on the mechanisms of displacement and condensation that define any particular dream-thought serves already as a rejection of the idea of the unconscious as a subterranean field of dark, inscrutable content. Rather, it is the formal compressions and displacements (to be understood as metaphoric and metonymic, respectively, when transferred to the realm of textuality), occurring at the imagistic surface of a dream-text, that provide a sense of its meaning. This is very far from Best and Marcus's conclusion, borrowed from the equally partial assessment of Carlo Ginzburg, that psychoanalysis, like Marxism, finds in "infinitesimal traces . . . the comprehension of a deeper, otherwise unattainable reality."[32] Macherey insists, as a Marxist in the field of literary theory, that those details are to be found at the surface, even though their haunting (again, *at the surface*) by a second or third possible meaning is itself enough to place in question the very metaphorics of surface and depth, one unapologetically retained by Best and Marcus. For those second and third possible meanings have no consistency, no substance, and no depth, except insofar as they are produced—actualized, if you like—by the immanent formal logic of a simultaneous articulation and disarticulation; as, again, in Spinoza, an apparently "buried" cause only ever inheres in its effects.

Another recent example of an anticritical practice of reading is to be found in Cannon Schmitt's nonetheless illuminating analysis of Joseph Conrad, "Tidal Conrad (Literally)."[33] Concerning himself with a "literal" reading of the nautical imagery that is distributed across much of Conrad's prose, Schmitt laments a "critical tradition that, as if taking its cue from Marlow or his avatar Pepper, values the deep and the figurative over the shallow and the literal."[34] Instead, Schmitt avers, one should take seriously the immediately perceptible and often technical references that a writer such as Conrad puts to use in lending his narrative color and detail. Schmitt does not, admittedly, wish to entirely leave suspicion behind; he concedes that "the figurative, repressed, ideological resonances of texts should not be abandoned; rather, they would be understood as incomplete if not worked out in complex relation to the sheer facticity of fictional worlds."[35]

By taking seriously the opening, say, of *Heart of Darkness*, where "the *Nellie*, a cruising yawl, swung to her anchor without a flutter of her sails,"[36] one would need to establish what a "yawl" literally is, what it tells us then about the nautical experience of dropping such a ship's anchor, and only after that search among the depths of this imagery for its figurative consequences. Schmitt christens this process, as deflating as it is, "denotative reading," and thus confesses a faith in the ability to sharply distinguish denotation from connotation, literal meaning from metaphoric mystery. But take Schmitt's analysis of the word "restraint" in Conrad, one that forms "an insistent refrain in *Heart of Darkness*."[37] Schmitt quotes Conrad's character Marlow reflecting on the puzzling failure of the cannibal crew of the steamer ship in the novella to kill and consume their masters: "Restraint! What possible restraint? . . . But there was the fact facing me—the fact dazzling, to be seen, like the foam on the depths of the sea, like a ripple on an unfathomable enigma."[38] Briefly entertaining the notion that the depth imagery of the passage may make of Marlow a quintessential symptomatic reader, Schmitt concludes instead that such depths are unimportant "in relation to what is superficially evident, the 'dazzling' 'fact' of realized restraint."[39] Here Schmitt seems to set up an equivalence between the kind of denotation he finds in the technical terms of seafaring—yawn, anchor, and so forth—and an apparently symmetrical literal meaning to be deduced from the term "restraint," one that may only then be supplemented by the term's figural permutations.

"Restraint," however, is no technical term, insofar as it has no immediately localizable or fixable object; indeed, it is a term that tends to be explained only in terms of its synonyms—"constraint," "control," "limits" for one of its most obvious definitions, "unemotional," "detached," "moderate" for another. Even if "yawl" and "anchor" might seem to bear less of a polyphony, might it not be that the very use of such apparently "blank" terms, terms close enough to what might be called jargon, may be intended as their own kind of allegorical realignment or displacement, such that it is in the very seeming *lack* of figurality apparent in such words that the reader finds herself searching all the harder for an elusive figural depth? Schmitt may be half right, then, but only in the sense that jargon functions to alert us to the fact that polyphony occurs precisely at the surfaces that may, at first blush, seem to tolerate only a denotative sobriety. Such a sobriety, I will argue in the chapters that follow, is best understood in terms of the constitutive constraints of literary form itself, in the manner in which those multiple forms of limitation—forms of restraint, one could say, the best exemplar of which is surely poetic meter—open the door, even if only slightly, to the very hermeneutic freedom that they may superficially seem to ward against. I will have cause to consider an especially fecund form of constraint in the final chapter, where the experiments of the "language poets," Ron Silliman in particular, announce, in their very apparent freedom from the usual normative demands of poetic form, the marked immortality of the latter.

It is, then, by rejecting the metaphors of surface and depth (of depths and shallows, in Schmitt's nautical terms), metaphors that traduce formal complexity at the same moment that they train the eye on narrative content at the expense of form, that the literariness of literature, the formativeness of form, may finally come into view; Schmitt, needless to say, clings to such a metaphorics as tenaciously as Best and Marcus do, even if the opposition is recoded for the former in the equally unstable distinction between denotation and connotation.[40] The contradictions that my speculative formalism attends to are not hidden away, but are simultaneously dissimulated and simulated in plain sight, as in the ripples that ebb and flow on a body of water. When, for instance, the ambivalent meter of a late poem by Mallarmé, strung anxiously between free verse and the prior lures of the alexandrine, underscores the productivity of formal constraint, the very freedom to be found in restriction, it does so nowhere but at the level of the line itself, in those tense silences between the beats that announce the rhythm of the poem surely as much as the words themselves:[41] "Mon doute, amas de nuit ancienne, s'achève / En maint rameau subtil, qui, demueré les vrais / Bois meme, prouve, hélas!

que bien seul je m'offrais / Pour triomphe la faute idéale de roses- // Réfléchissons . . . [My doubt, hoard of old darkness, ends in a whole stream / of subtle branches which, remaining as the true / forests, show that I've offered myself (quite alone, too) / the roses' ideal failing as something glorious- // Let me reflect . . .]."[42]

Here the interposed and unexpected punctuation (that exclamation mark, that protruding dash, strangely reminiscent of Gerard Manley Hopkins), as much as the enjambment and the culminating interruption of the meter, testify to the ghostly limits that are in question here, limits that produce the sense of their own transgression. Mallarmé's innovations may be read as the final consequence of the prior intermixing of poetic forms pursued by Victor Hugo, Verlaine, and Baudelaire, one that had as often as not pitted meter against content, scansion against accent, shadowboxing the seeming restrictions of prior Racinean metrics. Mallarmé was well aware of the fecundity of these tensions: "Verse is everywhere in language where there is rhythm," he wrote, "but in truth there is no prose: there is the alphabet, and then verses more or less tight, more or less diffuse."[43] That later theoretical phrase "the materiality of the signifier" only goes so far in capturing what it is at stake here.[44]

This holds true even for the pronounced rhythmic regularity of a Baudelaire, whose verse nonetheless presupposes, indeed *stages* through its periodic repurposing of prose, its own partial freedom from, or transgression of, poetry per se. And yet those prose poems always find a way to register their reliance on the prior restrictions of metered verse, not least through well-placed repetitions and casual, baggy rhymes. Consider, here, the repetition of "be drunken" and the covert use of rhyme; the introduction, in other words, of structural regularities into prose that is otherwise preoccupied with the virtues of the dissolute and the irregular. I've indicated rhyme in italics and repeated phrases in square brackets: "One must [be forever drunken]: that is the sole question of importance. If you would not feel the horrible burden of Time that bruises your shoulders and bends you to the earth, you must [be drunken] without *cease*. But how? With wine, with poetry, with virtue, with what you *please*. But [be drunken]."[45] As will be seen in the second chapter, Francis Ponge extended Baudelaire's appropriation of prose in a direction that finds in the tension between the conversational openness of prose and the constrictions of verse the very fount of poetic power.

Back to Best and Marcus, whose notion of a textual surface is far removed from the stark yet potent topological foldings of a Mallarmé or Baudelaire. As I've already established, Althusser and his comrades took inspiration in their own version of "surface reading" from Spinoza's metaphysics, one that proposes a single substance as constituting all that is. Such a monism precludes in advance the positing of any depth to be plumbed. Rather, the attributes and modes that modify substance are nonetheless part of that substance, to be traced through the wrinkles on its surfaces. It is of some surprise, then, given their denigration of that arch-Spinozist Althusser, to find in Best and Marcus's essay a strikingly Spinozist turn of phrase: "We take surface to mean what is evident, perceptible, apprehensible in texts; what is neither hidden nor hiding; what, in the geometrical sense, has length and breadth but no thickness; and therefore covers no depth. A surface is what insists on being looked *at* rather than what we must train ourselves to see *through*."[46] This seems little different from Pierre Macherey's patently Spinozist contention that "we must examine the work in its real complexity rather than in its mythical depth. Constrained by its essential diversity, the work, in order to say one thing, has at the same time [we may add "and in the same place"] to say another thing which is not necessarily of the same nature."[47] "Constrained by its essential diversity" is especially good: as much of what follows endeavors to prove and as I've already had cause to mention, it is in the very formal constraints that texts must pass through—in poetry, think of meter, in prose the normative limitations of genre—that their inner productivity is to be found, freedom from such constraints being paradoxically dependent, then, on the persistence of them.

This latter claim lies very far from the hermeneutics of suspicion fought by Best and Marcus. Rather, again from Macherey, "this [such a hermeneutics of suspicion] was precisely what Spinoza identified . . . as the confusion of causes and effects . . . [Instead] the enigmatic narrative gives the solution and the problem in inextricable simultaneity."[48] What Macherey via Spinoza insist on here at the level of temporality—the "mystery" of the text given at the same time as its solution—is true also spatially, whereby a narrative—Best and Marcus again—"has length and breadth but no thickness."[49] A simultaneously spatial and temporal realignment of our scholarly understanding of form is, then, very much at stake in the chapters that follow.

It would only be responsible for us to mark what one could call the "ruptural connection" between the position outlined here and those of earlier, aesthetic philosophies, perhaps most surprisingly with those of Schiller. The connection is ruptural because the broadly structural approach in what follows largely defines itself against the aesthetic approach, typified by Schiller perhaps more than anyone else, that would press artistic works into the service of a more general moral outlook, what Herbert Marcuse nonetheless strikingly redeployed as the "liberating force of the aesthetic function."[50] What imposes itself as an echo with past aesthetic approaches is to be found in Schiller's insistence that fictional language, at least at its best, is defined by "presentification [*Vergegenwärtigung*]," by the transformation of "what has happened" into the mode of the present.

The temporal and spatial simultaneity of articulation and disarticulation that is explored in this book also seems to require fictional language to draw up its materials into an eternal present, where text has always already begun, except of course that the moment of dis-articulation is always also the sign of an unanticipated *interruption*, disbarring in advance any sense of the text as essentially or absolutely synchronic or static. Such an apparently eternal but always already interrupted present confronts one empirically in those mysterious opening lines of Faulkner's extraordinary short stories, where, as Fredric Jameson observes, "they testify to the weakening . . . of the past-present-future system [of narrative] itself, by the dominance of an eternal present which seeks then to disguise itself as . . . narrative to be told and story or destiny to be revealed."[51] In such stories, the identity of the narrator, most often presented in an ambiguous third person, is kept hidden for enough time to instill a distinct sense in the reader of uncertainty, but also of the notion that the action has already been unspooling in a simultaneous, eternal "now," before the process of reading had even begun. But the expectation that the time of action is happening "now," in the seamless present already mentioned, can only be disappointed, not least because the very absence of any seeming temporal markers already raises time, to say nothing of history, as the crucial question to be answered.

Jameson refers us to the beginning of Faulkner's story "The Brooch" (1936): "The telephone waked him. He waked already hurrying, fumbling in the dark for robe and slippers, because he knew before waking that the bed beside his own was still empty, and the instrument was downstairs just opposite the door beyond which mother had propped upright in bed for five years."[52] The story begins *in medias res*, its narrative having already begun, an unspooling that is nonetheless vulnerably open to being seized by events to come, and from textual markers pointing backward in time. To be sure, the modernist event in prose narrative of which the above is one example bears out with a particular intensity the structural function that I am trying to identify here, one that, at the level of narrative point of view and as memorably evoked by Faulkner, reveals itself as a disquieting *impersonality*, a sense of events happening serenely if troublingly outside of the past/present/future train of narrative tension and release, if not for all that outside time and history *tout court*.

Insofar, however, as this notion of interruption as dis-articulation is simultaneous with that which it interrupts, the fictional "present" on my reading is very far from being narcotically fixed; instead, the present is already despoiled by the "future" as the site of an inevitable disassembly, and thus any pure present is, in advance, an impossibility.[53] And so even as I recognize a family resemblance with aesthetic discourses past, I must insist again on a fundamental difference. Whereas Schiller focuses on the *content* of fiction, whereby a narrated event from the past should be "made present" to the reader on its being narrated, the logic of textual temporality traced in what follows is of a formal or structural nature and may be construed as more fundamental even than the narrative mechanics of past, present, and future.

The latter distinctions have often been productively blurred by switches in tense, or by an author's refusal to divulge the narrative position from which their text proceeds, much as in the example of Faulkner's short fiction. This questioning of narrative position then resonates, albeit distantly, with Schiller's own distinction between the naive and the sentimental poet, the latter being one who self-consciously distances herself from her object, modernism emerging, ironically enough, as the later reproduction of Schiller's earlier excoriation of "sentimentality," typified for him, as inaccurate as he surely was, by Wordsworth.[54] My position, at any rate, is closer to that of Roland Barthes, for whom "there is no other time than that of the enunciation and every text is eternally written *here and now*,"[55] although there is too little acknowledgment in Barthes's still-bracing essay of the *barriers* to polyphony or to the multiplication of textuality, to those formal features that undercut the seemingly eternal plenitude of writing and of those "readerly texts" that Barthes so revered. Such a lack is as crucial to the account of literary form that follows as the uncanny temporal simultaneity already mentioned, a simultaneity that will be shown, in chapter 5, to be ever haunted by the ghosts of past and future historical possibility, even if only in their glaring absence.

The "New Formalism"

Back to the present critical "scene," from which I'd like to identify an approach to form that may more productively be read with and against my "speculative formalist" position. After this brief discussion of Caroline Levine's striking book *Forms*, the reader will find a sketch of the contents of the chapters that make up the rest of the book. Organized around four *ur*-forms—whole, rhythm, hierarchy, network—Levine attempts to reorient our focus away from literary form per se, and onto the ways in which social and political arrangements and literature alike are populated by jostling forms, none of which are ultimately able to fully gain precedence over the others. At the very opening of her highly suggestive *Forms: Whole, Rhythm, Hierarchy, Network*, Levine lays out what a standard formalist analysis of *Jane Eyre* might look like. A critic embarking on such a reading would attend to "literary techniques both large and small, including the marriage plot, first-person narration, description, free indirect speech, suspense, metaphor, and syntax."[56] Such an analysis would, it is implied, be likely to exclude social and historical questions. By contrast, Levine's New Formalism would trace the often-agonistic parity between those forms seemingly enclosed within the bounds of the literary text, and the forms and structures into which social life sediments. Levine draws our attention to the following passage in *Jane Eyre*, the action taking place after the ringing of a school bell at Lowood School. The girls "all formed in file, two and two, and in that order descended the stairs." Responding to a verbal command, the children arrange themselves into "four semicircles, before four chairs, placed at the four tables; all held books in their hands."[57] Critics, Levine writes, are used to "reading Lowood's disciplinary order as part of the novel's content and context . . . But what are Lowood's shapes and arrangements—its semicircles, timed durations, and ladders of achievement—if not themselves kinds of *form*?"[58]

This is only an initial example of the methodology employed across the book as a whole, meant perhaps only to set the scene, and Levine meets the first obvious objection rather well. "One might object," she writes, "that it is a category mistake to use the aesthetic term *form* to describe the daily routines of a nineteenth century school."[59] And yet as she rightly points out, "form" as a term has hardly been restricted to aesthetics. Rather, in its very generality, "form" has traveled through politics, through philosophy, through innumerable other domains, and it may nominate a particular object or describe a general property of a class of things. But does this historical usage justify treating with the same analytical brush Brontë's use of metaphor, say, and her description of the spatial outlines of a social institution? Levine argues her case forcefully, noting that "it is the work of form to make order. And this means that forms are the stuff of politics."[60] Thus, Levine's New Formalism, far from shutting out questions of social and political import, will rather widen their pertinence, to include the rhyming couplet as much as the disciplinary enclosure of space or the distribution of self-regulating bodies. As a consequence, "the traditionally troubling gap between the form of the literary text and its content and context dissolves. Formalist analysis turns out to be as valuable to understanding sociopolitical institutions as it is to reading literature. Forms are at work everywhere."[61]

But hasn't a crucial question been elided here? Even as Levine celebrates the "dissolving" of the barrier between text and context, she presumably wouldn't wish to claim that there is, as a result, absolutely no distinction to be made between the words that make up Brontë's narrative, and the arrangements of space that are her referent. Presuming this much, we are still to learn how it is that these two very different things are to be explained according to the same now highly capacious, perhaps *too* capacious, definition of "form." Even more importantly, how do these different forms come to relate to one another at all? To use a now unfashionable parlance, what is the theory of *reference* that underpins Levine's account? One thing is clear: for Levine, there is no unidirectional line of causality from context to text, as in the less reflective of historicist readings; indeed, there is an even more radical argument about causality here that I will come to shortly. We get something of a more positive answer with Levine's borrowing of the term "affordance" from design theory. Affordances, we're told, "describe the potential uses or actions latent in materials and designs." Thus, "a fork affords stabbing and scooping. A door-knob affords not only hardness and durability, but also turning, pushing, and pulling,"[62] and so on. Forms, on such a reading, are not merely reflective of a prior cause, content, or context; rather, they are active agents in their own right. Even literary forms, in their very abstraction, have affordances, one infers. But one wants to ask again how, precisely, one *specific* class of forms—literary forms—gain purchase on those other forms that jostle for attention? Or, in Levine's terms, what are the particular affordances that literature possesses, over and above the material and action-oriented uses to which other forms may be put to use—which is not to say that literature itself may not have its own, *specific* material and action-oriented consequences? I will return to this question in much of what follows, it being, I would wager, a problem rather often avoided in much recent literary theory.

The reader may have noticed the distinctly Latourian cast of Levine's analytical language, and it is a surprise that Bruno Latour is mentioned only twice in the main body of the text. Latour's "actor-network theory" has made much for decades now of how human and nonhuman "actants" enroll and resist one another in a great tangle of moves and countermoves. What I will come to call Levine's liberal-ecumenical vision of formal complexity shares some of the same limitations inherent to Latour's anthropologically inflected social theory. One encounters an especially Latourian inflection when Levine raises the question of causality:

> The first major goal of this book is to show that forms are everywhere structuring and patterning experience, and that this carries serious implications for understanding political communities . . . In theory, political forms impose their order on our lives, putting us in our places.

> But in practice, we encounter so many forms that even in the most ordinary daily experience they add up to a complex environment composed of multiple and conflicting modes of organization—forms arranging and containing us, yes, but also competing and colliding and rerouting each other. I will make the case here that no form, however seemingly powerful, causes, dominates, or organizes all others.[63]

I wonder whether the appeal to the theory/practice dichotomy here is more telling than it might initially appear. Latour has often deprecated the legacy of theoretical critique—of "critical theory," in shorthand.[64] In Latour's case, one surmises that this stems, in large part, from a distaste for Marxism especially, and while Lenin, Luxembourg, Althusser, Gramsci, Jameson, Roberto Schwarz, and numerous others have done much to complicate the model of causality inherited in the tradition, it would still be fair to say that doing without a theory of causality at all, as I think is implied by the final sentence above, would be unthinkable for every but the most "post" of "post-Marxists." And for all the usefulness of the language of overdetermination and structural causality, it is hard to imagine a major Marxist work of criticism in the last fifty years or so, from Raymond Williams onward, that could have gained much analytical purchase without this most central plank of truly critical writing. And one also wishes to ask who, including Marx himself, ever argued for a theory of literature or society that privileged one form apparently able to "cause, dominate, or organize all others"?

Levine's skepticism goes further. As well as lamenting the reductions of causal analysis, she also draws on Roberto Mangabeira Unger to lament any emphasis on deep structures or hidden ideological causes, ranging herself implicitly in solidarity with the trend for "surface reading" first announced by Stephen Best and Sharon Marcus.[65] Such a structural focus, Levine protests, "limits our attention and our targets to a small number of the most intractable factors, factors so difficult to unsettle that most people abandon the attempt altogether. What if we were to see social life instead as composed of 'loosely and unevenly collected arrangements' . . . ?"[66] Just as Marcus and Best rather crudely mischaracterize the "depth reading" that they wish to contest, so Levine risks recourse to the straw man here. After all, the best of structuralist reading, in both its formalist and Marxist manifestations, understands structure not in monolithic terms, but rather as, precisely, multiply caused and complex. But where structuralism would still, nonetheless, wish to maintain a nuanced but firm rubric of causality, Levine's ecumenicism—or, to be less generous, eclecticism—threatens, I think, to replace analysis with sophisticated description. The condition of a globalized capitalism is much as she intimates: hypersophisticated, hypermobile, making little of previously intractable barriers to temporal and spatial transport. But these are also, yes, surface features that frequently obscure the division of labor that conditions their existence. And what is to be gained by recoding our oppositional languages of analysis in the terms of those phenomena we wish to challenge? Might we further lose what little critical edge literary theory may still, potentially, possess by glossing it in the same quasi-Deleuzian terms as the site of what Levine calls "collision"—"the strange encounter between two or more forms that sometimes reroutes intention and ideology"?[67]

Levine's tracing of these different forms culminates in a concluding chapter on *The Wire,* David Simon's recent and much-lauded television series chronicling overlapping formal and informal economies in Baltimore. The series has been much talked about in academic circles, with various conferences, symposia, and articles focusing on its intricate plotting of the consequences of neoliberal urban restructuring, or on its complex relationship to canonical forms of narrative realism.[68] If, as is Levine's ambition, cultural studies must "take account of what happens when a great many social, political, natural, and aesthetic forms encounter one another,"[69] the multilayered character of *The Wire,* with its aggregation of multiple, internally heterogeneous institutions, scores of characters, and numerous distinct social spaces, would seem an ideal object for such a project. The series emphasizes both the grip that multiple institutional structures have on modern urban experience, and the scandalously uneven distribution of resources that such (post)modern cityscapes afford. Even as the series gleefully adopts and celebrates genre conventions, not least those associated with the cop show, Levine also sees in the series something of an updating of the best of nineteenth-century realism; "Not unlike *Bleak House,*" she writes, "*The Wire* expands the usual affordances of its medium by intertwining over 100 characters in multiple intricate sequences that overlap and reshape one another."[70]

As in the other readings that populate the book, Levine attempts to chart the ways in which forms both enable and frustrate each other's claims to autonomy. Its status as fiction, far from being a hindrance, in fact allows the construction of a social theory close to the original roots of *theoria,* to the ambition to extract from a spectacle generalizable knowledge of the world. With an eagle eye, Levine digs deep into the multiple localities or "wholes" that make up the space of *The Wire;* she is attentive, for instance, to events in the series' third season, where a police chief creates "Hamsterdam," an unofficial zone of drug legalization that shifts drug sales from their usual spots on street corners into a strictly bounded series of locales. But this apparently isolated and largely hidden social experiment soon rebounds on other enclosed wholes depicted in the series. As Levine writes, "Mayor Clarence Royce is momentarily impressed by the success of the zones, and his delay in shutting them down helps to bring about his defeat in the election, catapulting Tommy Carcetti into leadership of the city and eventually the state."[71] And thus, multiple intertwined structures—a spatial enclosure licensed illegally by a policeman operating outside his jurisdiction, the official police bureaucracy, the media, interlaced local and extralocal political hierarchies—collide, with effects as complex as the original interaction of the forms in question.

Here a specified and local space—the free drug zone—fans outward in influence, and the other forms it interacts with respond in turn. All of this one would concede, but in order to pass from sophisticated description to analysis, at least some recognition of underlying impetus, of causal push, is surely necessary. Levine makes passing reference to those scholars who have read *The Wire,* even in its commitment to local particularity, as an allegory of contemporary hypercapitalist deracination, but she implies that such a reading would necessarily mute those multiple other forms, those shapes or rhythms not entirely reducible to the economy, that populate the series. But why? To invoke a category such as capitalism is certainly not to deny the "affordances" of local forms, but it is to recognize the dialectical interaction of those forms with an absent totality that, partially but powerfully, structures them in perpetuity. To insist on such interaction as "dialectical" is already to agree with Levine's insistence that such particularities are capable of resisting, even displacing, their animating frames, but it also pushes us toward asking bigger questions, questions as big as the spaces that *The Wire* pictures. A theory of causation *must,* I think, underpin Levine's account, whether rendered explicit or not, not least because the language of forms "colliding" and "intermixing" already presumes a set of conditions within which such events could occur. My hope is that the details of this account will become clearer in subsequent work.

It may well be that Levine's analytical framework is too general to deal with the local causal interactions that she insists are too complex to "reduce." By this I mean that, in approaching any local object of analysis, the language of entanglement and affordance tends, not always but often enough, to obscure the very differences that it sets out to celebrate; the particular threatens to be lost by virtue of a paradoxically static language of generalized difference, one that turns around a few linked adjectives and nouns: "complex," "collision," "entangled," and so on. Consider the following passage, a remark on *The Wire*'s fourth season, the year that focused on the school system: "Each child's story emerges out of a complex collision of social forms that can never be limited to one or two dominant social principles—race, economics, the city, the family, politics, the law, or education—but takes shape amid the pressures of all these and their constantly colliding patterns."[72] Of course, there is never any fixed trajectory to social phenomena, no absolute pattern set in advance that would make the mapping process a foregone conclusion. But in practice, social forms, indeed aesthetic forms, are limited in their trajectories; retrospectively, one is often able to identify dominant factors that caused a particular event or made one thing more likely than another. To insist otherwise is potentially to blunt theory and disable political action.[73]

In the penultimate chapter, "Networks," Levine seems to admit as much; for example, she writes that "it is clarifying and practical to isolate a single network and pursue its impact, since when networks are thrown together they can seem messy or incoherent. But it is also misleading to treat them as separate."[74] I would insist that isolating a single or even a small sample of networks and interpreting their causal interaction is not necessarily to risk "treating them as separate." To the contrary, analytical self-selection, even a certain necessary blindness (de Man's conjunction of blindness and insight, perhaps),[75] is foundational to any project of inquiry, and it seems a fair assumption that, with all the constraints of the social and material world, such limitations are inherent there too. For all that, such a disciplined gaze does not require ignorance of the fact that, beyond the borders of one's analysis, there may well be further connections to be pursued, or latent links to be activated on the irruption of another social event. And it doesn't seem overly reductive to claim that the one thing that all the forms delineated in all their messiness in *The Wire* have in common is their being impacted, for the worse, by the effects of a feral capitalism, one whose contemporary surface complexity should not become an alibi for our losing sight of its increasing definition of, and disproportionately adverse impact on, the contemporary human condition.

One final brief comment on *The Wire*. In a number of the readings of literature that will follow, I argue that the very apparent separation of poetic form from its referents has the effect, far from undermining the poem's active impact in the world, of instead drawing an ever greater attention to the latter; through a kind of negative mutual constitution, the very disengagement between the two is the key to the sharpness of each and of their mutual resonance. Levine is fairly quick to pass over the generic status of *The Wire*,[76] arguing that a more directly sociological attention to its treatment of political form better gets at its relevance as a cultural object. But might we not expect a similar process of formal disengagement in a television serial that, after all, and in contrast with those who have insisted on its realism, makes quite the show of its generic borrowings? While I have no space to pursue this claim in any depth, I would suggest here only that the amplified, often absurd nature of those generic appropriations—think of the exaggerated, cartoonish aspects to lead detective Jimmy McNulty's self-destruction, a trope of the cop show if ever there was one—only makes the social "content" that much more compelling; as the Russian Formalists might have put it, these two impulses—formal artifice and social realism—are mutually estranging in *The Wire*, but this separateness, so warded against in Levine's analysis, is precisely what makes it such an accomplished televisual reflection on the deformations of capital. Somehow even the show's generic investments are warped by its subject matter, becoming outsized, even absurd, absorbing the excesses of the political phenomena in question even at points of apparent generic self-reference and pastiche. This infection of content by form will be one of the signal concerns of many of the readings that are the bedrock of this project.

Chapter Outline

It remains to give the reader a sense of how the following chapters relate to the general argument of the book. The first chapter deals in particular with the "digital humanities," a term used to capture the heterogeneous use of computation in recent humanities scholarship. Those with an ear to the ground of literature conferences and the academic press will have noticed the exponential growth, in recent years, of the use of digital techniques to track the mutation of literary content over time and space. Franco Moretti, one of the authors considered in chapter 1, is perhaps best known now for his exponential faith in such methods, techniques that, the reader is told, will deliver us from the illusory luxuries of close reading. For Moretti and others, we have too long been in thrall to the cult of close textual interpretation, "emanating," as Moretti has it, "from New Haven."[77] That such critics of critique tend to conflate theoretically minded "close reading" (often itself left undistinguished from I. A. Richards's rather different "practical criticism"), and the critical attention to form that marks the best of critical-theoretical reading, is enough reason for caution.

It seems prudent to locate the rise of the "digital humanities," and the potential threat it represents to the ecumenical vision of form and formalization that I'm concerned with here, with other, apparently less technically defined trends. Not the least of these is the New Historicism that has, since the eclipse of deconstruction, trained many an analytical gaze on finer- and finer-grained details of the historical life surrounding a text, resulting in less of an emphasis on the immanent formal productivity of literary writing "as such."[78] As chapter 1 and subsequent chapters demonstrate, there is no reason to suppose that a "high theoretical" approach to literary, philosophical, and even scientific form is in principled conflict with historicization as such, so long as history is itself understood as a complex and paradoxical kind of formalization, one that cannot be easily posed as a symmetrical correlate to a text conceived on equally limited terms. If New Historicists have sometimes threatened to impose on both text and history the same clarity and immediacy that earlier philosophical approaches had assumed defined the thinking "I," my intention by contrast will be to render history and text alike as complex forms, imperfectly and awkwardly interlaced in various agonistic combinations that elude the symmetrical priorities of Cartesian rationalisms and subjective humanisms past, and, for that matter, historicisms of the present day.

Put differently, it is imperative to avoid reproducing in contemporary terms the error implied by Alexander Pope's nonetheless alluring couplet: "The bookful blockhead, ignorantly read / With loads of learned lumber in his head";[79] Pope, needless to say, targets the reader whose contextual or historical understanding, her immense baggage of learning, blinds her to the knotty specificities of the text in question. The point isn't to discourage "learned lumber," whether it is of the historical, technological, or political kind, and neither is it to purify an ideal of the text-in-itself as radically impervious to prior historical or technological impurities. This book's ideal isn't that of Pope's *tabula rasa,* that of an utter and unmediated analytical receptiveness to textual forms preserved in aspic. Rather, the intent is to direct attention once again to the theoretical presumptions that necessarily underpin such shifts in understanding, such that one may proceed to a formalism disabused of such perilously unjustified prerequisites.

The second chapter reads two apparently far-removed French authors together: Francis Ponge, with his prose-poetry of everyday objects, and the earlier and hyper-rationalist philosophy of science of Jean Cavaillès. Ponge seemed to democratize the French poetic avant-garde by opening it to everyday objects, to cigarettes and oysters and oranges, while Cavaillès, by stark contrast, sought an epistemology that carved out a space for science as definitionally distinct from the realm of common experience, everyday objects, and sensory observation. But as I demonstrate, the two authors shared a suspicion for any delimitation of a pure space of perception impervious to its apparent linguistic or conceptual opposites. For Ponge, this meant registering in the formal paradoxes of his poetry the inability of language to latch neatly onto the object-world such that language's internal ambiguities and inconsistencies would be nullified in the presentation of things as they are; and this despite the surface logic of Ponge's poetry being precisely to present a phenomenologically pure account of things-in-themselves. It is this purposeful clash between such contrasting ambitions that lends Ponge's verse its delicious irony. Yet in this very impurity at the heart of his poetic project, Ponge demonstrates the only opening available to poetic reference, such a connection occurring ironically at the very moment when verse seems most unable to overcome its internal, formal, and apparently irrecoverable paradoxes and solipsisms.

Cavaillès's account of the formalization of scientific objects carries a strikingly similar charge. For the French philosopher, it is only on the resistance of conceptual language to the world, and with the simultaneous resistance of the dense stuff of the world to the symbol, that either may gain a nonmimetic and nonempirical purchase on the other. Cavaillès's name for this constitutive resistance of knowledge to its object, a resistance that announces nonetheless the asymmetrical connection of both, is "thematization," a term that, despite its birth in the philosophy of science, bears comparison with the Russian Formalists' "particularization," the latter a term pitched by such earlier formalisms against "generalization," or the ever-present temptation of the conversion of theory into mere empirical description.[80] These concepts will be further discussed in chapter 2.

One of the central if less obvious concerns of the book finds full expression in chapter 3, where the theoretical and rhetorical relationship between romanticism and modernism is explored. The traits generally attached to both "movements"—a faith in symbol, in nature, and in the possible adherence of humanity to both for the former, the self-conscious disconnection and experimental reconnection of all such links in the latter—are shown to be both staged and placed in question in the apparently neo-romantic poetry of Wallace Stevens and in the avowedly modernist philosophy of Alain Badiou. Stevens, I argue, has been ill-served by those who wish to find in his verse an expression, after the putative death of God, of a lingering faith in the transformative potential of poetic symbols; an expression of what Simon Critchley has called the "anxious atheism"[81] that seeks in poetry a site of postreligious, if not exactly secular, redemption. Neither, I argue, is Stevens a modernist in any received sense of the term, as multiple and contradictory as those received definitions have become. In this chapter, Alain Badiou's strictly modernist and, in its own way, formalist "inaesthetics" will serve as a foil through which the rather different formalism that I locate in Stevens can be illuminated. Stevens's verse evinces what I'm calling a speculative formalist interest in the simultaneous distance and proximity that the verse form, whether metered or free, forces upon its objects, such objects at the same time serving to distress poetic form from a topologically obscure "inside"—even as, to turn the screw once more, such objects are presupposed as *externally* opposed to the language that would, in an initial moment, seek to capture their inner essences. In the simultaneous recognition in Stevens of the formative and de-formative potentialities of poetic language, such potentialities to be understood as active both in the language and the material objects to be "captured" by the former, one may locate a poetic transcendence of the limited historical terms that philosophy, too, has so frequently been cast within.

Chapter 4 is the fullest exploration in the book of the legacy of deconstruction and its relevance to speculative formalism. Paul de Man's work is read as pointing in materialist directions that his adherents as much as his detractors have too infrequently identified.[82] Late essays by de Man on Kant and Hegel are interpreted as, far from marking a significant break with his earlier commitment to "rhetorical reading," making all the clearer what binds together those earlier and better-known writings. The position identified is one of a linguistic materialism, one that hovers at the precipice of arguing for the shared impurities of language and the material, only to finally settle on the better-known terrain of the distanciations of literary language proper.

The intent, then, is to push de Man's logic toward its inexorable end point, namely of a shared impurity and incompletion across text and context, word and world; such an account would recognize in those impasses the best evidence available that the world is as equally divided and paradoxical as the language that tries and fails to mimetically map it, such a world and its various historical archives equally held open, quivering in their incompletion. The consequences of such a conclusion for literary theory is explored in the fifth and final chapter through the uncompromising experimental verse of the so-called "language poets"; if my claim regarding the necessity of constraint or structured restriction in literary form is to hold water, I'd do well to put it to the test in a reading of verse that seems self-consciously to *rid* itself of such restrictions. History itself, and specifically the historical moment in the West defined by the widespread political claim that history had finally come to an end, will be shown to be an essential structuring force shaping the powerful minimalism of Bruce Andrews and his coconspirators; by implication, such formal logics will be shown to inhere in a back-and-forth between history and text that finally renders the distinction between the two porous, if not untenable. Here, finally, a specifically psychoanalytic account of literary time and history, one gleaned as much from Jean Laplanche as from Jacques Lacan, will help us bring together the structural simultaneity and historical density proper to speculative formalism as both theory and method.

A final comment is required. The reader will notice that the majority, if certainly not all, of the literary sources drawn upon in what follows are poetic, and this despite the more general term "literature" appearing in the book's subtitle. If it has often been claimed that poetry, more than narrative prose, compresses language, the better to reveal its less obvious but most crucial characteristics, this is only half the reason for my choice of sources, as contingent as that selection must, at least to some degree, be. As already mentioned, one of the express themes of this book is the productivity of formal constraints, of the manner in which seeming limitations on creative freedom in fact enable it all the better, not merely within language per se but in movements from language to the world. Poetry, with its illumination of explicit constraints—meter, most pressingly—is an especially useful wellspring for the elaboration of this thesis. (Needless to say, this is not to deny the constitutive constraints that apply to all instances of narrative, too.) But there is another reason, one that bears on the seeming centrality of narrative to, not only literature, but the psychic elaboration of subjective identity itself, a claim made with a striking lack of equivocation in Jameson's *The Political Unconscious*:[83] the irreplacibility of narrative, in other words, to the stories that, psychoanalysis has told us, the self tells itself about itself. It may be that poetry, with its self-conscious disruption of this narrative impulse (although prose poetry must be taken on its own lights, as will be seen in chapter 2), can act as a fever-chart of asubjective, even materialist impulses that are not so easily pinpointed in narrative, but that sit nonetheless at the eccentric center not only of all literary forms (narrative surely included), but also of variants of political and historical form. This, at least, is the thesis posed most explicitly in the final chapter and unevenly distributed across the book as a whole.

1

Clearing the Ground: New Digital Positivisms, the Fate of Literary Theory, and the Stakes of a "Speculative Formalism"

Humanities scholarship in the United States and the United Kingdom is perhaps more fragmented now than at any time in recent memory, at least since the popularization of higher education in the mid-twentieth century. Arguably, there has been no dominant school of thought or trend that has succeeded in converting significant numbers of scholars since the heyday of deconstruction in the early 1980s, a period that also saw the more modest ascendency of numerous theoretical subcultures, from postcolonial studies to psychoanalysis. Many of those tendencies had their roots in earlier interpretive traditions; deconstruction, at least as it was absorbed into literary studies, bore a closer debt to the attentive textualism of the New Criticism than has often been acknowledged. Psychoanalytic criticism, moreover, while largely framed by the mid-1980s within the terms of Lacanian metapsychology, had a previous and fecund life in the rather orthodox Freudianism of Lionel Trilling and in the slightly looser psychologism of Norman O. Brown.

All of this is to say that so-called "high" theory was, as often as not, a matter of the heightening and radicalization of previous trends, newly wrapped in the clothing of oppositional politics and in an attention to the marginal, to what had fallen out of hegemonic constructions of the canon. The fading of high theory, then, is to be understood less as the decline of a radically new, insurgent movement in the humanities. Rather, it marks the wider eclipse of older, variegated forms of analysis and critique that found their apogee, but certainly not their *inception*, in the moment of heightened theoretical self-understanding and reflexivity that characterized interdisciplinary humanities scholarship from the early 1970s to the early 1990s. Even as it is the task of this book to propose a new formalist apparatus for thinking literature, it may be beneficial to take seriously those emergent approaches in the literary humanities that have made great strides in recent decades, if only to clear the ground for what

I will propose should come, if not quite to *replace* them, then at least to complement them while nonetheless placing some of their central assumptions in question. In doing so, I hope to establish the foundation on which my "speculative formalist" approach will subsequently be constructed.

To give only a hint of the prodigious growth of neo-positivist methodologies in the humanities that will be my principal topic in this chapter, consider that, at the Modern Languages Association national convention in 2010, there were but twenty-seven sessions on the "digital humanities." After only three years, that number had jumped almost threefold, to sixty-six.[1] The concentration of grant funding in digital projects in the humanities is now well established.[2] There is, of course, a danger of confusing cause with effect here. One should make clear that the so-called "digital humanities" are to be understood less as a reactionary invader arising ex nihilo in the academy[3] and more as a symptom of broader social and political trends, a symptom nonetheless that is in the process of gaining its own autonomy, fortifying in turn the broadly antitheoretical currents that framed its emergence. I use the term "digital humanities" in an especially capacious sense, although I will limit my focus here to literary studies, the better to frame the discussion of literary form that emerges in the chapters that follow.

In grant applications and workshop proposals, the term "digital humanities" has come to mean various combinations of archival preservation, cataloguing, "text-mining" (a variant of "data-mining"), and the use of temporally and spatially broad-range content analysis.[4] My aim is not to deny the huge variation in motives and applications that are fueling the current vogue for computation, and neither is it to catalogue in minute detail the wide panoply of different techniques available to digital humanists. There will be an inevitable flattening of approaches in the analysis that follows, and I recognize that individual practitioners of the trends I critique often have laudable motives, and often combine their quantitative researches with qualitative finesse. Nonetheless, my aim is to identify and disassemble an ambient mood in the humanities, one that hangs over what is an admittedly catholic set of analytical procedures.

What I place myself in qualified opposition to here is thrusting, confident, often garlanded with money, and finds an especially welcoming home in those largely private universities that snap at the heels of the very top tier of institutions of higher learning, a tier still dominated in the United States by the Ivy League. Yale and Cornell were at the forefront of some of the more radical trends in theory prior to the emergence of the new orthodoxy discussed in this chapter, although they have since largely laid down the banner. In the United Kingdom, University College London has found an especially entrepreneurial advocate for hyperpositivist methods in Semir Zeki, who has put fMRI scans to use to explain the neuronal basis of aesthetic appreciation. His faith—for it is a faith—in the easy commensurability of aesthetics and neurology is best expressed, without further comment, in his claim that "the overall function of art is an extension of the function of the brain."[5] It is far harder to generalize about Cambridge and Oxford, the postfeudal structures of which generally militate against popular movements and fads; nonetheless, the presence of a "Digital Humanities Network" at Cambridge no doubt heralds things to come.[6] This growing equation of the quantitative with the professional makes Jonathan Gottschall's claim that the "young scholars . . . who should be questioning the yellowing scripts of their seniors dare not do so"[7] all the more questionable: there is no doubt a quanta of *jouissance* to be extracted from positioning oneself in a rebellious minority.

Although this chapter is principally negative (if not, I hope, emptily polemical), I will nonetheless give a glimpse of what I think an alternative, progressive trajectory in literary analysis might look like, a trajectory that will take greater shape in the chapters to follow. In doing so, I make clear my conviction that the technology as such—the scanners, digital records, and fMRI machines, the archival websites—is not at fault; far from it. The slimmest adherence to a historical materialist perspective, of which I am more than guilty, must convince that technological advancement almost always has a progressive and enlightening potential, even if such advancement is, in actuality, put to a less consequential use. There are undoubtedly highly significant ways in which data mining or patterning may be incorporated into humanities scholarship, and the truly profound benefits of the digitization of decaying archives hardly need restating.

My argument here will proceed through two case studies of digital approaches to literature, the first by Franco Moretti of the Stanford "Literary Lab" and the second by Stephen Ramsay of the University of Virginia, with a middle section drawing out the lessons of the undeservedly unfashionable Louis Althusser for any philosophically responsible approach to the epistemology of the humanities, to textual history and to the mutations of literary form. Moretti, in particular, will be shown to have committed to an often uncritical positivism at the very moment that he affirms an apparently critical *historicism,* albeit one that has come to place, in the manner that Althusser detected in the historicisms of his time—an inflated methodology where theory in its fullest and most useful sense once lay.[8] The firm linkage between a quasi-teleological historicism and the rise of the neo-positivists will, as a result, be a central preoccupation of this chapter. Ramsay has attempted to construct a genuine critical theory of quantitative methods in the literary humanities, one that resists the attempt to squeeze the digital turn into a narrowly empiricist frame. Even as I think we can learn much from his account of "algorithmic criticism," I will show that his constructions of criticism and science are both too abstract and underdetermined. Both scholars are of significant learning and influence, and my critique of their work here is not meant to be a "singling out." Rather, they strike me as especially symptomatic and thoughtful examples of a much broader and often less impressive trend.

I will both build on and distance myself from many of the extant critiques of the neo-positivisms accumulating in journals and in the academic presses in recent years. While the limits of space prevent me from comprehensively engaging with most of the readings published to date, I think it's fair to say that a majority have fallen into two broadly defined categories. The first laments the loss of humanist sensitivity in the face of technological anonymity, pitting a renewed, broadly neo-romantic aestheticism and recharged humanism against the growth of number crunching,[9] while the second understands the proliferation of positivist methods as another face of the neo-liberalization and corporatization of the university. This is not to say, of course, that the two aren't frequently combined.

My reservations about the first approach will become clear in my comments below about humanism and historicism. The latter argument is best summarized by a single quote from a panel, blessed with the pleasingly ominous title "The Dark Side of the Digital Humanities," that took place at the Modern Language Association convention in Boston in January 2013. The comment comes from Wendy Hui Kyong Chun of Brown University: "The humanities are sinking—if they are—not because of their earlier embrace of theory or multiculturalism, but because they have capitulated to a bureaucratic technocratic logic."[10] Chun is quick to defend aspects of the digital humanities that are not so easily mapped onto this broader attack on the corporatization of the university, but the pithiness of her perspective serves my purposes. I sympathize entirely with Chun's materialist optic, although what I will attempt here is much broader and more philosophical in its scope. Put simply, I wish to challenge the model of scientific rationality that underpins much that comes under the banner of the digital humanities and its cognate frameworks, a challenge that will actively seek alternative models, proposed in germinal form here and arrayed across the chapters to come, for thinking the scientificity of literary theory and criticism. This certainly isn't to say that practitioners of the digital humanities haven't considered the perils of scientism: Stephen Ramsay, my interlocutor in the latter third of this chapter, has been especially explicit in his contention that what he calls an algorithmic approach to literature "deforms" its objects, all the better, however, to open them out to pluralistic interpretative agendas.[11]

But such concessions leave intact the underlying epistemology that precedes them, or, at best, fail to consider the crucial conflict between the methodology employed and the wider, catholic form of interpretation argued for; this is the flaw that most undermines Stephen Ramsay's otherwise perspicacious work. But neither is what follows an attack on scientific rationality as such. Even as proponents of literary-critical positivisms so often falsely accuse critical theorists of disdaining science,[12] the crux of my argument here is that the vision of science upheld by the New Positivists is ahistorical and Anglo-centric in its theoretical assumptions (if not in its choice of data), and inadequate for dealing with formal objects such as literary and cultural texts, an inadequacy that should, but rarely does, put into question its very status as science if the latter is understood in its full complexity.

Why should this matter to those outside the walls of academe, or to those academics outside humanities departments? At least in the period following World War II, academia in Western Europe and the United States served as a haven, a laboratory of sorts, for the development of critical perspectives that, while often recondite and ponderous, took aim at the ramping up of capital accumulation occurring outside.[13] Of course, conditions in contemporary academia preclude one even speaking of a threatening "outside" to the university; as has been extensively documented, not least in the critiques of the digital humanities as neoliberalism just mentioned, the university now is frequently little more than a polite, more "cultured" site of a familiar drive to profit and expropriation.[14] One possible way, nonetheless, to clear a space for any light at the end of the tunnel is to more fully understand the predicament we're in, and to see how the latest trends in the humanities may be worsening a problem they set out to solve.

Moretti

The influence and prestige of Franco Moretti hardly needs restating. For those of us with a passion for Marxist literary history and criticism, Moretti is something of a paragon. His *Signs Taken for Wonders* is deservedly considered a classic of critical, comparative historical scholarship, one that engages literature not as a self-enclosed form preserved in aspic, but as a dynamic process that opens onto a reflection upon, and an urge to change, the conditions that serve or try to block its emergence.[15] Moretti's turn to quantitative methods, and his accompanying commitment to "distant reading," or the graphing of multiple sources of historical literary consumption in the place of the close reading of a small canon, has already provoked a slew of commentary—some of it positive and a significant portion less so.

Of the latter, the most persuasive critique to date has been authored by Christopher Prendergast, a careful essay published in the same journal, the *New Left Review* (*NLR*), that first hosted Moretti's three-part article "Graphs, Maps and Trees." The latter essays by Moretti will be my principal focus in this section, but I'd first like to lay out how and why my criticisms are distinct from most of those published since the original appearance of "Graphs, Maps and Trees" in *NLR* in 2005. Prendergast provides the most distinguished example of a critique that has since been reiterated in varying forms,[16] and I will contrast my approach with his as a result, while nonetheless agreeing with many of his conclusions. To preview, I contend that Moretti has adopted such an anemically empiricist and partial *definition* of science that science per se, in all its richness and heterodoxy, to say nothing of literature, suffers under his lights. Prendergast, and many of his fellow critics, have limited themselves to uncovering the aporia in Moretti's logic, of which there are many, but my broader case here will concern the glancing generalizations about the objects and purposes of literature that underlie Moretti's project and that render it especially symptomatic of a much broader tendency in the contemporary academy.

For Prendergast, the signal flaw in Moretti's appeal to the natural sciences for a model of literary history is his refusal to provide full, philosophical argumentation for his reduction of literary consumption to a singular model developed for quite different purposes. Each of Moretti's essays takes a branch of empirical social or natural science as a freestanding model for a new literary history, one that would, in its final synthesis, resist what he laments as the previous dominant trend of close reading, apparently limited to a selected few canonical texts in their varying historical contexts. The three sciences appealed to are quantitative history ("Graphs," the first essay), geography ("Maps," the second), and evolutionary biology ("Trees," the third). The focus of Prendergast's critique falls largely on the third essay, where the resources of evolutionary theory are put to use in charting the "survival of the fittest" in particular literary genres over time, with the detective novel taken as a central example. (My own approach will range freely and unevenly over all three essays.) As Prendergast notes, the apparent positivist glean of Moretti's impressive visuals is quickly obscured by some basic epistemological confusions.

Prendergast objects especially to Moretti's argumentative elisions around causality, and the latter's argument that it was "likely" Conan Doyle's innovative use of the "clue" in his detective narratives, more than anything else, that allowed his novels to attain a popularity denied numerous other crime writers of his time.

As Prendergast summarizes,

> Research into the varying modalities of the clue produces a hierarchically organized "tree" on whose top branch . . . there perches, and then somewhat precariously, only Doyle. Conversely, those writers who did not hit upon this "technical law" sank without trace in the dustbin of literary history. From this account is thus extracted an implicit syllogism: Doyle was to prove the most popular of the thriller writers; Doyle comes to use clues in a uniquely special way; therefore the way he uses clues explains his enduring popularity.[17]

Prendergast is quick to question the self-evidence of this syllogism, insofar as it relies on an implicit premise—the clue as an easily generalizable formal device—that prepares its conclusions in advance. Moretti's subsequent imputation of a causal relation between the "clue" (the tantalizing signs that lead the detectives down paths both fruitful and blind) and Doyle's dominance relies on a fictive model of the average reader and their patterns of consumption, expressed by Moretti as follows: "Readers discover that they like a certain device, and if a story doesn't seem to include it, they simply don't read it (and the story becomes extinct)."[18] Moretti assumes that readers who read detective novels do so because they are singularly attracted to their "devices," to the tricks and sleights of hand by which the author produces suspense and diversion—devices that, in a circular fashion, have already been foregrounded in Moretti's sifting of the possible variables that explain his "tree." Thus, what Moretti calls the "pressure of cultural selection"[19]—the abstract law that produces success and failure over large tracks of time—is, on his account, guided by the popularity of a single formal device—an ahistorically rendered one, at that, and one that seems arbitrarily foregrounded for especial consideration.

I'll return to this construction of reading, and its attendant subjects, presently. Moretti briefly considers one other possible variable in explaining Doyle's success over others, namely the more obviously Marxist explanation of the latter's social prestige and access to wide networks of distribution, but he dismisses these as available to any number of other detective authors of the time. The confusion of correlation with causation here hardly needs stating: Moretti's location of a *correlation* between the seeming popularity of a distinctive formal device, the clue—in fact already presupposed by Moretti's analysis as its founding axiom—and the wider popularity of a particular writer is just that, a correlation, potentially even a contingency. It would require the elimination of many more alternative causal variables for Moretti's single variable to be even remotely plausible as a cause in the fullest sense. But there's a much wider problem here, one not really explored by Prendergast, which is the very philosophical model of rationality that Moretti tacitly relies on, the very manner in which he constructs the text, the reader, and the historical time in which both exist as objects of analysis.

A first, and obvious, objection on these terms would be to the distant and uniform model of literary consumption that underpins the large scale of Moretti's optic. There are, of course, multiple instances in the writing of history when one must generalize beyond the complexities of individual subjectivities; how, otherwise, to explain the power and value of Marx's *Capital*, to name only one obvious and canonical example. But Moretti makes much of his refusal of the text's permutations as a central determinant (the individual text being an object that induces irresponsible, close "interpretation," and thus a blockage to any rigorous explanation of literary diffusion over time) while skating over the question of his derivation of individual reading mentalities and habits. Effaced here is a whole history of reader-response theory and psychology that one is meant to pass over in favor of Moretti's singular variable explaining the success of Doyle over his competitors in the "struggle for survival." It's worth noting that, in Moretti's response to Prendergast's criticisms, he invokes cognitive science as the domain where this variable might be more firmly confirmed. In at least partially conceding the weakness of the explanation given for the predominance of the clue as causative variable, Moretti assures us of "a small consolation," namely that "we have an idea of what may be 'in' the box [the box used as a figure here to invoke the mystery of causation]: the mental mechanisms—perception, processing, pleasure, cognition—through which a form interacts with its environment (and whose clarification may well come . . . from cognitive science)."[20] The light-footed manner in which Moretti switches his scientific allegiances here, from evolutionary theory to cognitivism, should make us wary.

To raise again Moretti's appeal to readers' appetites for the trickeries of detective fiction, one must wonder whether a vicarious appetite for the description of crime might not be an equally convincing subjective explanation. The point is that any number of explanations of this type are plausible, whether buttressed by the cognitive sciences or not, and one is surely unable to fully adjudicate without reference to the dense specificities of individual texts as they *coagulate over time into a genre.* To restrict oneself to the strictly extratextual is to disbar a potential answer to the complex questions of readerly subjectivity, and its multiply instantiated interactions with, and transformations of, the text in question, the text that in any theoretical framework deserving of the designator "literary" must surely be granted some autonomy and efficacy of its own, no matter how decentered, striated, or contradictory one might conceive it as being.

Moretti would wish to highlight in defense what he calls the "nonhomogeneous geography"[21] of his world-systems approach, where a nonunified space of analysis, in principle worldly in scope, meets multiple temporalities, all drawn together to reorient what might be meant by the contested term "world literature."[22] In the third essay, Moretti tracks the development of free indirect style in modern narrative across both spatial and temporal axes, from 1800 to 2000. The style, understood as an instance of literary form especially amenable to cross-spatial and cross-temporal analysis, is tracked as its modus operandi shifts from the "'objective' pole of its tonal scale"[23] to, dated around 1900 and part of the buildup to high modernism, its utilization in the exploration of the singular or the radically subjective. Moretti demurs from offering any real explanation of the shifts that he neutrally charts, ranging from the "silent, interiorized *doxa* of large-nation states" to the "noisy, *multi*-personal 'chorus'"[24] of the global South; the explanation provided leans heavily on the idea of the "dependence of morphological novelty on spatial discontinuity,"[25] which is to say the apparent necessity of an increasingly large and diffuse space of distribution for the fullest mutation of a style or device.

No doubt Moretti wishes this aspect of his quantitative project, the point where literary form at least gets a look in, to quell any skepticism as to his lack of care for the singularity of literature, what makes it a distinct cultural object.[26] Here there are no appeals to a privileged variable as the prime cause of a historical trend, as in the example of the detective novel above. Instead, one reads of the "perpetual uncertainty between history and form."[27] It may well be symptomatic that such a tone of caution creeps into Moretti's discourse at the moment at which he considers the up-close ambiguities of form as it shifts historically. But one should ask again whether the spatial and/or temporal correlation of a particular version of a literary style's emergence tells us much about *why* it emerges at that particular time and in that particular space. To get those answers would surely mean shortening the distance of one's gaze so as to understand the specificities of the political and historical moment in question; it would also mean resorting to a close reading of the texts in question, if only to clarify what the form or device being tracked across time and space *is*, and, just as importantly, how it interacts with other devices and styles within the same literary object, an interaction that is as important in judging the specificity of the original device in question as it is in clarifying its relationship to the others that surround it.

The New Positivism and New Historicism

In his rejection of close reading, disdained as a "secular theology" emanating from New Haven,[28] Moretti joins a significant minority in contemporary literary studies, gathering pace at least the end of the 1980s. As the New Historicism lapsed into something resembling the "old," the kaleidoscope of significance and a-significance, sense and non-sense generated at the level of the sentence faded just as starkly as on the more recent impress of digital techniques. This was not because the New Historicism explicitly disavowed the close reading of texts, but because it tended to pursue close reading only as a means to access the cultural variables that could subsequently be foregrounded at the expense of the text itself. Moretti is keen to endorse this eclipse of close reading. As he wrote in an essay responding to criticisms of his article "Conjectures on World Literature," "'Formalism without close reading' . . . I can't think of a better definition."[29]

One might respond that it was exactly close reading that made the various sins of the older formalisms (their holism and organicism especially)[30] potentially redeemable. It's worth pondering also whether what Moretti has achieved can be considered a formalism in any meaningful sense. To what extent does graphing the temporal and spatial distribution of a commodity count as a formalism if such a graphing pays no mind to the internal ambiguities of the form in question, the very ways in which that form is *formative* at the level of the sentence, the paragraph, the stanza, and so on? The analysis of free indirect style in the third essay perhaps comes closest to acknowledging the ramifications of form, what Moretti calls its "morphology," but in that instance what is tracked is the different uses of a form over space and time, rather than a theoretically precise construction of what that form *is* in textual terms and how it reforms itself not just over the large canvas of time that Moretti focuses on, but within the equally teeming borders of a single text, perhaps even a single sentence, line, or stanza, to say nothing of the transformations of that intimate level of form as it submits to and reconfigures the pressures of historical time.

Moretti's global positivism is only one star in a much wider constellation. Since the irruption of New Historicism,[31] the fine-grained mutations of a sentence in a novel or the subtle shift of rhythm in a poem have been much less likely to be invoked as the clue, no doubt one of many, that might give us a sense of its efficacy, or the ways in which it resists, rather than simply mirrors, its surrounding cultural and historical determinants. Instead, every possible causative variable outside the actual materiality of the *text* has been polemically foregrounded. There are reasons for this internal to the original theoretical manifestos that laid out the New Historicist stall. In his influential essay "Towards a Poetics of Culture," Stephen Greenblatt insists on the creed as a "practice" rather than a "doctrine," implicitly enjoining us to leave behind endless theoretical navel-gazing. Indeed, he makes much of his previous unwillingness to live or die by theoretical precepts, preferring instead to "go about and do [literary work], without establishing first exactly what my theoretical position is."[32]

There's something a little *belle-lettrist* in all this, resisting the vulgarizations of literature that inevitably come from its rigorous analysis. But presuming that Greenblatt believes that at least some positive theoretical reflection is necessary if literary study is not to repeat the errors of the "old" historicism, however they may be defined, it is nonetheless symptomatic that such a sketching out as is to be found in the essay is principally negative, reacting against other, more elaborately defined theoretical approaches. Of Fredric Jameson's cultural Marxism, Greenblatt writes: "History functions . . . as a convenient anecdotal ornament upon a theoretical structure, and capitalism appears not as a complex social and economic development in the West but as a malign philosophical principle."[33] What Greenblatt has overlooked here is that Jameson, far from merely paying lip service to history in the service of a broader theoretical abstraction, is precisely in the business of carefully rethinking what "history" might actually mean after the critiques of history as historicism that one finds in Althusser and elsewhere,[34] more about which anon. There may well be a problem with Jameson's thinking of history, insofar as it tends toward thinking history as a pregnant absence to be mentioned only in the terms of its uncanny effects, but it is certainly never anecdotal; that is surely Greenblatt's cross to bear.

That New Historicism generally, and Greenblatt in particular, have at least rhetorically resisted the lures of a totalized understanding of historical context is without question, but what remains, as unapologetically anecdotal as it so frequently is, lacks a sufficient sense of its a priori theoretical investments. Jameson himself has referred to this obscuring of a priori theoretical commitments as an insistence on immanence over the transcendence of abstract analysis and interpretation, even as transcendent principles—not least the very transcendentality of the injunction to reject the transcendental—persist beneath the cover of darkness. It might even be possible to refer to the very latest positivisms as just one more mutation in this process of the denial of the transcendental, using the digital technologies to, as Jameson puts it apropos of New Historicism, "keep the mind involved in detail and immediacy,"[35] the better to disbar the ungainly abstractions of theory proper.

It is, at any rate, the disavowal of the inevitability of a claim to the transcendental behind any interpretative act whatsoever that has, perhaps, produced in New Historicism its attraction to another internally heterogeneous school, the digital humanities, that has similarly made a virtue of its "detail" and eclecticism. Each relies on a vision of context often radically different in scale and composition, but both are nonetheless prone to what Dominick LaCapra has usefully described as "overcontextualization," a process that "often occludes the problem of the very grounds on which to motivate a selection of pertinent contexts . . . The farther back one goes in time, the less obvious the contexts informing discourse tend to become, and the more difficult it may be . . . to reconstruct them."[36] The "grounds" that LaCapra invokes are at least quasi-transcendental, insofar as they act as one of many conditions of possibility for the interpretation that results. Even as Moretti multiplies the possible scales, temporal and spatial, within which context may be constructed, their permeability to analysis is rarely questioned; instead, one gets a sense of the alluring and easy transparency afforded by the sharp technological lenses at his disposal. As he writes, "Distant reading, I have called this work elsewhere; where distance is however not an obstacle, but a *specific form of knowledge*: fewer elements, hence a sharper sense of their overall interconnection. Shapes, relations, structures. Patterns."[37] By contrast, it may be worth considering once again how obstacles can be productive; how the self-enclosure of a text, its formal indifference or even resistance to its context, might be the very source of its power. I'll have cause to consider a rather different account of the benefits of obstructive constraint in my reading of Stephen Ramsay below, and the productivity of formal constraints will emerge as a signal theme across the book as a whole.

Moretti has more recently, in an essay titled "Operationalizing," described the benefits of such digital techniques with reference to their "precision." As he writes, such techniques are "new" insofar as they are "precise."[38] Describing the process of measuring the space given over to certain characters in narrative texts, Moretti claims that this may "make some concepts 'actual,'"[39] or render a hypothesis as to the centrality to a novel's plot of a character or set of characters provable or disprovable. Moretti describes a similar technique used to measure the number of interactions that a character has with other characters in a given narrative. Even as he quotes the French philosopher of science Alexandre Koyré in the service of his argument, a philosopher for whom such questions are defined by the internal conceptual modulations of a particular science faced with the difficulties of its chosen objects, he risks missing how the kind of theoretical precision necessary for the analysis of a literary text may well be different from those of more empirically oriented disciplines.

Moretti, to be fair, has recently acknowledged (in the "Operationalizing" essay just cited) that, unlike the physical sciences, ideas in literary study move from theory to object; there is no ideal moment of neutral observation prior to the construction of analytical concepts. This recognition is, no doubt, an advance on the earlier, full-blown empiricism that conditioned "Graphs, Maps, Trees," although I would wish to emphasize in turn the dialectical movement across and between these different moments, neither of which can be said to fully stabilize into the poles of a dichotomy. What Moretti calls "operationalization," the activation of concepts in an empirical technique, "turns abstractions into a clear and, hopefully, unexpected elaboration of reality."[40] But one wonders about the resistance to "operationalization" itself, to such a conscription in an empirical analysis, a push-back that literary texts may be especially capable of. Such an approach would need to acknowledge that "precision," at least in literary studies, may well require the recognition of and reconciliation with the ambiguity, even the undecidability that the new digital techniques threaten to mute.

Texts when viewed from a distance, then, seem attractively delineable and open to analysis, as mere coordinates on a map, lacking in resistance to their enrollment in webs of historical causation, even as those webs are described, at least for the New Historicists, as conflicted, power-laden, nonunitary, in a rhetorical dressing that draws sparingly from Foucault. Rarely have questions been asked of late about the epistemological problem of aligning empirical history with the difficult formal terrain of a text's inner productivity, its dissimulations and readerly reproductions, its retroactive refigurations of its grounds (although the likes of Hayden White stand as powerful exceptions);[41] if Moretti's quantitative fireworks are one way to deny the actuality of a text, to dim its speculative resources, this fetishization of "context" is surely another. I would go so far as to suggest that, in its valorization of the "anecdote" or the especially particular historical detail, New Historicism has simply served to reverse the tacit assumption of older historicisms: where once it was the broadly conceived cultural and political surroundings that explained the contours of a cultural object, now it is frequently a single event or moment that is worked from within in order to explain a whole plethora of emergent cultural forms, forms thus denuded, as in the old historicism, of their formativeness, their capacity in the last instance to at least partially override their determining coordinates. The latest and most extreme expression of this is the growth of conferences and books that take a single year as their focus, the assumption being that it is enough to make the general emerge out of the particular in order to avoid the smothering of the particular by the universal.[42]

Back once again to Moretti, who takes a certain rhetorical pleasure in asserting his own particular kind of quantitative antihumanism—"human history is so seldom history," he quips in the third "Graphs, Maps, Trees" essay.[43] One can detect, nonetheless, a residual, "contextualizing" humanism that grounds his approach to history, one that seems stubbornly to have refused, as in Greenblatt, the lessons of the critiques of historicism that characterized the best of critical theory in the twentieth century. While the appeals that Moretti makes to Fernand Braudel in the first essay suggest that a broadly structural, cyclical vision of history will prove the most amenable to his aims, one finds, as his argument progresses, repeated appeals to a most teleological vision of correlation, even causation, between the consumption of differing literary genres and their historical importance.

Without specifying his analytical methodology (again, what understanding of readerly subjectivity is assumed here?), Moretti writes: "When one genre replaces another, it's reasonable to assume that the cause is internal to the two genres, and historically specific: amorous epistolary fiction being ill-equipped to capture the traumas of the revolutionary years, say—and gothic novels being particularly good at it."[44] The problem here is not so much the causal reductiveness of this explanation; there will always be an element of reduction in any attempt to make a causal connection across such broad swaths of space and time, and reduction is not in itself an obstacle to nuanced analysis—indeed, it is sometimes its necessary condition. Neither is the problem the immediate assignation of causality to what seems to be a mere correlation, although the move is far too quickly made. Rather, it's the tacit, humanistic assumption that history progresses toward a *goal*, cultural form perspiring on cue to changes in the political temperature—changes that are to be charted from the perspective of their already having *happened*, and thus, one may say, from the purview of the victors.

There's an irony to be detected in Moretti's admonition that literary academics should avoid the temptations of German and French metaphysics;[45] arguably, it is an implicit Hegelianism that fills in the gaps in causal explanation that riddle Moretti's analysis. Moretti defends himself from such accusations by highlighting the equal importance of divergence as well as convergence in his analysis, which is to say the equal analytical weight placed on moments of disparity as well as parity in the distribution of literary trends. As he writes during his discussion of detective fiction, "Is divergence a factor, in literary history? These first findings suggest a cautious Yes."[46] But to measure the reversal of a teleology is not to undermine the assumptions on which that teleology is built. Divergence as it is understood in evolutionary theory, whereby populations gradually accrue differences over time, seems fated to lapse into a negative teleology when wrenched into the service of literary history.

Consider the interpretation of the aforementioned Braudel's historiography that peppers Moretti's first essay. There Braudel is described as offering a vision of the *longue durée* that is "all structure and no flow," structures serving to "introduce repetition into history, and hence regularity, order, pattern."[47] Other scales of analysis when filtered through Braudel offer Moretti the sense of fluidity that this emphasis on structure may otherwise preclude. But Braudel and the *Annales* school are not immune, in their use of apparently new scales of historical analysis, to the teleological errors of previous historicisms; as Miriam Cooke has phrased it, Braudel's work is characterized by a tension between "the teleology of temporal fixity and the randomness of spatial fluidity," with teleology "winning out in the end."[48] As she also notes, this has much to do with Braudel's importation of a sense of a broader historical permanence and linearity associated especially with the resonant figure of the Mediterranean and derived from the structure of the Greek epic as its necessarily occluded origin. One may speculate that the telescoping capacities of the digital make this kind of quasi-dialectical history—from structure and fixity to fluidity and back again—especially attractive to the New Positivisms, providing as it does readymade frames within which to slot endlessly proliferating data. But there is none of the true plasticity of the dialectic in this shuttling back and forth between fixed coordinates, a shuttling that seems to fix the poles in place that it might otherwise seek to overcome.

Moretti goes on to argue that the simultaneous disappearance of a cluster of literary forms can be explained in terms of the succession of generations, of the replacement of one generation's cultural tastes with that of another. But again, while it may well be true that different generations will consume different cultural products, why one genre rather than another should be appreciated by specific generations, in all their internal multiplicity, is not answered by the fragile correlations established by the research of Moretti and his collaborators. One may think of this, again, in terms of scales of analysis.[49] Moretti remains at such an abstract scale, of reified patterns of consumption and distribution, that he is prevented in advance from being able to understand the more obscure kinds of cultural forms that pool between the cracks of their ostensible networks of distribution. "Books survive if they're read and disappear if they aren't," Moretti claims,[50] but what he really means to say is that the expanding *market*, under certain historical conditions, supported the sale of some books over others at different times and under different conditions.

Prendergast is on point, then, when he tasks Moretti with treating the market as an equivalent, within the realm of culture, of the nature that is the concern of evolutionary science, assuming in turn a similar predictability to evolutionary patterns in literary history.[51] And here one encounters another parallel between the new digital positivisms and the New Historicism, namely the reliance on the language of the market in place of a refined and precise analytical language proper to the complexities of literary texts; as Prendergast notes of Greenblatt, "History itself is conceived . . . through models and metaphors to do with the market, the social as a space of transactions or deals between players in the marketplace."[52] Suffice to invoke Marx, again, on the tendency to naturalize the "insights" of one discourse (in his example, political economy, in Moretti's case quantitative modeling) as if they were unproblematically generalizable across craggy, unsurpassable discursive borders. But even to stick to the positivist model that Moretti endorses, one would need a more tiered and mediated account of how global consumption *influences* markets as much as it is led by them to make good a number of the claims that Moretti advances.

Emily Apter is surely right when she laments the "dangling participle" in Moretti's world-systems approach to the diffusion of global literatures, the favoring of "narrative over linguistic engagement" and the lack of "an approach that would valorize textual closeness while refusing to sacrifice distance,"[53] but the problem is a far wider one, one that pertains to now-dominant constructions of history, text, and method in the humanities. As unlikely as it may seem, it could be of use to resurrect Althusser's stringent critique of teleological historicisms and positivisms in order to access the broader ramifications of the shift in academic culture that Moretti embodies in impressive miniature.

Althusser and the Limits of Moretti's "Materialism"

If Moretti's vision of quantitative, large-scale analysis seems predicated on an unapologetically empiricist, if not quite positivist, variant of scientific rationality, what alternative models might one appeal to if one is not to lapse into prior humanisms or reject entirely the appeal in humanities scholarship to the resources of science? Implicitly, Moretti's impatient positivism imposes a forced choice: either the testable insights of broad-brush quantificatory analysis, or a muddle-headed, idealist textual solipsism that reifies the individual book over its multiple contextual histories. But there are other ways of approaching the scientificity of literary form and history that refuse such a binary and that significantly deepen what might be meant by literary-critical rationality. Jonathan Gottschall refers to such previous attempts as "authentic antisciences" that have "inoculate[d] themselves against negative evidence."[54] But what kind of "evidence" is particular to the field of literary forms, and might it be the neo-positivists such as Gottschall that have imposed on culture epistemic models that smother its complex internal nature—silencing, in other words, what might make it a distinct object for a kind of scientific appraisal and analysis?

In *Reading Capital*, Althusser outlines with some precision what he takes to be the central philosophical error of empiricism as it is applied to the science of history. In doing so, he constructs his own account of how objects and subjects of scientific knowledge relate. "Knowledge," Althusser writes, "never, as empiricism desperately demands it should, confronts a *pure object* which is then identical to the *real object* of which knowledge aimed to produce precisely . . . the knowledge [of]."[55] Knowledge is never the simple transposition of predicates or essences from a single, stable object in the world to a progressively unfolding, external account of its unchanging structure, a structure lying passively in wait for discovery. Rather, "knowledge working on its 'object' . . . does not work on the *real* object but on the peculiar raw material, which constitutes, in the strict sense of the term, *its 'object.'* . . . That raw material is ever-already, in the strong sense Marx gives it in *Capital*, a *raw material*, i.e., matter already elaborated and transformed, precisely by the imposition of the complex (sensuous-technical-ideological) structure which constitutes it as an *object of knowledge*."[56]

There is a profound argument here that sidesteps the false choice of a full-blown empiricism or a full-blown rationalism, an argument that the undue haste with which Althusser's exposition proceeds may tempt us to overlook. For Althusser, the object of knowledge is always already, from the moment that one approaches it scientifically, an *impure* object, neither "real" in the sense of being empirically self-present, symmetrically situated in an empirical field external to the subject, nor Platonically pure, absolutely abstracted from the "raw material" of the empirical field. "Raw material," for Althusser, is another name for the messiness, the impurity that all knowledge is confronted with and that scientific processes of purification can never fully expunge; indeed, to expunge that impurity would be to confront the scientific method with its exhaustion. One must be cautious here; Althusser is very far from endorsing the commonsensical, humanist view that conceptual rationality is compromised and humbled by the density of the phenomenal world. Rather, scientific conceptuality must itself bear and incorporate the internal, dialectical impurity of the objects that it analyzes.

Thus, the labor of science is, by definition, never over; it is, as Gaston Bachelard averred, something that has no absolute purity of origin; it is something that "continues but never 'begins.'"[57] To have ever "begun" would suggest an orientation to an ending, the implicit teleology of which discounts in advance the constitutive complexities with which scientific knowledge must deal, and that are re-produced and refined by their conscription within a scientific project. Parenthetically, it is within the epistemological dynamism of Bachelard and Althusser's take on the elasticity and impurity of scientific form that later, so-called poststructuralist accounts of the impossibility of absolute origins, as much as absolute ends, are to be found.[58]

Here, one may usefully supplement Claire Colebrook's recent reflections on Paul de Man's brand of materialism, a materialism that was "neither empirical—that is, available to experience—nor ideal (a consequence of the human organism's way of mapping its world)."[59] By the same token, Althusser's epistemology would wish us to dialecticize our understanding of scientific knowing in a manner that refuses either strong constructivism—scientists construct their object of knowledge even as they think they are receiving its truths empirically—or Moretti-like positivism, where the efficacy and agency of the object itself is discounted in favor of its statistical capture, its passive inscription in a technological or teleological apparatus. Rather, texts on an Althusserian account sit always in complex relation with multiple intersecting fields of ideological, empirical, and conceptual forces, forces that are, in turn, *refigured*, no doubt often ineffectually or incompletely, by the text's own internal resources of speculative possibility.

Such intersecting, impure fields are irreducible to what Greenblatt's New Historicism would wish to call "context," a term that, for all New Historicism's attempts to distance itself from a notion of unitary historical causality, nonetheless implies a more or less symmetrical division between a text and its surrounding determinants, and a retrospective causality moving from culture to word. This is not, again, to suggest that Greenblatt and his collaborators have self-consciously produced a reified, unified vision of historical causation; far from it. But the anecdotal eclecticism that is the true final product of much New Historicist scholarship does little to avoid what Greenblatt himself, erroneously and fatally, accuses Marxism of, namely invoking capitalism (or, indeed, any historical context) as a "unitary demonic principle."[60] The Marx that emerges in Althusser as well as in Jameson and others is precisely a thinker of the heterogeneity and nontotalizability of any historical moment or conjuncture. But such thinkers are also keen to grant the *object* of contextualization its due, its right to be contradictory and uncanny and difficult, in dialectically reforming the "context" that is, from a certain angle, the (Aristotelian) material cause of its existence.

Althusser's predecessor in this dynamic philosophy of science, Gaston Bachelard, phrased this dialectical productivity of the object of the scientific gaze in its agonistic duel with its "context" as follows: "We must first posit the object as a subject of the problem, and the subject of the cogito as a consciousness of a problem."[61] To translate this into my terms, the object is always subject to a "problematic," to a field of forces, forces that help make and remake that object over time. The object will, in turn, subjectify, or at least alter, the forces in question in such a way that any clean separation of the knowing subject and the passive object evades in principle the dynamic, dialectical interchange between object and field, text and world. One may evoke once again, here, the notion of "scales" of analysis. For while Moretti may protest that this textual-dynamic approach to the scientific apprehension of literature excludes his explicit focus and intent, namely the global, extratextual mutations of cultural distribution and consumption over time, the opposite is the case. Imagine, for instance, a study, using all of the tools of scalar computation available to us, which combines the close reading of a text's internal contradictions with an external study of the quantitative *and* qualitative shifts that aided its composition, shifts that are put in sharp relief again upon the text's own multiple interventions into the interpretive communities in which it subsists. Such a study would need to underline rather than efface the productive disjunction between qualitative and quantitative methodologies, the fault line between the gathering of data and the actualization of literary form that occurs on its being read.

There are, of course, scholars who have attempted precisely such a creative combination, albeit without the critical epistemology that I gesture to here. One thinks of Jahan Ramazani's masterful *A Transnational Poetics*, in which there is no disabling contradiction—only an enabling one—between the attentive close reading of individual texts and the mapping of their temporal and spatial trajectories.[62] One could mention a plethora of other texts. But such works often seem a little too complacent in their assumption that the ideological trappings that cling to positivist analysis can be dispelled purely and only by telescoping back and forth from close to distant reading; I noted another version of that telescoping earlier in Moretti's stalled dialectic of temporal structure and spatial fluidity. In the final section of this chapter, and in advance of launching more fully into the positive literary-theoretical claims that will occupy us for the rest of this book, I'll turn to the work of someone who has more responsibly than most raised precisely these questions of the disjuncture between literary-critical interpretation and the quantitative process of data analysis, albeit in a way that, in the final analysis, falls short of its commendable goals.

Reading Machines—On Stephen Ramsay

The publication in 2011 of Stephen Ramsay's *Reading Machines: Toward an Algorithmic Criticism* heralded a significant advance on previous critical and theoretical reflections on the digital humanities. Ramsay, in contrast to Moretti, wishes to advance a theory of digital humanities practice that is attentive to the epistemological peculiarities of its object, to the productive gap between quantitative positivisms and the formal ambiguities of literary language. His aim, as he writes, is to "locate a hermeneutics at the boundary between mechanism and theory,"[63] which is to say in the interstice between the boosted methodologies of the digital and the prior, conceptually oriented critical humanities, with their emphasis on textual undecidability, the motivations of gender and race, and on the multiple meanings produced by the juxtaposition of different literary devices. Ramsay is important to our account insofar as he wishes to save digital interpretation via the very critical-theoretical claims that, I have been arguing, the digital humanities risk brushing aside.

Ramsay's approach is, to be sure, substantially informed by the earlier work of Lisa Samuels and Jerome McGann. The latter have influentially advocated for what they call the interpretative "deformance" of a textual work, for the ways in which the rearrangement, diagramming, or foregrounding of certain nonsemantic aspects of the work over others reveals "how its pretensions to meaning are not so much a function of ideas as of style."[64] Such an argument is premised on the claim that all interpretation is, at least to some degree, a replacement of the original text with a new one. Critics, as Ramsay has it, "who endeavor to put forth a 'reading' puts forth not the text, but a new text in which the data bas been paraphrased, elaborated, selected, truncated, and transduced."[65] Ramsay would wish to highlight the ways in which quantitative methods perform their own "defacement" of literary texts, opening those texts to what remains a fundamentally subjective, subsequent practice of interpretation. As such, the "algorithmic criticism" that Ramsay advocates for is one that uses quantitative methods for ends that are assuredly not to be located in the narrow digital parameters that define the mere beginnings of such a process.

Underpinning Ramsay's theory is the notion that "the digital revolution, for all its wonders, has not penetrated the core activity of literary studies, which . . . remains mostly concerned with the interpretative analysis of written cultural artifacts."[66] Instead, the radical disjunction between what could be called the quantitative ontology of digital methodologies and the subtleties and nuances of literary analysis must be admitted, even if the former may give us access to aspects of the latter that were up to now unavailable. Digital textual analysis, then, "must endeavor to assist the critic in the unfolding of interpretative possibilities."[67] The evidence that might be accrued from the data mining of texts and so on "is not definitive, but suggestive of grander arguments and schemes."[68] The technology available to the digital humanist interested, for instance, in crisscrossing discourses of gender in the fiction of Virginia Woolf (an example employed by Ramsay himself, as will be discussed below) may take advantage of the "rigidly holistic"[69] manner in which computation transforms the text, allowing a sound empirical assessment of repeated phrasings and words, the better to ground the necessarily speculative work of interpretation to come. "It is one thing," Ramsey avers, "to notice patterns of vocabulary, variations in line length, or images of darkness and light; it is another thing to employ a machine that can unerringly discover every instance of such features across a massive corpus of literary texts."[70]

At the root of this argument is the thesis that the artificial constraints of computation, stripping away the usual boundaries of the text within which multiple interpretative strategies usually bloom, is paradoxically enabling, allowing less obvious meanings to emerge across multiple sources. Such constraints, compared elsewhere in the book to the formal experiments of Raymond Queneau and the Oulipo group, are rendered equivalent to "what the Russian Formalists called *ostranenie*—the estrangement and defamiliarization of textuality."[71] For Ramsay, "the narrowing constraints of computational logic—the irreducible tendency of the computer toward enumeration, measurement and verification—is [*sic*] fully compatible with the goals of criticism."[72] This is because "critical reading practices already contain elements of the algorithmic."[73] Here, Ramsay evokes again the "deformance" thesis of McGann and Samuels, whereby the very act of interpretation, in its selectivity, deforms or even re-creates the text in question. This is as true, for Ramsay, for older interpretative practices as it is for those enabled by computation.

While a cursory reading of Althusser's comments on the distinction between the real and theoretical object discussed above might suggest a striking parallel with Ramsay's claim, whereby the real object qua text is replaced by the text produced by an act of interpretation, some caution is required here. For whereas French epistemology is as concerned to emphasize the push-back of the real object on attempts to conscript it within the terms of an interpretation, a push-back memorably termed a "co-efficient of adversity" by Bachelard,[74] Ramsay, while acknowledging the fundamental discrepancy between the act of computation itself and the subsequent act of critical interpretation, nonetheless considers the gap easily and unproblematically surmountable. In bridging that gap, one gets little sense from Ramsay of how either the object itself or the critical possibilities attendant to it have changed, how the movement from a computationally enabled disfigurement to a computationally enabled critical reading have altered the internal composition of the text, not simply in an empirical sense, where one is left with data sets that bear an obvious and marked difference from the original text, but in a *theoretical* sense, where the formal possibilities available to interpretation have radically shifted. Indeed, when Ramsay gives us a glimpse of how his deformative criticism might function in practice, what results seems little different from standard liberal-humanistic content analysis. Thus, in his use of "information retrieval" to transform Woolf's *The Waves* into "lists of tokens" in order to establish the most and least distinctive words uttered by each of the novel's characters, one finds a "gender divide" among the characters in their language use, supporting the insights of numerous earlier critics.[75] Characters associated in the narrative with contemplative occupations like writing are shown to use words associated with thinking; thus, "for Bernard, the aspiring novelist who some say is modeled on Woolf herself, the top word is 'thinks.'"[76]

Here, the constraints of computation, rather than enabling a more experimental criticism, seem merely to have constrained Ramsay's critical range, allowing him only to confirm, through endless lists of information, insights already adumbrated by past close readings of Woolf's novel. That this is a symptom of what Herman Rapaport has usefully referred to as the trend to "replace interpretation with information"[77] is surely without doubt. But the reason for Ramsay's fall back on humanistic character analysis must also be related to his theoretically underdetermined notions of constraint and defamiliarization. While he makes reference to the Russian Formalists, there seems little in common between what Viktor Shklovsky referred to as the effect of "particularization" attendant to literary form, and the readily predictable deformations of the computer that so preoccupy Ramsay. Indeed, Shklovsky actively opposed what he called "generalization" in literary criticism, defined by its "creating, insofar as possible, wide-ranging, all encompassing formulas,"[78] in favor of what he called "particularization" as the essence of art. Art, on this reading, is "based on a step-by-step structure and on the particularizing of even that which is presented in a generalized and unified form."[79] It is precisely this effect of singularity, of the moment at which a text shakes loose from its context and effects a spontaneous change in the interpretative temperature, that Ramsay and Moretti's lists and graphs constitutively foreclose. Instead, they remain firmly within what Shklovsky disdains as "generalization," the straightening out of a text's formal folds, incommensurabilities, and contradictions into neatly manageable data sets.

Ramsay's analysis of the necessary disjuncture, then, between objective computation and subjective interpretation is mitigated by the recrudescent humanism that enables him to distinguish so easily between the "subjective" and the "objective" in the first place. For what Althusser, Bachelard, and Shklovsky insist on in their different ways is that any separation of subject from object is an agonistic, ongoing process, subject to the resistances of the object and to the ideological valences that color the subject's perspective and that taint, in turn, the object as it is reconstructed in practices of analysis. In shorthand, the capacious, active formalism of Althusser et al. would wish to underline the dialectical dynamism that threatens always to render impure the very distinction between subjective and objective, the establishment of such a distinction being the perpetual and always only partially successful labor of science itself. Contemporary literary studies, in its rush to embrace the reified objectivism of the digital, may have much to learn from a reconsideration of the sources of the critical theory that it seems so keen to leave behind. What should result is a speculative and critical formalism, one that respects the ambiguities and stubbornness of its objects of interpretation, objects that may prove to be less readily assimilable to the clean lines of technological positivism than has recently been assumed, even as such an approach would flinch from rejecting technology *tout court* as an aid to analysis.

The positive details of such a formalism will be outlined in the chapters that follow, but for now it is worth mentioning that, as well as attending to the multiple effects of specific literary devices when considered up close, such an approach must also take account of what Peter Osborne has adroitly called "the utopian horizon of global interconnectedness,"[80] a horizon that only capital, in its contemporary manifestation, seems able to create. This, then, would be the "distant" optic that is so often bungled in the approaches discussed above, an optic that will be explored in more depth in the conclusion. Osborne distinguishes between modernity as the periodization of avant-garde possibilities and the contemporary as the distinctly postconceptual moment of an abstract globalism. Such a globalism can "exhibit the structure of a subject (the unity of an activity) only objectively, in [its] product, separated from individual subjects and particular collectivities of labor."[81] It is surely this abstract objectivity, one that nonetheless attempts to produce a sense of the subjective as its static opposite, that one finds in differently coded forms in Moretti and Ramsay's positivisms. Ramsay, for example, uses the opposition between contemporary digital techniques and older, subjective humanisms as a means of arguing for the easy compatibility of the former with the latter. But the consequence of the positivism that underpins these new methods seems to be precisely the shallow, objectified or reified subjectivity that Osborne so acutely diagnoses, one that is deaf to the dynamic interpenetration of subjective and objective forms that mark all relatively autonomous acts of artistic production. Identifying this as a problem is the first step toward producing an alternative critical theory of the contemporary in its relation with literature, one that might truly be able to encapsulate the peculiarities of the admixture of subject and object, form and history that literary language has the potential to manifest with especial power. It is to that task that the rest of this book will turn.

2

Francis Ponge, Jean Cavaillès, and the Vexed Relation between Word and World

There is more than one way to "return to objects," to reignite the fires of realism, if indeed such a task is truly worth pursuing. The internal divisions within so-called "speculative realism," a new philosophical movement defined more by what it is against than by any shared positive content, attest to this. If the philosopher Graham Harman, the founder of "object-oriented philosophy," is concerned principally with a generalization of Kant's limitation of our access to things-in-themselves, such that it is not only humans but all objects that relate partially and incompletely with other objects,[1] the French theorist Quentin Meillassoux restricts his version of the Absolute to mathematizable primary properties, in a manner that, as Peter Hallward has observed, threatens to collapse the material makeup of a thing into its logical qualification.[2] Paul Levi Bryant, inspired by Harman, has done the most to expand an object-oriented approach to questions of politics, ethics, and aesthetics. One senses in his work a genuine and admirable fear that the expansion, once again, of philosophical attention to something like Kant's noumena may well lead to a lessening of attention to the depredations of contemporary politics, at a time when those depredations are so horrifyingly acute.[3]

No doubt the turn to the nonhuman, to the animal, to objects, to the Anthropocene, has much to do with frustration over the apparent failures of critical theory to effect fundamental change beyond the ivory tower. Alain Badiou's abstract, Platonic communism offers little succor to those of a realist or hyper-rationalist bent who would, no doubt, point to his ascetic subtraction of radical leftism from the messiness of economic relations as a further symptom of this malaise.[4] Despite this prevailing mood, I want to argue here for a critical reinvention and displacement of the modernist moment in theory, one that draws on recent structuralisms and that takes sustenance from literature, understood as a privileged means of posing the question of formalization, albeit one that, especially in its poetic guise, reveals much about the complex *failures* of forms, the better nonetheless to appreciate their efficacy. Here the apparent distance between the imperative of scientific formalization and the questions of the so-called "linguistic turn," a gap insisted on most recently by Badiou, will be put into question, even as the impossibility of collapsing the one into the other will be equally insisted on. Badiou has argued that the philosophy of language most associated with literary theory and the continental tradition in philosophy can be christened a kind of "*idealinguisterie*," or an idealist privileging of the linguistic, and as a result any contemporary materialism worth its salt would act to discredit such idealisms as its foundational move; "today it is *idealinguisterie* that the materialist assault makes into its cause."[5]

To the contrary, just as language should not be understood as merely the passive vehicle for an already existing object-world, so even less should it be construed as the ruse of finitude preventing us from accessing, à la Badiou, the infinite, the evental, the radically new. Rather, one should think of language as an immanently interleaved aspect of the world in all its moments of stasis and rupture, even and perhaps especially when language seems most solipsistically withdrawn from the possibility of reference or representation as they are commonly understood; through mimesis, in short. Language, in other words, makes its fullest contact with the world at those points at which it seems most unable to perform the representative tasks it is usually tasked with. Mimesis, of course, has a rich and complex history in literary and philosophical history, and one should note here in passing a definition of the term that comes a little closer to my position. As John D. Lyons and Stephen G. Nichols Jr. write, "The other view of mimesis does not emphasize the independent existence of the object represented, but rather focuses on the gesture of the person or subject who undertakes to displace our attention from the world of pre-existent objects to the work itself."[6] But in what follows, it is not so much a turning away from the object and onto the subject that concerns us. Rather, literary form, in its agonistic interactions with the outside world, can be said to access a similarly resistant and antimimetic logic (imagined as inherently subjective in the second view of mimesis above) to be found in the world itself; such a model of literary meaning ranges itself against mimesis in both the most common sense, whereby form merely passively mirrors content imposed on it from an external source, and in the second sense, where the subject reigns over, even serves to construct, a world whose being "in-itself," again in the Kantian sense, nonetheless remains inaccessible.

By contrast, speculative realist and object-oriented approaches, in their polemical haste, threaten to jettison crucial aspects of prior approaches in theory that give access to this paradoxical property of linguistic reference. Perhaps the most important of these is reflexivity, itself a component of form and formalization when the latter are treated expansively. Reflexivity can be said to operate at two related levels: first, it makes us, as subjects, aware of the position from which we are producing knowledge, thus alerting us to the hierarchies that our knowledge practices threaten to reproduce. The assumption of a "flat ontology" as in Bruno Latour and Bryant,[7] where every object and relation are assumed, at least potentially, to have the same ontological power or resonance, threatens to mask the hierarchies that, in advance, condition both the reality of things and the kinds of knowledge we're able to ascertain about them. Second, and at a more formal level, reflexivity attends to the impurity of the distinctions that both language *and* materiality embody and perpetuate, shared imperfections that allow the very nonmimetic interaction between language and world that is otherwise foreclosed by the nonmimetic destabilization that makes up one essential part of linguistic structure. The human/language/object/body quadrumvirate, and the awkward and asymmetrical movements between them, will thus form a central focus of my attention in this chapter.

My recognition of the commutability of linguistic and worldly boundaries will, I hope, be shown to have rather less to do with the refusal of the autonomy of objects or subjects (as per the criticisms of Latour and the "speculative realists"), and rather more to do with underlining a necessary paradox for thought, one that is enabling rather than disabling. It is, that is to say, in the precisely *non*-mimetic occlusions, impurities and slippages between the perceiving subject and the objecting object, that the fragile, relative autonomy of each may be affirmed. Jacques Lacan alighted on this notion as he developed his theory of the object proper to psychoanalysis, or more precisely his account of how object and subject interact: "The division in . . . the subject is verified in the fact that an object traverses him [*le traverse*] without them interpenetrating [*sans qu'ils se penetrant*] in any respect."[8] There is a resonance of the object on the subject, in other words, without the latter ever finally recuperating or incorporating the former in any way that would imply the mimetic representation of the object in the subject, or the subject in the object.

The same, I argue, holds true for literary language and its apparent outsides, where it is in the seeming inability of literary signs to glom entirely onto the world that a nonmimetic, agonistic relation between word and world is achieved. In a later chapter, I'll show how Paul de Man ingeniously rethought Kant's theory of the sublime, precisely to highlight this shared linguistic and material dehiscence. Here, I'll trace this affirmative formalism of the impure and the incommensurable as it travels across the sensitive poetics of Francis Ponge, as it is reformulated in the apparently severe philosophical rationalism of Jean Cavaillès, and as it is reinscribed in the parodic pseudo-romanticism of Wallace Stevens's extraordinary poem "Anecdote of the Jar." On the way, I'll have cause to consider Fredric Jameson's recent reflections on realism, and his much earlier critique of formalism, especially insofar as it engaged the work of the Russian formalist Viktor Shklovsky, first encountered in the introduction. The latter, finally, will be shown to have constructed a much more generous, capacious account of literary form than he has most often been associated with, one in significant agreement with aspects of the formalism that I am in the process of outlining in this book.

I'll begin with an analysis of Francis Ponge's prose poem "The Oyster," before turning to the underappreciated epistemological writings of Jean Cavaillès,[9] the better to appreciate how the latter's invigorating rethinking of the interaction between material objects and conceptual and linguistic structures may enrich contemporary theoretical discussions in literary theory and elsewhere around objects and form taken in the round. No doubt a reading of French poetry through and alongside formalist philosophy of science will strike the reader as eccentric, but as I hope to show, there are striking and challenging convergences between the various instances of poetic form and formalization that this book is concerned principally with tracing, and the revival of a broadly rationalist philosophy of science in France in the middle years of the twentieth century. To make such a connection is not merely of historical interest; intellectual history is not my purpose here. Rather, I hope that the view of form and formalization that emerges when Ponge and Cavaillès are read together will gain an autonomy of its own, as the first iteration of a speculative formalism that this book will, in subsequent chapters, picture anew from multiple angles.

Francis Ponge and the Poetics of Formalization

At first blush, the prose poetry of Francis Ponge, a French poet active from the 1930s to the 1970s and much loved by the French philosophical avant-garde, seems eminently "object-oriented," to evoke the currently fashionable appellation already mentioned above. Famously concerned with a poetic encounter with everyday objects, Ponge initially seems intent on subordinating the metrical complexities of verse to the neutral insistence of the object-world, such that the formal possibilities of poetry are radically tamed according to their most basic representative possibilities and in deference to material objects themselves. Nonetheless, in an interview from 1974, Ponge makes clear that his intent, to the contrary, was to revitalize poetic form through recognition of the fundamental and creative receptivity of humanity to its world. The "things themselves" on this reading, the oysters and rain and dogs and cigarettes that populate Ponge's poetic universe, are ultimately at the service of the rejuvenation of language itself, and the (human) users of it as they strain language through a uniquely human capacity of reinvention.[10] Here lies, then, no "object-oriented poetry." At least in partial accord with Husserl's phenomenology, an obvious early influence on Ponge, the object itself is downgraded in favor of the penetrating power of a transcendentally oriented frame of reception, in this case poetic language. Consider Ponge's poem "The Oyster" from 1942:

> The oyster, about as big as a fair-sized pebble, is rougher, less evenly colored, brightly whitish. It is a world stubbornly closed. Yet it can be opened: one must hold it in a cloth, use a dull jagged knife, and try more than once. Avid fingers get cut, nails get chipped: a rough job. The repeated pryings mark its cover with white rings, like haloes.
>
> Inside one finds a whole world, to eat and drink; under a *firmament* (properly speaking) of nacre, the skies above collapse on the skies below, forming nothing but a puddle, a viscous greenish blob that ebbs and flows on sight and smell, fringed with blackish lace along the edge.
>
> Once in a rare while a globule pearls in its nacre throat, with which one instantly seeks to adorn oneself.[11]

I'd like to attend to the opening line: "The oyster, about as big as a fair-sized pebble, is rougher, less evenly colored, brightly whitish." Such unassuming, declarative prose is common to Ponge. This is one instance of Ponge's concern for the "literality" of which Barbara Johnson wrote so incisively, literality intended here to convey both the bluff simplicity of intent behind Ponge's verse, but also its attendance to the grain of the letter, to the unpredictable materiality of poetic signs. Here, then, are manifest two aspects of the "form" that will be my concern across this book; as I signaled in the introduction, "form" will just as likely name the inflection of literary language, its tenor, as much as more classical formal devices. What holds the different facets of "form" together, in my account, is that they seem to point inward, toward a kind of self-reference, and therefore away from reference to the world. As I'll show, it is this inwardness that in fact makes the peculiar kind of reference that literature performs a possibility.

Johnson's reading of "The Oyster" in her *Persons and Things* refuses to take at face value Ponge's seeming adherence to a sensuous phenomenology of objects. She focuses in particular on "The Oyster's" final, short paragraph, where Ponge invokes a pearl lodged in the oyster's throat. Pearl is here used in its verb form, "to pearl," in Johnson's supple translation above rendered as "a globule pearls in its nacre throat." For Johnson, this personification testifies that the poet and the object in question are burdened with an excrescence or encrustation which is in itself a figure for their inability to be pure unto themselves, neatly separated from one another, the one coolly observing the other's impassivity.[12]

The inability to swallow, here, images the failure of either the oyster or the poet attempting to capture it in poetic form to keep themselves pure of interference, whether internally directed, in the shape of a pearl, or externally, in the shape of the poet's inability to extricate himself from the conflicting imperatives of his chosen mode of expression. Of course, the two become one when one understands the pearl as the figurative concentration of the impasses of both language and the material, of the internal inability of the material world to close upon itself, and in the anxious failure of poetic language to break out of its own tendency toward self-reference. The pearl, in other words, in its concentration of the figural tactics of the verse, becomes as much a formal feature of the poem as it is an emblem of its "content." And one may ask, with Paul de Man, whether any poetic position of neutral understanding, where object could map perfectly onto word, would be an advantage at all, or whether it would be a kind of alienation, where the object would be granted, in de Man's terms, "quasi-divine powers which, in turn, reduce the subject to the awestruck bafflement of a will entirely alienated from its works."[13]

Lukács made a similar observation with respect to the nineteenth-century novel, where he noted a strong divergence between "interiority and the outside world," where interiority registers as "a cosmos . . . self-sufficient, at rest within itself."[14] De Man and Lukács's formulations each concern a perilously self-expanding category, the object in de Man, the subject in Lukács, as each smothers its opposite number. De Man usefully permits us to wonder how to even distinguish the object-world from its accompanying signs, let alone grant it any autonomy, if the gap between it and the subject, or it and language, is finally closed. One encounters in Ponge, by contrast, a model of *formalization*, of the dynamic attempt to give poetic form to an object-world, that succeeds through a certain kind of failure, through the necessity of an impurity (figured by that glistening pearl) that uses alienation to its own advantage. At stake is a noncorrelational spark that becomes possible when both poetic language and the material world are imagined as necessarily shot through with impurities, such impurities preventing the swallowing of one by the other while permitting, nonetheless, their ruptural connection.

In the case of the oyster, its impurity in the shape of its secreted pearl is, of course, what lends it its singularity, its value; as Ponge writes in the final line of the poem, it is that "with which one instantly seeks to adorn oneself"—and yet, one infers that such an object is finally unpossessable by the poetic subject, insofar as the latter is incapable of treating the object in its autonomy, without already making it a thing to be incorporated. Thus the poet, while casting his gaze outward, finds himself as imbricated in the compromising impurities of language (the frustration inherent in wanting to get at something in-itself, but only having language with all its formal inscrutabilities at one's disposal to do it) as he is in the apparent "neutrality" of the object of his gaze, an impurity figured in the poem through, again, the direct personification of the oyster and its "throat," a personification that arrests poetic language's quest to achieve an objective measure of its target. And yet somehow, in that very failure of poetry's mimetic task, a trait proper to both subject and object—the inability of either to be fully unto-themselves, an impurity that then permits their fragile connection—is evoked and then spun out in its consequences. Ponge is something of a Benjaminian here: just as Walter Benjamin prized the furtive languages to be detected in materiality itself, a kind of inherent object-language to be tended to and revivified,[15] so Ponge wishes us to refuse any simple external relation between word and thing; rather, poetry for Ponge is a "rough job," as the first paragraph of the "The Oyster" has it, one that points toward the necessary imperfection attendant to any communication between literature and its worlds.

Here, language is less a purely human substance or capacity cast out onto the world, but is rather something that exists both inside and outside us, and potentially within the object-world itself. As such, the oyster is less an absolutely withdrawn thing that eludes linguistic capture or the net of human consciousness; rather, both forms overlap in their very incommensurability, in their frustration of the other's substantiality and autonomy, and this at the moment when the poem itself comments on its own frustrated mimetic ambitions. Such a frustration occurs not through the successful mapping of one onto the other (their mutual embedding, to recall Caroline Levine's terms as explored in the introduction), but rather in a kind of missed encounter, of what Hart Crane, in a poem otherwise concerned with the human usurpation of nature, wrote of through the image of creatures eluding their fossilization in poetic verse. It may be worth a brief parenthesis to take the measure of Crane's account of this tussle between word and world.

Crane begins: "Moonmoth and grasshopper that flee our page / And still wing on, untarnished of the name."[16] Of course, even as those insects flee fixation in a poetic structure, and so "wing on" in their vitality, they appear to us nonetheless. They do so, however, only on the condition that they are able to elude any absolute *nomination*, any reduction attendant to the total envelopment of life by word. Crane continues: "Because we are usurpers, and chagrined- / And take wing and scar it in the hand / Names we have, even, to clap on the wind; / But we must die, as you, to understand."[17] The "usurpers" in question, one surmises, are the wielders of language themselves, humans whose hubris is partly conditioned on their ability to fix the world in their image with the glue of linguistic structure. It is the act of naming, that is to say, that defers world to word, that performs its own kind of suppressive violence on its objects: "And take wing and scar it in the hand."[18] The wind, even, can't escape the domination that issues from our linguistic colonization of the world: "Names we have, even, to clap on the wind."[19]

But the truly profound move comes in Crane's insistence that "we must die, as you, to understand"—humankind, that is to say, with all its own struggles with language and representation, must also suffer at the hands of the symbol, such that it is less human agents who are in charge but rather language or understanding itself, language to be understood then as an affliction that subject and object must bear alike. Like Ponge's poem explored above, this verse actively comments on its own formal strategies as they unfold; it contains a metatext, explanatory of its own ruses. One is reminded again of Paul de Man's comment as to the alienation that would result from the pure subordination of subject by object; for de Man, recall, to grant the object-world an absolute autonomy would reduce "the subject to the awestruck bafflement of a will entirely alienated from its works."[20] In Crane's more complete vision, however, it is both subject *and* object, the world and its human observer, that are divided from within by the threat of nomination. Ponge, in a slightly different register, would also have one appreciate the shared incompletion and alienation that cuts through language and through world that language may otherwise be assumed to merely pacify—to "usurp" and "to scar," in Crane's well-judged words. Yet finally Crane offers, in his concluding stanza, a vision that one would be forgiven for thinking utopian, and thus indicative of a resolution, a denial even, of the very tension and incompletion that, in my account, defines the constructive effect of literary language: "I dreamed that all men dropped their names, and sang / As only they can praise, who build their days / With fin and hoof, with wind and sweetened fang / Struck free and holy in one Name always."[21]

A beautiful picture of man, world, and beast, this, almost Rousseauian in its charge, but one that nonetheless remains a *dream*, troubled in advance by the prior stanzas that hang ominously over such a vision and remind us that the very need to conscript the world in the structures of the word prevents in advance any real possibility of symmetry or harmony between the two. This may be a particularly dramatic instance of how prior lines can, in their general effect, induce a formal, and thus not simply thematic, effect on what succeeds them; there is something of an effect of massification here, a process whereby what, in the moment of reading, may have been taken as content or theme hardens into a formal device as the eye leaves it behind. That mass now cloaks all that succeeds it, darkening it as it were.

Crane's poem, I would wager, stages the very undecidability between naming and description that Jacques Derrida saw in Ponge's verse;[22] as men "drop their names," the poem reaches a fever pitch of description—"With fin and hood, with wind and sweetened fang"—but the name, with its threat of fixity, is ever-close behind; "Struck free and holy in one Name always," a divine or Godly nomination that frees in the same moment that it homogenizes or cancels out the lively natural difference that the poem has otherwise celebrated. There's a much-commented-on optimism to Crane's poetic vision,[23] of course, and one would be forgiven for locating such a moment of uplift in this final stanza, but I'm not sure that this culminating, divine dream of unity between human and world, both thus free from the binding effects of naming except through the universal name of God, can be read apart from the heavy melancholy that hangs over the preceding lines, inducing by the poem's end a kind of massified formal pressure, lines that, in their heavy thunder, ironize in advance those that seem to mop the poem's anxious brow in the final stanza.

Despite this, one should settle on a less negative conclusion from such a seeming moment of disabusement, insofar as it is only in the *inability* of word and world, subject and object if you like, to respect one another, to somberly reproduce the qualities of the other, that a fragile resonance between the two may be possible. Crane's willingness to hold together a sense of canny plenitude, of a stealthy poetic expansiveness, evading the constriction of nomination, and his equal recognition of the inevitable and necessary *return* of such a linguistic imperative, is what raises the poem to greatness. The shared vulnerability produced by the inability of either word or world to tame the other becomes their only possible connection. Here utopia and dystopia coincide; the incompletion of Crane's ecological vision should have us appreciate the "scarring" of word and world alike, a vision that Crane's poem communicates almost despite itself, in the face of its fantasmatic, nay fetishistic drift toward images of unity and cohesion, and as much in its metatextual commentary on itself as in its initial level of form and content.

Back to Ponge, where everywhere in "The Oyster" the poem's rhetorical devices enter into battle with its surface desire to describe rather than address the thing in question, to do justice to what Ponge would wish the reader to initially glean as the object's nonpoetic "neutrality," its passive dwelling before the poet qua subject—the better the ironic effect, then, when the very impossibility of such a neutrality comes crashing into view. Thus, in the very first line, the use of "brightly whitish" to image the rough coloration of the oyster sets a pattern of arrestingly contradictory juxtapositions; indeed, contradiction assumes the status of a formal device in Ponge, and the clash of contradiction will be a signal instance of form, one often and perhaps mistakenly taken to be a question of "content," in all that follows. Just as it is the oyster's very dullness of color that makes it bright, so the whole oyster itself, as a figure of closure, of ungraspable, black interiority, a "world stubbornly closed" in Ponge's words—such an opacity is called on to provide "a whole world, to eat and drink."[24] An absolute, closed off interiority runs up against the desire for a boundless exteriority, whereby "the skies above collapse on the skies below," leaving "nothing but a puddle"—an exteriority, of course, to be internalized, to be incorporated—literally, that is, to be eaten.

At such moments, the viscous impurities of the object to be captured in description assume a precarious parity (if not quite a correlation) with the impurities, the forms of incompletion, the aberrant resonances, of the language that is, ostensibly, merely doing the describing. At stake here is a problematization of description and mimesis per se, one that has implications for the elevation of sophisticated description that, one suspects, will be the upshot of the appeals to "surface reading" that were investigated in the introduction. Just as, for the French philosopher of science Gaston Bachelard, the object to be formalized in a scientific project may *object*, may become the condition in its very objection for any further act of formalization,[25] so poetic language in Ponge embodies the constitutive incompletions, the pearl lodged in the throat, characteristic of its apparent referent, an objectification that disbars neutral, symmetrical description in advance.

Poetic language, that is to say, is objectified at the very moment that its objects resist their incorporation into the neat folds of a poem. Conversely, the objects of poetic attention undergo a linguistic conversion at the moment at which such objects seem to persist prior to and in defiance of the ambition of poetry to ensnare them. Such objects, then, are infected with and transformed by the attempt to capture them, although what results is far from any Hegelian transmutation of substance into subject. Rather, the very possibility of a mimetic correspondence, of any smooth transport of one into the other, is blocked by the paradox that finds the one resisting the other at the moment of their seeming unification, an incommensurability that nonetheless enables the properly *non*-mimetic force of literature as it evokes its seeming outsides. When Derrida, in his "Signéponge," comments that one "never knows whether

[Ponge] names or describes,"[26] one may conclude that is in the very indeterminacy of the distinction that his poetic power resides. To "name" is to performatively bring the object into being, whereas to describe such an object is to presuppose that it preexists any poetic attempt to transcribe its essence. Derrida finds in Ponge the admirable resolve to refuse the forced choice: poetic language both names *and* describes, insofar as the linguistic construction of the object soon meets those aspects of the object that force themselves back on language itself, rendering both contingent and unstable. One is reminded, again, of Hart Crane's muted horror at the prospect of nomination, except here the name loses some of its suffocating power in the dissolution of any firm distinction between name and representation, and in the encounter with the resistances of the object itself. Such indeterminacy dramatizes the broader aim of this chapter, namely to retain the reflexivity of the "linguistic turn" while accounting for the obstinancies of materiality that rely on, and find a nonmimetic resonance with, the languages that may otherwise have wished to drown those very same resistant objects in the acid bath of representation.

Ponge's poetics is shot through with an ironical, reflexive sense of its own constitutive inability to perform such a one-way, representative function, to faithfully reproduce the absolute density and independence of its objects; this is the metatextual level I've already had cause to note. Here the echo with Benjamin's aesthetics trails off: whereas Benjamin had at least some faith in allegory's capacity to revivify and resacralize language, both allegory and symbol fall short in the failures of form that are nonetheless in the service of poetic production in Ponge. Benjamin wrote of allegory as that which gives rise to expression per se: "Allegory . . . is not a playful technique of images, but expression, just as speech is expression, and, indeed, writing is."[27] For all that, allegory at its best announces a kind of disruptive creation for Benjamin, one that produces a fragile unity where otherwise language may be seen to fall back on an atomistic ineffectuality, on the mere endless nominalistic agglomeration of words and sentences.

The reader may recall my discussion of Baudelaire's prose poetry in the introduction, where the strategic repetition of key phrases introduces a formal rhythmic pressure that may otherwise seem to have disappeared with prose poetry's rejection of the line break. Here I'd like to briefly emphasize a more general formal feature of prose poetry, one that is very much at work in Ponge's poetics and that underscores the "argument" about poetic reference that I've been tracing in his verse. One of the recurrent claims of this book is that the marked absence of a particular formal feature can, when that absence interacts with present formal features, have its own marked effect. The very formal status of prose poetry, suspended somewhere indeterminate between prose and metered verse, is an especially striking example of this. As one scans Ponge's lines, one's expectations remain attuned to poetry's usual formal features, such that the absence of much of those, meter especially, heightens the paradoxes and indeterminacies that are already there to be found. But it does more than this: it also makes any formal feature that does repeat itself into significance in the verse that much more efficacious; the absence of what one expects to find, that is, makes that which *is* encountered especially acute in its formal effects. Such formal effects may well be senseless on their own, but in their conversation with the indeterminacy of the generic status of prose poetry and in their interaction with the poetry's own "argument" about poetic reference, they prepare the ground for the poetry's intervention in the world. One of the most interesting of such unexpected formal features in the otherwise apparently leisurely and forward-moving "The Oyster" is repetition, to which I'll now turn.

Ponge reacted angrily to the accusation of anthropomorphism[28] (that "stubborn" closure of the oyster, for example) by emphasizing that, in choosing words that contain the letters -*tre* across the poem, his intent was to rhyme the internal uses of such an arbitrary collection of letters with the name of the object, "L'hui*tre*" ("The Oyster"), that ends in *tre* and that forms the poem's title. In consequence, the oyster being described as "stubbornly closed" (in French, "opiniâ*tre*mont clos") has rather less to do with anthropomorphic projection than it does with the choice of a word, *opiniâtrement,* that, from the purview of the poem's content, has a purely arbitrary connection, a sense-less and partial echo, with the poem's title. Thus, the *formal repetition* of a contingent, in itself sense-less formal unit -*tre,* implies an attempt to reach out of the internality of the poem to its external title, its "name," to again invoke Derrida's distinction between "naming" and "description"—a name, moreover, that resonates as much as an insult in French as it does as a neutral description of the poem's object. Yet such a move outward from the poem to its title relies on a purely senseless repetition internal to the poem itself, one that is more obviously, if superficially, explained by virtue of the anthropomorphic projection of poetic language on its object.[29] Repetition may be added, then, to my growing list of formal devices outside the more recognizable grouping populated by voice, diction, metaphor, metonymy, and so on.

This is another way of saying that the primary function of poetry for Ponge is not to *make sense for a subject or make subjects of its objects,* is not to inspire the spark of recognition in a perceiving consciousness or endow that consciousness on its objects, is not to conjure interpretation. Poetry persists luxurious in its very failure to carry a unified sense from object, through language, to consciousness, and thus somehow to furnish a text readymade to be interpreted. There's a limited echo here, too, with Graham Harman's evocative (I would argue *poetic*) analyses of the necessarily indirect relations between withdrawn objects:[30] on my model, linguistic forms and object forms are, by necessity, unable to fully know one another. But the lack of a suitably nuanced account of subjectivity in Harman's object-oriented ontology is overcome if one proposes the human subject, as well as language and the external object, as encompassed in a far broader set of processes of *formalization*, processes that are motored by the resistances of objects, both material and linguistic, and in processes that are never "flat" or easily delineable in the manner that Harman and his acolytes so often presuppose.

Before I leave poetry behind, if only for a moment, it might be of interest to address directly the question of poetic meter, one of the constrictive formal conditions that, for this book, are central to any account of poetry's power. Consider briefly the example of Mallarmé. In his *Mallarmé: The Politics of the Siren*, Jacques Rancière convincingly rebuts the common notion, propagated most insistently by the poet himself, that Mallarmé's poems are austere machines of purification, banishing the referent in the name of a poetics of purity.[31] To the contrary, Rancière detects in Mallarmé's verse an attempt to summon what he calls "a real presence of absence,"[32] a kind of nonrelational referentiality, one that concentrates all the powers of poetic figuration in order to connote the most interstitial, recalcitrant qualities of a nonetheless knowable reality. When Mallarmé, in his *Divagations*, argues for the viability of meter as against the full embrace of free verse, he does so not as a concession to tradition but because poetic meter, again a crucial instance of poetic form, concentrates the essential contingences of language, provides them with an amplifying frame, so as to better open poetry out onto the heterogeneous, onto its wild outsides.[33] Or, better, Mallarmé insists on the usefulness of holding together meter and its negation, as a necessary and generative contradiction that both language and its supposed referent rely on. Mallarmé's syntax is equally responsive to convention, the better to hint at the freedoms that only the tense holding together of structure and free-play may afford. Barbara Johnson captures this beautifully: "Mallarmé's syntax is never confused; it is, as he says, profound and scrupulous, as decentered as possible without being cut loose from the gravitational pull of incompatible grammatical possibilities."[34]

In a similar vein, Quentin Meillassoux's recent book on Mallarmé argues that, by encoding numerical figures in his most radical verses, Mallarmé "produc[es] a *poetic* reconciliation between regular verse and free verse . . . Rather than proposing . . . a division of roles between the two forms, he would have produced . . . a Verse capable of bringing about their effective synthesis."[35] Here the very lack of a synthesis or resolution between meter and its negation, meter's always having the potential to be "set free" or canceled out, operates as the condition of any positive poetic meaning at all; in the case of prose poetry, of course, a more radical absence of meter only amplifies again the formal conditions of the verse. Might there be a way of accounting for objects that is similarly attentive to the constitutive de-formations of form, without hypostatizing the category "object" as the final arbiter of one's commitment to a metaphysical, and thus precritical, realism? How might the relationship between scientific concepts and their objects—arranged not in parallel, but in awkward configurations of constitution and negation—mirror or problematize that between poetic language and its outsides? In the next section, I'll read the late, indeed posthumously published, work of Jean Cavaillès, a French philosopher of science and *resistant* killed by the Gestapo in 1944, as a resource that may spark a distinctive de-formation of our understanding of objects across science and literature, the better to realize the formative effects thereof. Such an optic may be reframed as *poetic* insofar as it, like Ponge's ambiguous prose poetry above, wishes to find in the very impossibility of any transitive movement between the essence of things and their linguistic apprehension the possibility, nonetheless, of their fragile resonance.

Jean Cavaillès and the Poetic Vacillations of Scientific Form

As noted in the introduction to this chapter, reading French poetry alongside the rather austere tradition of French historical epistemology, a revivification of a broadly rationalist approach to the development of scientific knowledge that predated the emergence of structuralism in France, may naturally strike the reader as unexpected at best, and unnecessarily perverse at worse. From most sides of the contemporary academy, and for all the eager talk of interdisciplinarity, the worlds of poetry on the one side and the physical sciences and mathematics on the other are kept firmly apart, along lines most famously documented by C. P. Snow.[36] If Bruno Latour's "actor-network" approach to the anthropology of modernity has sought to level the playing field of human and nonhuman actors, it has done so with only a cursory glance at literature, and at the risk that description is valued over critical analysis. Despite this, what follows is decidedly not an attempt to argue for the tidy compatibility of critical approaches associated with literature and poetry and those to be found in continental theories of scientific knowledge. One of the unfortunate tendencies of the contemporary valorization of all things "interdisciplinary" and "postdisciplinary" is the assumption that traffic between already established structures of knowledge is smooth and untroubled. Recent publications attempting to meld neuroscientific and psychoanalytic insights, for example, have paid too little attention to the epistemological problems attendant to the conflation of what are, philosophically speaking, two highly distinct kinds of theoretical object, the brain and the unconscious.[37]

As such, my reading of Cavaillès in what follows takes as axiomatic the opposite assumption, namely that squeezing between the dividing lines of contemporary knowledge is arduous, and requires an especially reflective process of translation and re-translation, one that has much to learn from the literary process of wrenching the singular meaning of one national language into the very different terms of another.[38] Such a perpetual translation is, I would argue, itself a kind of formalization, an ongoing articulation of divergent materials within an emergent, structuring frame of legibility, one that may never achieve completion lest the process of translation, and thus of meaning per se, were to shudder to a halt. And in line with the defining claims of this book as a whole, the emergence of such a frame is, within its own constitutive conditions of possibility, to be expected to *fail*, again according to its own immanent criteria, and in productive and enlightening ways. Think of the grit in Ponge's oyster, the figure for the necessary ways in which poetic language overreaches its object, precluding the possibility of any neat correlation with the world. The emergence of such an unstable holding structure for two otherwise divergent structures of knowledge—here, poetry and the interaction between scientific claims and their philosophical apprehension—can be taken as an allegory for the very speculative model of form that this book endeavors to produce, a model that, to repeat, wishes to hold together constitutive moments of both formation and de-formation, of articulation and dis-articulation, thought in their agonistic interaction and in their refusal of any moment of sublation.

I might sharpen my position here by contrasting it with the claim of a storied French psychiatrist writing in the same period as Cavaillès. In an essay from 1936, Eugène Minkowski sought to resolidify the distinction between science and culture that, in the broadest sense, that which follows would seek to trouble. Minkowski's "Prose and Poetry (Astronomy and Cosmology)" aimed to limit the totalizing ambitions of science while nonetheless seeking in philosophy a partner for poetry, the latter collaboration thus better equipped to detail those aspects of life that are irreducible to the stern rectitude of the scientific gaze. As he wrote, "Science knows only the [scientific] attitude. It has as its domain the cold and naked facts stripped of all poetic raiment," and "Science dissects, opposes, proceeds by means of abstraction, generalizes. At its touch, life comes to a standstill."[39] One would be hard pressed to find a more direct expression of that resilient humanist canard, namely that where science trades in austere abstraction, poetry and the arts console and inspire from a location beyond the frozen tundra of empty "facts."

It would be easy enough to enumerate numerous poets and novelists, many of them writing long before the development of self-conscious artistic avant-gardes in the waning years of the nineteenth century, whose practice would resist such an easily parodied view of the purpose of art. It is of more interest, however, to locate in the work of another French epistemologist, Jean Cavaillès, a superior accounting of science that is able to forgo the reductions of positivism and humanism alike, Cavaillès then becoming an unexpected resource, speaking from somewhere beyond C. P. Snow's "two cultures," for the analysis of the speculative structures of poetry that I've already begun to expose.

Much of Jean Cavaillès's *On Logic and the Theory of Science*, written while the philosopher was imprisoned by the Nazis and providing for us the most thorough treatment available of his philosophical position, is concerned with a critique of transcendentalism in the philosophy of science and in the theory of knowledge more generally. Targets include Husserl's phenomenology, which is accused of illegitimately retaining a variant of Kant's transcendental subject and thus, like the initiator of transcendental philosophy, reducing the norms of scientific progress to the subordinate properties of a sovereign consciousness. Logical positivism, according to Cavaillès, is equally guilty of silencing the proper autonomy of scientific knowledge, making do instead with tracing the modestly scalable logical principles that a local study of science might afford. Of more import to my argument is Cavaillès's bracing commitment to a philosophy of what I'm tempted to call *structural immanence*, which is to say a mode of thought that traces the internal movements of conceptuality as they help produce the objects that they are seen, at first glance, to merely represent or codify.

The reader may well have noticed the parallel with Ponge's poetics as laid out above. Like the latter, Cavaillès would discard any symmetrical opposition (one often assumed to be seamlessly bridgeable) between the signs that make up scientific knowledge's inner conceptual world, and their seeming "outsides." Positivist approaches would condemn as compliant such apparent "outsides" in their capture by a conceptual language, while transcendental tendencies in philosophy would rather have us think the external world as molded by, even determined by, the machinations of cognition, by the operations of what Cavaillès calls "the absolute of a consciousness whose presence and essential structure—which is consciousness in itself—are an irreducible which no rational content defines."[40] In response to the frequent accusations of formalism (no dirty word in this book, of course) leveled at rationalist philosophy of science, Cavaillès turns the tables—to the contrary, it is the supposition of a transcendental, ordering consciousness that blasts scientific knowledge out of history and into the purity of an ideal form of unchanging reception serenely impervious to the content that it nonetheless always and successfully recuperates.

Just as Ponge would refuse the privilege traditionally accorded the poetic genius qua subject in her possession of both language and the objects that language successfully comes to represent (a privilege that denies the grit in Ponge's oyster, so to speak), so Cavaillès reinvents form as elastic, responsive, sensitive to the interruptions of subject and object that define the nonlinear accumulation of scientific knowledge. To quote him again at a moment of especial dialectical sensitivity, "The [scientific] synthesis is coextensive with the production of what is synthesized,"[41] or the knowledge of an object is coextensive with the partial *construction* of that object. Ponge's poetics stages a similar paradox, whereby the very resistance of word and world is at the same time the partial construction of each by the other, such a formal paradox then bleeding into the very imagistic and allegorical texture of individual poems themselves.

The speculative generativity of form that cuts across both Ponge's poetics and the account of scientific knowledge in Cavaillès both records and helps incite an ever expanding topological complexity, one that refuses in advance any clean inner/outer distinction. Instead, the language that serves to capture its object—at the moment of the synthesis of knowledge alluded to by Cavaillès above—is, from the perspective of a more distant, encompassing scale, somehow *a part of the object that it is otherwise assumed to merely represent.* This is another way of saying that, for any speculative formalist approach, the world is as penetrated by the conceptual and the linguistic as the linguistic is very much of the world, such that the catachresis implied in such a formulation begins to seem inadequate in advance of its conclusion—inadequate, not least because the easy commutability between terms implied in the above fails to capture the agonistic *resistance* of one to the other.

Merely reversing the terms, this is to say, shuttling merrily back and forth between the linguistic and the material, would only go so far in doing justice to the simultaneity of the intransigent *event* of materiality, and the equally evental irruption of language—or, to put it again in terms borrowed from Cavaillès, "There is no meaning without an act, and no new act without the meaning which produces it."[42] Repeating that the one is only grounded with the other, in a concession to the relativity of conceptual terms that would barely approach the sophistication of, say, a Saussurean recognition of the differential constitution of meaning, would in fact do much to solidify either term, setting in stone what one had wished to make liquid; and this is sometimes the error of Paul de Man, whose ingenious readings of poetry I have otherwise taken much inspiration from. And suffice to notice here also the New Historicist appetite for a similar and ultimately impotent reversal of terms—think of Louis Montrose's alluring but ultimately shallow construction "the historicity of texts and the textuality of history."[43] One needs to go much further: the grit and fervidity of the encounter between the two terms is, far from the scene of their easy substitution back and forth, the key to a relation established as a result of a shared intransigence, not any neat exchangeability.

By invoking the language of the event, one shifts further again from a representative model of reference, older models of reference otherwise seeming to rely on a static opposition between the world of signs and the world of things. I would argue that we go one step further, too, than the undoubtedly suggestive use of Lacan made by Shoshana Felman, as when she insists that "what *can* be read (and perhaps what *should* be read) is not just meaning, but the lack of meaning; that significance lies not just in consciousness, but specifically in its disruption."[44] The emphasis on the constitutivity of nonmeaning is crucial, for sure, and the general Lacanian insistence on the generative relation of non-sense to sense inflects every turn of my analysis,[45] but Felman demurs from pushing her analysis beyond the closed circle of language, and of consciousness and of the unconscious insofar as they are linguistically defined. What if we were to observe a similar two-step of sense and non-sense within the objects of poetic capture themselves, such that it is in poetry's very failed ambition to mimic that world, to render it meaningful, that the impurities and non-sensicalities in both come ever clearer into view? I'll have cause to approach such material impurities in depth in chapter 4, a chapter that concerns in particular Paul de Man's repurposing of what he insists is Kant's materialism, Kant's registering of the blank sublimity of the material world.

Cavaillès, for his part, also insisted on the roles of multiplicity and interruption, but in a manner that read such indeterminacies as implicated in the elastic properties of scientific form itself, even at its most seemingly ascetic. Even more importantly, Cavaillès wished to preserve the potential of the forms of materiality or the linguistic to *fail*, to overshoot their targets, all the better to do justice to the impurities, internal inconsistencies, in both. Such a view of the unpredictability of the objects of knowledge is not in itself an argument for the relativity of all knowledge or for the chaotic unpredictability of the scientific endeavor; far from it. Just as importantly, the unity of the knowledge that results from the encounter of materiality and concepts, of world with word, does not inevitably take the form of a stifling uniformity or conformity, impervious to the breach of future novelty. As Cavaillès bluntly phrases it, "unity does not mean uniformity."[46] Unity, here, signifies the different levels of structurality that even the most apparently random singularity must be framed against if that singularity is to be conceptually legible, if it is not to fade immediately from view.

There is no contradiction, then, between the notion that the development of a scientific theory proceeds via singularities, via excesses that initially overrun the symbolic resources of the most stout of scientific hypotheses, and the idea that such singularities are nonetheless to be understood as already structured, so long as the "structures" in question are read as necessarily flawed, shot through with impurities that are then received as such structures' conditions of possible existence. As Cavaillès phrases it, "the singularity as origin, and form, the actual meaning. This is likewise the source of a distinction which, when projected into the absolute, would extend from one end of the general sequence to the other, like a continuous flaw through the nodes of the particular distinctions."[47] Such a flaw is the mark of the impurity and instability that scientific and poetic modes of formalization must bear, even as one may subsequently realize their necessity. That necessary unpredictability of both language and its objects, an instability conducive to singular events, is, then, the ground for the very subsequent emergence of stability. Cavaillès argues as much, as when he distinguishes between

> two dimensions in particular . . . a realm of singularities . . . and the set of sequences in the strict sense which, although they are indispensable only to the extent that they actually demonstrate something and as a result cannot be renewed in their integrity, present a kinship of type according to groups, a mark of the unity of movements which can be manifested in the abstract.[48]

"A mark of the unity of movements"—Cavaillès's language is precise here in registering the lack of any absolute contradiction between unity and movement, between the accretion of structure and form and the generative interruption of the new. It is surely one of the great errors of contemporary theory to assume, against the emphases of Cavaillès's subtle account here, that any focus on structure and form is necessarily to repudiate any account of change. As Ponge's poetry also shows, the apparent refusal of the object to be poetically (or, one should here add, scientifically) apprehended is the ground on which one "finds a whole world," a "firmament" to be swallowed whole. Equally, the pearl that clogs up the apparent unity of the object to be ascertained turns out, in the final analysis, to be the very condition of any knowledge of that object in the first place, and thus to any perceivable unity; without it, that firmament would remain smothered in darkness, would never be forced open in the first place.

Wallace Stevens and the Transport of Capacities

To reassure the reader that such a position is not merely the eccentric concern of French poets and philosophers, consider the following lines from Wallace Stevens, an exemplary poet of the mysteries of form whom I will discuss in much more detail in the next chapter. In his early work "Anecdote of a Jar," a lyric that is at first glance a kind of Heideggerian celebration of the productive dissonance attendant to the enframing and containing of space, Stevens writes:

> I placed a jar in Tennessee
> And round it was, upon a hill
> It made the slovenly wilderness
> Surround that hill
>
> The wilderness rose up to it
> And sprawled around, no longer wild
> The jar was round upon the ground
> And tall and of a port in air.[49]

One immediately notes the transfer in capacities between the jar and its surrounds, such that the jar's roundness begins to infect the "slovenly wilderness" that it has invaded, the disorderly spatial distribution of the wilderness increasingly bent to the tighter and smaller spaces of the alien, intransigent object now stubbornly situated in its midst. But the traffic isn't entirely one-way: by the end of the quoted verse, the jar itself is now "tall" and itself a "port in air," a conduit for its outside, its smallness now puffed out, disfigured according to the greater dimensions of the hill that it dwells on; even as it appears to have transformed its environs, one learns that it is now also, at one and the same time, in greater conformity with them.

That this is no contradiction for Stevens, that the power of the jar comes as much in its conforming to its surrounds as in its dominance over them; that the two movements, withdrawal and expansion, happen at one and the same time—these findings are enough to place in question any reading of the poem that might have enjoined one to choose object over landscape, or landscape over object. Moreover, the regularity, even severity of the meter that pulses through the poem is in ironic contrast to the sense of transfiguration and change that its lines evoke, and yet one senses that a freer formal structure may have perilously muffled the productive battle between austerity and withdrawal, expansion and power that the poem so strikingly stages. Commentators, of course, have frequently underlined the seemingly parodic quality of the antiromantic sparseness of Stevens's portrayal of the movements of an object within space, the asceticism of its structure seemingly in stark contradiction of its romantic sources with their faith in the poetic transformation of consciousness and its objects; the specific reference is, of course, to Keats's "Ode on a Grecian Urn."

There is more going on here, however; there is a formal, and thus philosophical and not merely literary-historical, argument for the ways in which objects and their structures interact, and it bears on the comments made at the very beginning of this chapter with respect to reflexivity. Stevens demonstrates that such a virtue is not necessarily the consequence of a maximalist effusion of content or affect or stream of consciousness, characteristics so often associated with the postmodern turn in both narrative fiction and poetry. Rather, the most seemingly austere of poetic forms, even the drip-drop predictability of the meter found in "Anecdote of the Jar," may serve as the ground for an elastic reflexivity, a dynamic interchange or plasticity, that courses through what is only at first glance a reduction of poetic possibility to its simplest possible components.

If Stevens's jar is an object defined in agonistic relation to the mutable structures within which it sits, an object that is gradually penetrated by the shifts and rhythms that surround it, it perhaps isn't going too far to read it through the singularities theorized by Cavaillès and as discussed above. There the interruptions of scientific conceptuality are always also part of the structures that they come to grate against, only for those singularities to then replace such prior structures with structures of their own. Stevens's object is no more the absolute exception to its surroundings than those surroundings are somehow able to easily overcome or define the jar as fixed in its properties, or as the property of the landscape within which it is encased. Object and landscape try to dominate the other, just as poetic language for Ponge tries to dominate the oyster, but the very failure to do so, the very inability of either agent to rid itself of the qualities of the other and thus to imperiously trace the characteristics of the other from a position of dominating distance, is precisely the mark of their nonmimetic, formal affinity. One is not so far here from Alexandre Kojève's hugely influential, anthropological reading of Hegel's *Phenomenology of Spirit*, disseminated to the leading lights of French theory in his seminar in 1930s Paris.[50] There Kojève privileged the portion of the *Phenomenology* that narrates the battle between two nascent consciousnesses, a struggle for recognition that ultimately results in the (seeming) subordination of one over the other. In Stevens's poem, however, there is no resolution to speak of, or, better, the very irresolution of the fight between old and new, between landscape and object, stands as its own kind of poetic resolution, its own kind of solution to the question of how new and old might settle into a kind of fraught coexistence.

It is, I hope, not too much of a leap to suggest that what is allegorized in Stevens's poem, beyond the general scene of the incursion of the new within the terms of the old, is more specifically the relationship between history and poetic form. Far from being a mere externality, where history interpellates verse as its passive and compliant "content," the landscape as a figure of history rhythmically folds upon its object in such a way that the latter, in turn, incites and provokes its historical "outsides." The end result is surely the refusal of any absolute inside/outside or history/text distinction, such that history and poetic form are asymmetrically intercalated in much the same way as, in Ponge's account of the oyster, poetic language registers something of the world only at moments when poetic figures and devices, anthropomorphism especially in Ponge's case, signal a curling back of language on itself. Here I must complicate Jameson's influential argument, in his *The Political Unconscious*, that history can be understood as "the content [literature] has to take up into itself in order to submit it to the transformations of form."[51] On my account, there can be no immediate assignation of form to text and history to content: Jameson will of course recognize the dialectical interlacing of both, but my account of form here would rather imagine history itself as a formal process, as therefore always and already interacting with literary form as its asymmetrically posed other, an other that history would wish, against all likelihood, to possess. I'll confront the question of form, history, and politics again in chapter 5.

Stevens again: "It [the jar] took dominion every where / The jar was gray and bare / It did not give of bird or bush / Like nothing else in Tennessee."[52] At first blush, this final stanza seems to undercut the sense of permeability between object and landscape, between text and history, that the first two stanzas propose; the jar or poetry itself, it seems, has definitively won the day. In fact, Stevens would finally affirm that his object, far from having cancelled its surrounding landscape or its historical determination through a total solipsistic denial of those surrounds or contexts, is rather being embedded *in* those surrounds precisely by virtue *of* that apparent withdrawal, figured here by its being "gray and bare," as far as possible from the seeming fecundity of the nature within which it rests. "*Seeming* fecundity" because nature itself, recall, was marked at the beginning of the poem as "slovenly," as close enough to the bareness and grayness that the reader is told is the condition of the jar by the end. At issue here is Stevens's deliberate undermining of any broadly romantic vision of nature as wild and fertile plenitude; by the final lines, jar and landscape are connected insofar as they're *both* withdrawn, both drained of wildness and life, "of bird and bush." It is in the gradual affinity between the "slovenly" wilderness and the asceticism of the object that penetrates it that what Deleuze would have called their disjunctive synthesis is realized.

I should comment here, too, on the parallel but nonetheless divergent ways in which Stevens and Ponge put anthropomorphism to use against its usual intentions. The "slovenly" wilderness in Stevens imposes an apparent passivity, a flaccidity, on the landscape into which the jar intervenes, but only to then dialectically revise this sense through the ways in which the wilderness comes to infect the jar itself, such that the invading object is made "tall," such that it becomes massive, as grandiose as landscape itself, "tall and of a port in air." The effect here is one of imposing a granite monumentality on both invading object and its determining spatial and temporal outsides, even as both twist around each other in a dialectical dance that one assumes will never end. And yet, as I've noted, by the *poem's* end both landscape and jar have assumed a position of self-negation, slovenly, gray, neither "of bird and bush," all the better to effect a kind of fragile synthesis between the two. Such a synthesis could justifiably be described as tragic, insofar as it is achieved not through the successful, positive incorporation of an object in its context, but rather in the withering of both, in their mutual depletion. For Ponge, the anthropomorphism of the oyster—to resort to my usual example, its "stubbornness"—is one that points back to the impure linguistic conditions that, far from consisting symmetrically apart from their object, rather come to infect the very physical contours that they would otherwise seek to represent and thus neutralize. Both poets, then, use the attribution of human features to inanimate objects in a manner that subverts our usual expectations of that device's effect, namely its apparent ability to make poetic content easily assimilable to a representational and recuperative reading—one that would be easy to swallow, so to speak.

Here I must supplement Frank Lentricchia, who, while recognizing the disunity lurking within the relation between jar and hill in Stevens's poem, nonetheless succumbs to the conclusion that it is only the *jar* that is doing the dominating, that is to be understood as the sole author of the "flaw," to invoke Cavaillès's term, that inflects the movement between object and world: "The original structural opposition of 'jar' and 'wilderness,' an opposition of nouns as substances, modulates into an opposition of verbs or actions: jars 'take,' the wilderness 'gives.' Jars take power—'dominion' . . . Who is responsible for this power? Certainly not 'I'; the jar did it."[53] Stevens's jar stands in, here, for Lentricchia's more general interest in the drive to domination and purity that transfers from modernity, with its structures of surveillance and capillary power, into the aesthetic modernism that Stevens is here conscripted to represent. But my reading would emphasize the opposite, namely the forms of destabilization that both modernist verse and nonpositivist philosophy of science would insist on as the very condition of the *new*, the latter a term not finally reducible here to any ideology of aesthetic autonomy, to say nothing of any totalized and totalizing vision of power and domination. It is the very ironical *lack* of autonomy of either jar or landscape, that is to say, that causes either, in all their figural richness, to move, to incite one another to movement.

Again, what Cavaillès, Ponge, and Stevens demonstrate is the benefit of a nonrepresentational, noncorrelational account of how distinct forms—objects and their surrounding structures, the material world and the poetic languages that would stretch to capture it—agonistically meet, indict, and (in)cite one another, apparently at the point at which they fail to adequately mirror one another's internal complexities, or at the point—think of Lentricchia's reading of Stevens—where one seems to have got the upper hand over the other. We pass a certain way down this path by recognizing the tendency of poems old and new to lay bare their own reflexive processes of composition, thus allowing verse to present both the content of its intended objects and the arduous process of the attempt to picture them. Ted Hughes recognized this integral aspect of poetic creativity in an interview with the *Paris Review*, where he spoke of "the sense in which every poem that comes off is a description or dramatization of its own creation."[54] The temptation to avoid here is to hive history, as the "dramatization" Hughes speaks of, off into its own domain, leaving "form" as static and internally self-sufficient, or else as entirely determined by its historical other. Rather, what the Russian Formalists referred to as the *ostrananie* proper to literary language and what I've called its inherent reflexivity refuses to remain within limits prescribed by its outsides.

Rather, the "description or dramatization of its own creation" is also the dramatization, the reflexive incorporation and disincorporation, of those historical forces that could be called, with Lacan, "ex-timate"—simultaneously both inside and outside—the contours of any given literary object. I'll have reason to engage once again with this most knotty of problems—the precise status of history vis-à-vis form—in the chapters that follow, but especially in chapter 5.

Cavaillès, Thematization, Reflexivity

It remains to approach the most important concept employed by Cavaillès relevant to the model of literary form and formalization explored in this book. To repeat, such an articulation is not meant as a mere scholastic exercise, the bringing together of unlikely bedfellows in the service of intellectual history. Rather, it is my wager that a strikingly new account of form may emerge in the interstices between apparently incommensurable discourses, especially insofar as those discourses are both fundamentally concerned with the interaction of word and world, object and structure. The concept that runs most productively through both traditions, as already mentioned above, is that of *reflexivity*, when understood in an especially capacious sense. On being imported into a theory of formal structures, be they scientific or poetic, reflexivity points us toward how the structurality of structure consists in its instability, in the productivity unleashed by the frictional, agonistic, and thus never static relation between an object and the symbols that would, in vain, wish to correspond with it. Cavaillès's name for this paradoxical form of generative impasse or productive misprision is *thematization*.

In its broadest sense, "thematization" names the transition in a science between one paradigm and another. Specifically, thematization captures a particular kind of abstraction, one that pushes the horizons of scientific knowledge beyond the particular set of objects with which it had otherwise been concerned. Jean Ladrière, a French philosopher of mathematics writing in the shadow of Cavaillès's influence, writes of thematization as follows: "In relation to a certain sector of experience, the act of thematization is itself carried out in a characteristic horizon which is necessarily beyond the horizon which is to be retrieved."[55] In other words, an act of novel scientific comprehension, the setting up of a new structure of sense, necessarily oversteps the relational limits, the set of possible combinations, that the prevailing horizon would seem to force on its objects. But there is a key difference between these two

French philosophers, otherwise so united in their antipositivism and in their commitment to a nonempirical, rationalist epistemology of scientific knowledge. For Ladrière, the process of abstraction proper to thematization must be understood as a progressive distancing from the inchoate world of experience from which the scientific is subsequently built. As he writes, "Science itself is not the first layer of experience; it is not an absolute beginning. It constitutes itself in starting from perceptual experience, thanks to a thematization of a special type."[56]

For Cavaillès, by contrast, structurality goes all the way down; to invoke "perceptual experience" as an originary moment foundational to science, even if that science would progressively leave that foundation behind, is to risk the foundational errors of phenomenology that Cavaillès is so resolute in opposing in his "On Logic." Such errors arise when a transcendental consciousness and its percepts are posited as the source and goal of all knowledge, as both the origin and exception to the structures that emerge in their wake and on its ground. For Cavaillès, the invocation of a perceptual origin allows the easy recourse, at the moment that knowledge reaches an impasse (an antinomy in Kant's language), to the very same origin as a false solution, a stitch with which to artificially heal dilemmas that, in their very intractability, are, when left alone, productive of the new. Here, of course, Cavaillès strongly departs from Kantianism and its antinomies, insofar as the latter would see in such impasses nothing but error and confusion, the inevitable but misleading limits to reason's ambitions. Apparent defects in knowledge are, on such a model, turned over to the aid of an imagined perceptual origin, and allowed then to fall back on the easy salve of foundation, the better to disbar in advance questions that, in truth, are situated very far beyond the simplicity and immediacy that one may associate with an imagined realm of pure perception, or with the empirical as a fantasized domain of immediacy. When held stubbornly in view, such paradoxes may provoke a creative if initially senseless breach with that which is currently understood as true, reproducing in turn previous conditions or structures in the light of the incursion of genuine novelty.

This is another way of reiterating a lesson already learnt from Ponge, namely that it is in the very senselessness of form that the conditions of any new sense might arise (recall Ponge's distribution of the senseless unit "*tre*" through "The Oyster," a paradoxical spot of nonsense that propels the poem around it into sense); to invoke a sense-laden origin, tied to a primary consciousness, is to deny the essential grounding of sense in non-sense, and thus to obscure the poetical moment proper to all acts of scientific knowing. Such a moment may be labeled poetical only if one insists that poetry, far from being a kind of Heideggerian key with which to unlock and disperse the technological objectifications of contemporary science, instantiates instead a kind of *ur*-reflexivity proper to *any* attempt, including those deemed scientific, to sieve the intractability of the world through the equally obstinate matrices of language.[57]

As Cavaillès writes, "If empirical history [as a meaningful origin] is used to reveal essential sequences, it is on the wrong side, not as a forward movement, but through the myth of the return of the past."[58] Even as such mythologies of the origin inevitably arise for beings limited in time and space, the processes of formalization that the sciences reveal when closely attended to are defined by a different logic, one that tends toward a rejection of the easy opposition between experience and language, or between sign and object, to say nothing of that between past and present. Such a refusal is, to be clear, of a kind with Ponge's insistence on the zones of non-sense that, even on the articulation of poetic signs and the world, point to the necessary and constitutive gap that persists between the two; to deny such interzones of nonmeaning that may poke through even the most abundant sites of apparent communion with the world is to be tragically tempted to find the absolute origin of sense outside language, with the result that understanding of both word and world, to temporarily maintain what is now surely an inadequate binary, is impoverished.

It seems appropriate, at this juncture, to acknowledge an obvious objection to my position, namely that, by imagining some nonmimetic connective function of literary signs, I have smuggled through the back door an even more tenacious essentialism than the one I have sought to replace. It is true, of course, that to imagine the object-world as bearing within itself some kind of buried linguistic structure or stability, one then located by an equally nonmimetic poetic structure, would be to revert to a kind of quasi-Heideggerian metaphysics. One can imagine the obvious catechresis, or suspiciously easy exchange of terms: "the textuality of materiality, the materiality of the text." But it is not *meaning* that courses through the objects that are the targets of literary capture, as in some kind of newfangled pan-psychism, but rather the *non*-meaning, the *non*-sense that inheres in their persistence; here, for both language and the world it seeks to tame, any meaningfulness to be established must gain its anxious grip on an ever-shifting and always-threatening ground of nonmeaning, a foundation that unites both a condition of possibility and of impossibility. Literary possibility and impossibility are held together in a tense standoff, one that has little enough to do with the mere reversal of terms already rejected above. In chapter 4, I'll explore how Paul de Man devoted himself in the latter years of his life to an account of just such an explanation of the agonistic foundation of non-sense to sense, one that nonetheless falls short of the ambitions of this book.

What might Ponge have to tell us about this nonoriginary "thematization," this nonoriginary and nonmeaningful destabilization of the levels proper to the world and its registration in language? Here his poem "L'orange" (1942), quite possibly his most powerful commentary on the tragedy of the human-language-object imbroglio, will be of particular use. Perhaps more than others of Ponge's celebrated encomia to everyday things, Ponge's poetic apprehension of the orange works hard to keep us off the scent of its formal strategies, not least because of the abundant sensuality of its content, almost queasy in its potency. In a string of praise that surely should, in its very excessiveness, raise our suspicions as to its sincerity, the poet breathlessly finds himself "unable to find words to express the admiration evoked by the covering of this tender, fragile, pink oval ball inside its thick moist absorbent blotting paper of which the extremely thin but intensely colored epidermis with its bitter oil is just ruddy enough to catch worthily the light that reveals the perfect form of the fruit."[59] There's a striking and deliberate contradiction here between the intensity of the sense experience to be imparted and the self-conscious clumsiness of its formal registration, in that curiously punctuationless rush of words, the very lack of metrical weighting here producing a strange, onrushing rhythm in its absence. No doubt the agglomeration of adjectives is meant, on some level, to replicate the breathlessness one would experience on perceiving such a ripe and rich piece of fruit, but I would argue for a different reading. Just as Ponge, in his "Oyster," had us appreciate the necessary artificiality of the poetic ambition to encompass the world, the better for us to notice that the word and the world coincide in their noncorrelation, so here the "perfect form" of the fruit points us irrevocably to the mimetic inadequacy of the language that would hope to cleave to that form, that language tripping over itself to find a form adequate to its object.

The reader is already pointed in this direction by the opening of the poem, where one finds a comic expression of sympathy for the orange's "yearning to recover its content after having been subjected to the ordeal of squeezing." Such, presumably, would be the figural state of the fruit should it ever be entirely subsumed within language, and one would be forgiven for thinking that language itself, then, dominates entirely the object that is finally only the plaything of the former's sadistic impulses. And yet what issues from this seeming execution or exhaustion is the juice itself, the gloriousness of which may be said to provoke the orange's masochistic celebration of its own disfigurement, such a disfigurement having revealed what was most precious in the object in the first place; tellingly, the orange in Ponge's poem "rejoic[es] its executioner."

The masochism of the orange, then, is counterposed to the sadism of language; the latter's inability to preserve its object reveals what is most unique and important in the object itself, its juice, and one is reminded, once again, of Ponge's oyster and its secreted pearl, revealed only by the shucking open of lips that otherwise would wish to remain chastely shut. Perhaps Ponge's poetry of objects is best understood, then, as a somewhat devilish celebration of different instances of material and textual violence, of the ineluctable smothering of the autonomy of objects by the caprice of human language with its anthropomorphic excesses. But it is the question of why such a forcing should nonetheless produce a nonmimetic accounting of its object that I'm principally concerned with here.

Back to Ponge's excitable celebration of his object in the fourth stanza, where one reads of the "admiration evoked by the covering of this tender, fragile, pink oval ball"—one would be forgiven for finding here a parody of the neo-romanticism that it would otherwise be tempting to associate Ponge's more general poetic project with. For all that the dramatic evocation of sensual rapture might tempt the reader to associate Ponge with a project to fuse poetic consciousness to the plenitude of things, and thus to deny the seemingly ascetic priorities most often associated with at least the sharp outer edges of modernism, the poem instead cannily undercuts its own sensuality, reimposes the gap between word and thing in the very apparent immersion of word in world, of the poet in the sensuous folds of the thing he describes. It's worth asking why Ponge would have us revel in the failure of his poetic strategy. Is this just the playful, family-friendly surrealism that, again, Ponge's verse may tempt its reader to consign it to? More is at stake: midway through the poem, Ponge adopts the image of an opening, of a yawning forth, that brings to mind the stark revelation of a world, a "firmament," that the very closure of the oyster's shell, in the reading of "L'huître" earlier, couldn't help but teasingly produce.

Ponge writes of the "glorious color of the . . . juice which, better than that of the lemon, forces one's throat wide open as much to pronounce the word as to swallow the liquid." Here, once again, something is "forced open" in Ponge's imaginary (think once more of the shucked oyster), a movement that allegorizes as much the resistances of language, the necessity of signification to be forced against its will, as it does any creative expansion, of the opening of aesthetic possibilities. The violent image of having one's throat forced open to pronounce the word associated with the object that one is ingesting—the mouth forming as a result an exaggerated and strained "O"—threatens to take the reader rather far from the easy, bold-colored testament to nature's bounty that the poem might otherwise winkingly seem to convey. Language, to put it another way, sticks in the throat of Ponge's imagined gourmand, just as there seems something perilous and unhealthy even among the exuberant colors and juices of the sugary object lying passive in wait of language's devouring. Needless to say, this is another instance of Ponge inserting a metatextual commentary into his verse that both affirms and records the formal strategies of the "primary" poem to be read. Once again, Ponge emphasizes here the queasy mucosity of the throat, the movements of the esophagus as an involuntary expression of pleasure—its opening and closing at the pleasurable acidity of the orange's juice—and the throat as the site of a bodily impasse, as vehicle of the grit that clogs it up and makes its movements slow and pained, and yet somehow more expressive for all that of the impasses of poetic language and its objects.

The word that forces itself on the mouth and the throat is, significantly, the name of the object that would pass through those openings; think, once again, of Hart Crane's fear of naming, given here an especially powerful and embodied form. As a consequence, we're left at the end of the poem wondering which came first—the gasp to swallow the juices of the fruit or the contraction of the throat that attends the speaking of the object's very name, a name that is, of course, in a distinctly Pongean irony, the poem's very title. I am reminded again of Derrida's profound remark that one never knows whether Ponge is "naming or describing" his objects, although in light of "L'orange" it may well be the object of poetic language just as much as language itself that forces on the reader such an ambivalence relative to the division between nomination and description. Ponge freezes his poetic image at the point at which a name might be formed, deferring the full netting of the object by the poem. The question to be labored over here isn't the essentially theological one of which came first, the word or the world; rather, it is the question of what happens when the gap between poetry and its objects of concern, the quick overcoming of which Ponge's serene authorial comportment seems to imply as its very founding assumption, is rather held open in its impurity, precisely as a result of the linguistic strategies that issue forth from that very founding stance of poetic serenity and authority. That the body should take center stage here is crucial; for Ponge, the impasses of language are written on the body, in the involuntary corporeal contractions that poetic language and the object of that language alike may inflict.

Or, better, for Ponge there is no contradiction between the ironical smirk that seems to motivate his rapturous description of the fruit, suggesting as it does an apparent indifference to the mimetic ambition one may otherwise be forgiven for seeing everywhere in his verse, and his desire, no less important, to get at the world and the body in their uneasy and overwhelming densities, in their unlikely contractions and yawning openings. By holding himself ironically apart from things, he finds himself confronted by a similar distance that inheres in things themselves and the bodies that must incorporate them. For such a vertiginous unease is as much to be found in the messy mystery of the fruit itself as it ripens and decays, and yet even more so in the mucous membrane of the mouth; this latter should now be reframed in the light of Freud's theory of the erogenous zones, those parts of the body that are simultaneously open and closed to contact with the outside and that impose on the subject its founding inability to fully differentiate itself from its others; this very inability, nonetheless, the only opening the subject has to the pleasures and pains of building an identity.

The point to take away is that poetic language is barred in advance from short-circuiting this necessary ironic detour, what in Cavaillès's terms one might call an originary reflexivity or "thematization" of all knowledge, in order to get at the thing itself; such would be the idealistic dream of vulgar materialisms past—or "surface readers" present. Rather, it is only through an uncannily material, corporeal, and reflexive self-reference that poetic language may touch the real. My analytic takes its distance here, I would argue, from earlier attempts to think poetic language and the body as somehow implicated, the one doubling the other. In the poetry of the so-called Victorian "spasmodics," and just as much in the quasi-corporeal verse of Elizabeth Barrett Browning crowned by her *Aurora Leigh*, the weight of poetic language seems something to be replaced by the language of the body, or at least the one is set up to be ecstatically fused with the other.[60] In Ponge, there can be no final collapse of the distance between language and body—such a collapse being a concession to something like representation. Rather, the resilient gap between the body and the word is redoubled at the level of both body and language; the body, more specifically the mouth, is twisted by the formal force of language, language itself then being infected and contorted by the body, Ponge unable to convey the shape of his object without referring to "the extremely thin but intensely colored epidermis with its bitter oil." Orifices are less ecstatic here than they are leaky; sputtering gaskets that testify to the fleshiness of language and the susceptibility of language to the flesh, such a portability not indicating, for all that, any gelatinous merging of one into the other.

In his recent, magisterial study of literary realism, Fredric Jameson encounters a similar queasy rapture in Zola's famous descriptions of imperial Paris. The evocation of Paris's Les Halles market in the first chapter of *Le ventre de Paris* is cited by Jameson as an especially compelling example of what he calls the "relationship between the perceptual and language or naming"—shades, again, of Derrida's distinction between description and nomination, as referenced above.[61] Zola's picturing of Les Halles climaxes in his raptured description of "boxes of whiting, like opal reflections in a mirror; and baskets of smelt—neat little baskets as pretty as punnets of strawberries and giving off a strong smell of violets. The tiny jet-black eyes of the prawns, in covered baskets, were like thousands of beads scattered across the piles of soft-toned pink and gray; the spiky lobsters and crayfish, striped with black and still alive, were dragging themselves about on their broken legs."[62] There's little of Ponge's sense of irony here, and the narrative form (very different in its grandiloquence from the deceptive sense of modesty produced by Ponge's recalibration of prose in poetic form) allows Zola to spin out his apparently mimetic apparatus into a loose and billowing temporal frame, one that nonetheless rises in intensity as it nears the "spiky" lobsters with their cruelly broken legs. Jameson initially locates in Zola's prose a progressive urge to categorization or nomination, such that "the enormous lists and catalogues would seem to be subsumed under generic categories and everyday commonsense universals: from life to the edible, from the edible to plants and animals, from the latter to meats and fish,"[63] and so on.

Yet "there exists a second movement that undermines [such categorization] and secretly discredits it—a tremendous fermenting and bubbling pullulation in which the simplicity of words and names is unsettled to the point of an ecstatic dizziness."[64] But far from Zola leaving his reader at the mercy of a phenomenal immersion in this "pullulation" of things, Jameson concludes that "the unexpected result is that far from enriching representational language with all kinds of new meanings, the gap between words and things is heightened."[65] Here one encounters both similarities and differences with Ponge. In the latter's "L'orange," one sees an ironical and distanced reflexivity induce, in its very highlighting of the gap between word and thing, a sense of the material and corporeal effects of those things themselves, while in Zola Jameson traces how an apparent proliferation of names and categories gives way to the phenomenal excess of things themselves, only then to find that such a proliferation itself *reinstates* the very gap between word and thing it might otherwise have been expected to have overcome. My reading of Ponge could be distinguished here by noting how, in "L'orange," the dialectical end point of this transition between word and thing is the very perturbation of things themselves and the bodies that incorporate them, things to be accessed only after first passing through the linguistic, reflexive distance that might otherwise seem to impose an unimpeachable wall between language and its possible referents; this being the initial naive sensualism, the "sense certainty" in Hegel's terms, that must by necessity be overcome. Jameson, by contrast, locates in Zola's heightened naturalism a perpetual back-and-forth between perception, nomination, and thing that is formally undecidable and that nonetheless seems to conclude with the restatement of the unbridgeable gap between word and thing that Ponge, in my reading, surmounts at the moment at which his poetry recognizes its very ironical necessity. Repeated, once more, is something of the anxiety of Crane's poetic evocation of nature and the name, although here names and categories seem to sharpen a prior perceptual excess, a dizziness that threatens always to harden into stasis.

In any case, there is no clear line of influence or priority here between word and thing, even as both invoke and convoke a similar physical reflex (as in the "O" that the mouth forms to name Ponge's orange), and even as Ponge in poetry and Zola in fictional narrative would wish to remind us of the gap between world and thing even at the moment that such a tenacious polarity has apparently been transcended. The unpredictability of the transport between one and the other, reminiscent of the more agonistic battle between jar and wilderness staged by Stevens in the poem discussed above, shoots an impurity through both language and the object in question, the only aspect of either that might then ensure any connection between the two. That impurity, recall, is expressed as much in the seeming withdrawal of word from thing, a gap never entirely bridged, as it is in any successful, elastic intertwining of one with the other; yet Ponge, at least, seems to get somewhere across that bridge in his perverse celebration of mimetic impossibility.

Against my emphasis, a certain strain in contemporary theory, and surprisingly one often in avowed fidelity to Derridean deconstruction, has preferred to define the literariness of literature in terms of its ceaseless and successful motion, by reference to the in-principle endless mutability and commutability of both literary form and content. Consider Nicholas Royle's theory of "veering," of a kinetic and uncanny "swerve" that can be found across broad swaths of literature and defines the best of our experiences with texts, those improving moments when poems or novels reverse our expectations and thus establish their importance and durability. Far from being just a phenomenological account of the experience of surprise that surely any reader has had when overtaken by the cunning of a particular text's defenses against expectation, Royle contends that "veering" may help us decide what is to count as great literature. "The compelling but also the most resistant to reading, are the most veering. A masterpiece is always a veerer."[66]

Crucially, Royle is quick to associate this notion of a central or constitutive shift with terms familiar from deconstruction. "You cannot pin down a veerer," Royle writes, "any more than you can categorize the place of a supplement or finalize the relationship between literature and the secret."[67] "Supplement" and "secret" are, of course, key terms for Derrida, who worked to assiduously parse the necessity and impossibility of both concepts within various structures of intelligibility. Royle, it seems to me, is very quick, perhaps too quick, to associate such a conditioning impossibility or intransigence with endless *movement.* What of those moments when literature, far from being an endless kinetic blur of impossible to predict twists and turns, may actually define itself in its *refusal* of the reversals that Royle thinks are the key to greatness? Might the very tension thus generated contain the condition for any subsequent movement of literary sense? On my account, literary form may be able to locate itself in the intransigence of the material world only as a consequence of such a stubborn intransigence, in its own diffident closure upon itself. I wonder how Royle would account for the dialectic of permanence and frustrated movement that Stevens so stunningly evokes in his "Anecdote of the Jar," where traits of impermeability—precisely, of the *lack* of movement—are shared between foreground and background, object and landscape, precisely as the key to the power of each, and, allegorically, as the fount of poetic language itself in its cold war with history. Against the contemporary critical valorization of all things endlessly generative, affective, or accelerated, a speculative formalism would find in closure, in shutdown and constraint, sources of unexpected fecundity.

To conclude, I'd like to consider the most bracing critique of formalist approaches to literature to appear in the last five decades or so, one that has come to us from the Marxist tradition, even as it was precisely the imperative of Marxist politics that pushed Louis Althusser and others to such a nuanced, quasi-formalist (or, as I've called it, "postrationalist")[68] approach to literary language and scientific structure alike. Fredric Jameson remains our most persuasive critic of the seemingly ahistorical drift of formalist analysis, and I will briefly contrast the formalism introduced here with the reading he influentially advanced in one of his very first books, *The Prison-House of Language*—the title, of course, revealing much about the critique worked out across the book as a whole.

Writing of the Russian formalists, and especially Viktor Shklovsky, Jameson notes their insistence on a sharp distinction between ordinary language and the language of literature. Literature for the formalists is designed to estrange us from our everyday surroundings, such surroundings most pertinently to include ordinary language itself. As Jameson puts it, "The deeper implication is that poetry is not a merely specialized part of everyday language, but constitutes a total linguistic system in its own right."[69] Jameson goes on to insist that, far from imparting a general or universal theory of literary language, Russian formalism (and the structuralism that emerged in its wake) needed to accord an undue privilege to self-consciously modernist, poetical texts, insofar as they best exemplify what is subsequently, and without full justification, claimed to be a universal feature of such language, namely the capacity to shock us out of what Heidegger famously called our "ready-to-hand" relationship to the world, our tendency to scan the aspects of the world around us only in terms of their potential use.[70]

Jameson's critique turns, especially, on the charge that the theory of prose developed in particular in Shklovsky's now-classic work is unable to deal with the especially *modern* staging of change and instability that the novel, as a genre, seemed machine-tooled to evoke. As Jameson writes, "Defamiliarization was originally a method derived from lyric or at least from lyrical perceptions, and in its application to plot it retains traces of its relatively more static origins."[71] "Only pre-existing things," Jameson continues, "objects, institutions, units of some kind—can be defamiliarized"[72]—as if it were only the frozen or static thing or belief that can be shaken up, forced into a new awareness of its contingency. The novel, Jameson seems to suggest, bears within it an especial capacity to register the already mutable character of things that lyric poetry, in the modesty of its mostly subjective purview tied to the illusions of the sovereign "I," cannot achieve. Quite aside from Jameson's uncharacteristic acceptance here of a literary form's claims to its own ontological exceptionality—the novel, in this instance, as claiming an exclusive capacity to become the oracle of modernity's speed, its melting of all things solid into air—I should underline, too, the indefensible equation of poetry (more specifically, lyric) with synchronic atemporality; as my reading of the articulation of poetic and historical time in chapters 5 will make especially clear, there can be no clean separation of poetic form from history and vice versa, a separation most redolent, ironically, of the most basic criticisms of formalism that it is Jameson's wont to complicate. And we may wonder, too, whether estrangement itself may be sometimes better achieved, not through the kinesis of narrative action, but through the very kinds of stasis that I've already begun to insist are crucial to any full understanding of poetic form.

At any rate, my reading of Stevens's "Anecdote of the Jar" above, if nothing else, may serve to trouble the following from Jameson: "Only pre-existing things . . . can be defamiliarized." Stevens's jar only truly comes to be, only assumes its full potentiality, on the equally formative and de-formative impress of the landscape within which it is placed and with which it then tussles; defamiliarization, that is to say, goes all the way down in Stevens's verse, through and between foreground and background, past and present, even via the employment (gently parodic, to be sure, in "The Anecdote") of a traditional, lyric rhythmic balance and decorum. As such, it may be useful to explore a different reading of Russian formalism than that given by Jameson, if only to highlight the indispensable resources to be found in those formalisms that have tended to be mislabeled, by Jameson among others, with the tags of synchronism and static ahistoricity. As will be seen in the brief reading of Shklovsky that follows, Russian formalism contained in germinal form a number of the facets of a renewed, speculative formalism that I'm proposing as essential to any creative analysis of literature today.

Within a disquisition on rhythm in literary writing in his *Theory of Prose* from 1920, Shklovksy writes: "There are those who think that the purpose of art is to facilitate something or to inspire or to generalize. Lacking a sufficient number of steam hammers, these people enlist the help of rhythm to do the job."[73] Rhythm should be taken here as a literary function conducive to standardization or what he goes on to describe as "generalization"[74]—a process of passive formalization that might wish to sort oysters, rain, cigarettes, all of Ponge's deceptively "thingly objects," and squeeze them into forms that then come to dominate them, ironing out their crinkles.

In an intriguing passage that I've already pressed into service, Shklovsky opposes such a "generalization," defined by its operation of "creating, insofar as possible, wide-ranging, all encompassing formulas,"[75] to "particularization" as the essence of art. Art, on this model, is "based on a step-by-step structure and on the particularizing of even that which is presented in a generalized and unified form."[76] It's hard to square this insistence with the common understanding of Russian formalism, as reducing texts to mechanism, aesthetic feeling to structural necessity. Shklovsky's emphasis on particularization is, I think, key to extracting the potential for a formalism of impurity from an author too often suspected to be arid in his lack of concern for context, for the unpredictability of a textual structure as it unfolds over time. First, a "step by step structure" as Shklovsky describes it is one that is necessarily open-ended. Such a structure is comparable to the vision of the scientific advanced by Cavaillès; far from being closed, mute, and shut off from the ambivalence that might give rise to change, scientific codification proceeds, and is productively interrupted, by the unpredictable incitements of its objects. Quentin Meillassoux provides an apt summation of this doubleness of form by reference to poetic meter, where meter, far from being only constrictive, "singularizes better and further than the absence of meter."[77] The active kind of formalization that Shklovsky adopts, that is to say, is one that finds in limitation and constriction the conditions for an at least partial poetic freedom.

A "step by step structure," for Shklovsky, is one that pays due heed to the formativeness of form, to risk a tautology I've already toyed with, while encompassing the potential for literary structures to hold together radically heterogeneous elements; such a holding together and a production of heterogeneity is presented, crucially, as *noncontradictory*, indeed as the key to any understanding of literary form as such. To cleave to an analytics of particularity, or "particularization" as Shklovsky has it, "singularization" in Meillassoux's account, or even "thematization" in Cavaillès's sense, is not to deny the existence of general kinds of formal utterance, but to find within those generalities the singularities that prevent them from fading into the background: their very own secreted pearls, so to speak. Form becomes here not something immovable, ahistorical, but a moving principle of articulation and disarticulation, something like what Paul de Man had in mind when he wrote, in a discussion of Schiller and Kleist, of the aesthetic as "not a separate category, but a principle of articulation between various known faculties, activities and modes of cognition."[78]

I would need to add, of course, that such an articulation does not leave untouched the objects that it conscripts, and that those objects or figures have much to say in return, much to *object* to. This agonistic conversation between the respective elements of literary language reposes once again a question asked with admirable eloquence by Michael Sprinker, who wrote of the "tension between the aesthetic as a model of transcendental cognitive power and the aesthetic as a historical and ideological social practice."[79] Such a capaciously enlarged theory of form, where the topological indetermination between structure and its objects is taken as the condition of their very interaction, might aid us in rethinking in turn the articulation of historical causation and cultural autonomy, a question that has its genesis in Marx's own reflections on Greek art in the *Grundrisse*: "But the difficulty lies not in understanding that the Greek arts and epic are bound up with certain forms of social development. The difficulty is that they still afford us artistic pleasure and that in a certain respect they count as a norm and as an unattainable model."[80] I hope the comments above on reflexivity, on poetry's dramatization of its own engagements and disengagements from its outsides, may at least lay the ground for the renewal of such a critical conversation, one that recognizes the simultaneous situatedness and quasi-autonomy of literary form. The subject will be raised again in the chapters that follow.

With this in mind, I should acknowledge a question latent in my comparative reading of Ponge and Cavaillès, namely whether there is an absolute difference between the kinds of objects that scientific languages and poetic languages arrange and are arranged by. Shklovsky's insistence on the particular, on particularization as the condition of form proper to literature, helps us, finally, to resist the forced choice of scientific universalism on the one hand, poetic nominalism on the other. The "particular," perhaps, is the necessary pearl in the oyster, the impurity that enables the opening out of the oyster's flared shell on to the universal outside. Science and poetry remain, at the end of this chapter, fundamentally different domains, but they share, in their projects of formalization, an ability to motivate their materials in a direction irreducible to conceptual or linguistic solipsism on the one hand, mimetic reflection on the other.

3

Alain Badiou, Wallace Stevens, and the Paradoxical Productivity of Poetic Form

It is hard to imagine two more apparently opposed philosophical approaches to the poetry of Wallace Stevens, indeed to poetry as such, than those of the contemporary theorists Simon Critchley and Alain Badiou. For Critchley, the later Stevens is emblematic of a more general poetic capacity, namely to present the world in its "mereness," its placid, human-affected but nonetheless independent existence. For Badiou, the poet instantiates what Stevens himself described in the title of one of his poems as art's "description without place," which is to say its capacity to create worlds out of active linguistic engagement; a description that, one might say, creates a place without being put *in* its place. Such a power would trickily precede its object, would even force its object into appearance. While it won't be the main focus of this chapter, Badiou's general philosophy of art is of a piece with his political philosophy, one that maintains an unapologetic fidelity to *les événements* of May 1968 in France and focuses on the rare occurrence of such events insofar as they radically transform and rearrange the coordinates of the possible, producing a universalizable truth in their wake.[1] Through an encounter with Badiou's writings on Wallace Stevens, with occasional counterpoint from Critchley, I hope to gain a sense of the concrete consequences of Badiou's so-called "inaesthetic" writings. The aim, nonetheless, is not to give a comprehensive account of Badiou's philosophy of art. Instead, through an immanent critique of his account of Wallace Stevens, to be interspersed with my own set of readings of the poet, I hope to demonstrate how the "speculative formalist" approach of this book may provide keener insights, otherwise lost to what is still a bracing and often innovative reinvigoration of French philosophy's engagements with literature.[2]

Appearance on Badiou's account—and poetry, for Badiou, is a linguistically fueled form of creative appearance—is its own affirmation; there is an absolute and positive equivalence between a poetic sign and its effectivity, and poetry is thus unresponsive to any notion of hidden essence, any attempt to subordinate appearance to a more primary reality.

Badiou departs here from what has become a standard claim made of Stevens, namely that his poetry underscores the world's fallen passivity and its subsequent tending-to by the finite but determined human mind. On such a reading, what exists behind the degraded veil of appearances is the creative and sustaining impetus of the human will. One reads in Stevens's well-known poem "The Idea of Order at Key West" of a "she" who

> . . . sang, the sea,
> Whatever self it had, became the self
> That was her song, for she was the maker. Then we,
> As we beheld her striding there alone,
> Knew that there never was a world for her
> Except the one she sang and, singing, made.[3]

One is tempted to detect here in the poet a variant of the subjective idealist who would wish to make the world bend to the imaginative whims of consciousness. It is not, however, a minded form of creation that Badiou ascribes to poetry, as will be seen anon, and the forms that come under poetry's command are not meekly pliant or entirely overdetermined by subjective caprice. As Stevens remarks of the sea earlier in the poem:

> its mimic notion
> Made constant cry, caused constantly a cry
> That was not ours although we understood,
> Inhuman, of the veritable ocean[4]

But as I'll outline below, Badiou's approach, in its affirmative positivity, risks neglecting the productive incommensurability between human meaning-making and the materiality of the outdoors—the "inhumanity," in Stevens's terms above, of literary and material form both—that is recognized (and perhaps also, at times, obfuscated) in Stevens's poetics.

For Simon Critchley, it is Stevens's postromantic reconciliation with the world, with the *angst* attendant to its lack of a divine supernatural realm, that allows poetry to "take the place of religion as that medium which offers the possibility, or at least pursues the question, of life's redemption."[5] The kind of redemption that Stevens proffers for Critchley contrasts sharply with Badiou's secularized Pauline streak. Instead of embodying the inherent evental potentiality of artistic practice, Stevens for Critchley begins from the world as it affronts us in its immovable placidity, from the necessity of our passing through its stubborn, thick-grained *there-ness*, a transport that will only then allow poetic language its ability to transfigure or heighten reality in its nonetheless equivocal complexity.

In this chapter, I will argue for a reading of Wallace Stevens that tempers Critchley's Heidegger-inflected neo-romanticism, whereby the fallen-ness of things can be partially redeemed in poetry's capacity to, as Critchley puts it via Stevens, capture "mere being as it is."[6] Equally, I will divert from Badiou's gathering of the resources of poetic language under an eccentrically Platonic conception of truth, one that remains Platonic despite, of course, Plato's well-known aversion to representational poetry. Badiou will be my main foil in what follows, and I will take the philosopher, despite his innovations, to repeat aspects of an older trend in Wallace Stevens criticism, namely to argue for the poet as what Critchley calls a kind of "anxious atheist"[7] who sought to forge a temporary bridge between the mind of a disabused modernity and its recalcitrant objects. As will be seen, Stevens's verse offers a different optic on to the problem already posed to us by Ponge in the previous chapter, namely how to understand those poetic voices that seem concerned with the effusive presentation of worldly plenitude in their content, and yet who undercut such moves at the level of their form. By understanding how it is through the disarticulation of form in poetry that the latter may come to successfully evoke its various worlds, we move a step beyond the conventional distinction between form and content just employed, a distinction that always seems in the final instance to defer to content over its elusive other. As in the previous chapter, "form" here will generally name those aspects of Stevens's poem that are self-referring, that initially seem to undercut rather than amplify meaning; as before, I will be especially concerned with moments of contradiction and paradox, the better to find in such apparent moments of literary inwardness a transport outward, an eccentric reference to the density of things off the page. Just as often, and not unlike Ponge, Stevens will be shown to provide a poetic metacommentary on this process; as a result, I will foreground the "argument," the metapoetic reflection on poetry's conditions of possibility that threads through much of this verse, without neglecting Stevens's own employment of the formal strategies that he so often comments on at the level of what we may risk still calling poetic content.

Given my specific focus on Badiou's renovation of an older trend in Stevens's criticism, one that alights in particular on the idea of Stevens as (reluctant?) inheritor of romanticism, a thorough survey of contemporary Wallace Stevens criticism is neither possible here nor entirely apt. Nonetheless, it is worth mentioning that, in the turn to material history and eco-criticism that has defined much commentary on Stevens since the waning of the deconstructive school, the emphasis on the poet as a kind of modern naturalist has often served to mask what is, in fact, a familiar call for him to bear the load of a pseudo-romantic unification of idea and world, world and word. This is what is found, for instance, in Robert Pogue Harrison's essay "Not Ideas about the Thing but the Thing Itself."[8] There Harrison writes that "'idea' and 'nature' are essentially homologous in the thought of Wallace Stevens . . . Nature is the birth, or coming into being, of the idea itself."[9] There is, in other words, a thorough and absolute unification of word and world in Stevens, and it is with the vehicle of nature that such a harmony may be found. It is hard to reconcile this notion with Stevens's insistence, say in his "Description without Place," that "Even the seeming of a summer's day / Is description without place";[10] even the apparent immediacy of the plenitude and presence of summer is already refracted by an originary dislocation, and so cannot be located in any definitive encompassing horizon, one that would invoke a determinative place where idea and world might cohere. Rather, in a moment of poetic metacommentary,

> Description is
> Composed of a sight indifferent to the eye
>
> It is an expectation, a desire
> A palm that rises up beyond the sea
>
> A little different from reality.[11]

What Stevens archly underplays here as a "little" difference, the constitutive crack between word (description) and world (reality), between "expectation" and reality, is, I have been arguing, exactly what allows poetry its nonmimetic contact with its material outsides. It is this noncorrelational reference that Harrison's and others' contemporary relocation of Stevens within a kind of poetic naturalism forecloses.

Something stranger, less ameliorative, is at work in Stevens's verse, then, something that bears on any attempt to reimagine once again what literature may have to tell us about the necessary paradoxes of language per se and its outsides, or the ways in which the paradoxes of the world exist, awkwardly, in language, and, perhaps more crucially, vice versa; how, in other words, to detect similar formal mechanisms across literature, as an especially compacted and libidinized form of language, and materiality as its apparently elusive other, when both are understood not as distinct fields ranged in symmetrical opposition, but rather, as seen above in my reading of Ponge, as impurely crisscrossed structures that spark in affinity even as they appear to shrink from one another. Such structures abound in paradoxes and dead zones as much as they refuse the rhetoric of the rhizome, the network, or the plane of immanence; the analytical language of flux and fluidity, mixture and network, as popular as it is,[12] fails to capture the stubbornness of poetic form, its minimalism. Caroline Levine, as I noted in the introduction, is surely right to emphasize the constitutive lack of fit between literary form and its various "contexts," such that currently predominant forms of historical determinism in literary studies, in their tacit acceptance of a tidy fit between form and context, neuter the estrangement proper to literary form's principal function. But I'd like to enquire again after *how* poetic form generates such possibilities through its holding together of order and disorder, negativity and the positive.[13]

In consequence, my argument is incompatible with a comment made by Badiou in an interview about the film *Magnolia,* directed by Paul Thomas Anderson: "If you want to bring about . . . something that takes a stand on a possible meaning of generic humanity, the path has to be that of *construction,* not deconstruction."[14] As I think Stevens's poetics exemplify fully, there is no construction *without* deconstruction, or alternately, poetic form is both formative and de-formative at every instance of its manifestation. If deconstruction was always in danger of ennobling the deformative *over* the formative, I think Badiou lapses too frequently into the opposite, into what Benjamin Noys has usefully named "affirmationism."[15] Intriguingly, this is not always the case in Badiou's ontological writings, especially of late, where stasis and inertia, if not the negative in quite the productive way I intend it, play a crucial if reactive role.[16] Stevens, as will be seen, wants us to appreciate how the quasi-solipsistic closure of poetic form, its very failure to faithfully capture the colors and affects and irritations of the world, is precisely where it is most likely to make contact, however brief, with its apparent others.

Where I will even more decisively depart from Badiou and Critchley is in my rejection of the residual and largely unexamined romanticism inherent in both authors' philosophies of poetry, a residue also appreciable in Harold Bloom's pathbreaking work on Stevens, where poetry can be said to resacralize, in a secular tongue, a godless world.[17] This, it is fair to say, is one of the accepted truths of Wallace Stevens criticism. Critchley and Badiou, for all their apparent differences, reflect the two sides of this neo-romantic totality, with the former arguing for the quiet pathos of acquiescence in the face of the fallen world, and Badiou projecting a faith in the power of poetic language to recover the epic or heroic tendency otherwise lost in the attempt to translate the expanses of epic verse into the alienated spaces and temporalities of modernity. In the analysis of

Badiou's reading of Stevens's poem "L'esthétique du mal" that follows, the figure of the soldier performs this alternately tragic and heroic function for Badiou, in some ways of course the same function viewed from different angles of approach.

Both sides of this coin, the anxious and the resigned on the one and the heroic and thrusting on the other, are implicitly reliant on the prior expansion of the aesthetic as a philosophical category that may lay claim to art for its own, for all that Badiou otherwise insists on the autonomy of artistic practice as an independent condition for philosophy. Badiou tries to secure such an autonomy through the neologistic concept of "inaesthetics," intended to register the self-sufficiency of art as a condition of truth, irreducible to its ever being a product or protectorate of philosophy per se; as he writes, "By inaesthetics I understand a relation of philosophy to art that, maintaining that art is itself a producer of truths, makes no claim to turn art into an object for philosophy."[18] Perhaps, though, it is in Badiou's very rhetorical insistence on the autonomy of the inaesthetic, its refusal to be colonized by philosophy, that unexpectedly produces something of that colonization by stealth.

For if poetry, included in the more general category of art, is to act as one of the conditions of philosophy without being reducible to it, there is the nagging temptation to inflate a discourse that mediates between that condition and philosophy proper, and what is that discourse if not the hypostatized domain of the "aesthetic" that has been passed down to us from Baumgarten onward, a domain that, in the final analysis, clings to philosophy for its legitimating terms of reference. But the "aesthetic" is doubly inadequate for my purposes, insofar as Stevens's poetry, and perhaps modernist poetry more generally, austerely subtracts at the level of its form from the ideology of the sensible that is surely one of the defining features of romanticisms both English and German. Stevens's poetry is equally indifferent to the ideology of taste that is a sensuous romanticism's means of discrimination, taste becoming, finally, the rubric by which a criticism at the cusp of modernism's unapologetic sorting strategies could evoke such hierarchies despite its more general aversion to moral absolutes or rigid, objective measures of truth. This is not to deny the numerous references to sensation and feeling at the level of Stevens's poetic content, of course, but the attempt by Bloom and others to portray Stevens as the "dependent heir"[19] of the romantics threatens to dissimulate the crucial and determining dislocations to be found at the level of his use of poetic form. Badiou's own concept of truth, it's worth highlighting at this stage, is equally disdainful of both the objective and the idea of "measure," something it shares with high romanticism, broadly conceived. "Each truth is a process," Badiou writes, "and not a judgment or a state of affairs."[20]

The point at which my position comes closer to that of Badiou can be found in his, at first glance rather inscrutable, assertion that "the infinite of language is the powerlessness immanent to the poem's effect of power."[21] Power*less*ness precisely insofar as poetic language is only ever the singular presentation of an idea, or as Badiou sometimes phrases it, a singular "presentation of presence" itself; poetry can never universalize the idea in the way that mathematics, in its generic indifference, can. I would want to reorient Badiou's statement to mean something slightly different, a recasting that would hinge on the apparent contradiction implied by the claim that the powerlessness immanent to the poem has something centrally to do with its effect of power. It is in poetry's determinative inability to present the whole, an inability written into the very productive constraints exemplified in poetry by the marshaling of language into meter, that it gains momentary access to the similar failures of completion and rational totalization that define its referents, referents otherwise assumed to lie submissive in anticipation of poetic representation; Stevens, needless to say, instantiates for us this paradox better than most.

Earlier critical accounts of the success of art in producing such a worldly effect have often relied on the notion of "imagination," as a capacity that, in sharp distinction from its use in Kant as that which might synthesize otherwise disparately situated impressions, nonetheless finds an alternative principle of clarity in the unlikely figure of the dream. Such an instance of imagination, it has been argued, contributes to the production of the reality that it might otherwise only have been assumed to register unconsciously; think, most obviously, of Freud's account of how dreams stage and help solidify the coordinates of our fantasy lives, such coordinates becoming a necessary frame through which reality itself becomes explicable. On such an account, the dream, as the subtraction of a perceiving subjectivity from a narrowly empirical waking state, becomes the condition for the partial construction of, and insight into, something more fundamental about reality as such. Nietzsche insisted on the necessity of such a dream-state for an understanding of art, as when he wrote of "the fair illusion of the dream sphere," as "a precondition of not only all plastic art, but even . . . of a wide range of poetry."[22] But Nietzsche also wished us to "behave toward the reality of the dream in much the way the philosopher behaves toward the reality of existence,"[23] which is to say that one must treat the apparent codes of fiction, here embodied by the dream, as real structures to be conscientiously parsed, the better to discern the fictional lens through which any knowledge of such a reality must travel. This may be rephrased again by saying that it is in the apparent solipsism of a dreaming "imagination" that reality is, paradoxically, to be most richly discerned; as the Lacanian cliché has it, truth has the structure of a fiction.[24]

Or to risk a reversal, it may be in the very resistance of nonfantasmatic material worlds to their capture by the demands of imaginational poetic structure, the imperatives of such worlds' compressive, constrictive force, that produces the fleeting contact of the act of imagination and the sheer facticity of wordly density. Clearly, one need not choose between a precritical realism, whereby the self-sufficiency of the world proudly sits impervious to subjectivity, or the philosophically loose nominalism that threatened to define deconstructive literary theory as it entered its dotage. Stevens nicely phrases the dilemma in his "Notes toward a Supreme Fiction":

> Is there a poem that never reaches words
>
> And one that chaffers the time away?
> Is the poem both peculiar and general?
> There's a meditation there, in which there seems
>
> To be an evasion, a thing not apprehended.[25]

A poem that never reaches words, that has everything to do with things-in-themselves, is as much a fantasy as a theory of poetic language as that which would "chaffer" the time away entirely within its own solipsistic bounds, indifferent to the density of things. To hold oneself within such false terms is to evade poetry in the fullness of its consequences.

The soldering together of opposite momentums that I take here to be characteristic of poetic form—articulation and disarticulation, formation and deformation, presence and absence—should be distinguished too from how they appear within romanticist aesthetics, or at least that variant of romanticism best expressed in Samuel Coleridge's famous encomium to "the balance or reconciliation of opposite or discordant qualities: of sameness, with difference; of the general, with the concrete; the idea, with the image,"[26] and so on. The symmetry and sense of synthesis here is precluded by the incommensurability that I think is the mark of poetry's intervention, an incommensurability that nonetheless serves as a condition of possibility as much as, in fact *more than*, impossibility. For Coleridge by contrast, the opposites in question are to be understood as the product of an underlying unity, namely the aesthetic, itself in turn the conceptual holding pen of the unpredictable but nonetheless connective movements of poetic symbol. In what follows, incommensurability and asymmetry come first; whatever precarious shell of symbolic unity that might then encase them is only ever a temporary stabilization at the level of content of a prior formal impasse. But again, that impasse is not to be conceived of as flux or rhizome or the virtual or the abject or even the trace structure of *différance,* for those terms do little to capture the curious, minimal *rigidity* of poetic structure, its imposing and yet fecund constraint, evocatively imaged by Stevens in the figure of the Rock in his poem of the same name: "Its barrenness becomes a thousand things."[27]

But it is not just the constitutive blankness and rigidity of literary signification that is evoked in this late poem; equal attention is given to the blank solidity of the world, its apparent refusal to match seamlessly with our symbolic designs. As Stevens writes at the beginning of the poem:

> It is an illusion that we were ever alive,
> Lived in the houses of mothers, arranged ourselves
> By our own motions in a freedom of air.
>
> Regard the freedom of seventy years ago.
> It is no longer air. The houses still stand,
> Though they are rigid in rigid emptiness.[28]

In these lines, autonomy, the ability to arrange ourselves "by our motions," freedom in a word, is now, from the purview of the poem's present, a mere illusion. One is led even to suspect that it was an illusion all along, an hallucination produced by memory's inherent tendency toward nostalgia. The houses, however, remain; materiality persists, albeit in rigid emptiness, a nonsymmetrical analogue to poetry's own uncanny emptiness, its "barrenness." Later lines, however, might seem to support the arguments of those who wish to find in Stevens a postromantic path to poetical reconciliation with the world. In a section pointedly titled "The Poem as Icon," Stevens writes:

> The fiction of the leaves is the icon
>
> Of the poem, the figuration of blessedness,
> And the icon is the man. The pearled chaplet of
> spring,
> The magnum wreath of summer, time's autumn
> snood,
>
> Its copy of the sun, these cover the rock.
> These leaves are the poem, the icon and the man.
> These are a cure of the ground and of ourselves[29]

Icons, of course, are famously contested things, sometimes taken to be lethal in their ambiguity, an ambiguity that issues from their bold claim to represent that more often considered unrepresentable. Historically, some have found in icons' picturing of divinity a path toward knowledge of God. Others have seen an attempt to undermine, via blasphemously earthly and material means, the proper exceptionality of the divine. But I don't think divinity is Stevens's topic or target here, not directly at least. Rather, it is a certain vision of nature, nature of course often standing in for the divine in multiple poetic traditions. The leaves that give color to the rock but ultimately "cover," which is to say mask, its blunt materiality, are one figure of iconicity here; another is "man," another is poetry itself, all of these an apparent "cure" for the lack of autonomy, the loss of freedom, diagnosed in the poem's first stanza. But the rock persists in its autonomy, perhaps as starkly as those words, "spring" and "snood," that Stevens isolates on the page, giving them a material mass and weight; these elements smuggle in a sense that any attempt to render nature immaterial, ephemeral, even heaven-directed is belied by those elements' very density and groundedness, their material interiority.

There is no attempt in this poem to claim that the rock's definitional "barrenness" is negated by the leaf's iconic presence, or indeed by poetry's seeming properties of transfiguration, and an apparently life-affirming season, spring, noticeably denied its usual capital *S* here, is rather lent a certain austerity by its aforementioned isolation on the page.[30] Word and world both, in their impassivity and even intransigence, resonate upon one another in these lines, in a manner that makes a virtue of the apparent distance between them. As Stevens writes toward the poem's conclusion:

> The rock is the gray particular of man's life,
> The stone from which he rises, up—and—ho,
> The step to the bleaker depths of his descents . . .[31]

The rock remains, not just as a disturbingly blank impediment to our attempts to turn nature into a passive, symbolic prosthesis, but instead as the condition of our making sense in the first place; that condition of possibility from which we may rise, but also the condition of impossibility that marks our mortality in advance and that prevents any mere mapping of word onto world, of the ambitions of human sense-making onto the canvas of the natural world.[32] And as a "gray particular," the rock is no symbolic stand-in for a generalizable or purely transcendental horizon. As uncanny particular rather than universal, or perhaps as the intransigently material particular that is always to be found within the apparently immaterial bounds of the universal, the rock should be taken as allegorical of the formal excess, the excessively particular element, that conditions every putatively universal structure of meaning or any comprehensive approach to the world. Insofar as it remains always troublingly external to "man's" projects of representation, it is also outside those projects and of and in the world itself, the internal supplement that prevents nature ever forming an organic and impermeable totality unto itself. This then would serve as a good example of how Stevens, not unlike Ponge, saw fit to force explicit arguments about form into those aspects of his poetry that one would normally think belong to their content; in so doing, Stevens demonstrates the potential instability of the very distinction between the two. Turning back to Badiou, I'll be interested to trace how the philosopher, in his implicit romanticization of Stevens's poetics, risks obscuring these especially innovative aspects of Stevens's project.

The Figure of the Soldier

In his recent book *Philosophy for Militants,* Badiou treats the theme of heroism in its division between, on the one hand, a premodern figure of religious sacrifice, and the modern figure of the last man on the other, an explicitly "nihilistic" evocation. The "paradigm of all heroic figures," he argues, at least in the revolutionary times of 1789–1976 (the end of the Cultural Revolution in China), has been that of the soldier.[33] Badiou goes on to conflate this figure as it appears in epic, and in what he describes as "romantic and post-romantic lyric poetry."[34] The nostalgia that we witness on cinema screens and on television for the figure of the warrior is, for the philosopher, a sign that the figure of the soldier, as an explicitly revolutionary symbol, has decomposed. "Can we hope, once more," Badiou pleads, "after the death of the paradigmatic soldier, for something like the true appearance of being and affirmative thinking?"[35]

Note here the quick equation of being with affirmation; being, at least insofar as it is attached to the rupture of the event, artistic or otherwise, must affirm itself outside the laws of its surrounding world, even as it emerges in the interstices of that world. Badiou turns to Stevens's poetry to get at something of this notion of the soldier as what he calls the hero, in a construction that the philosopher all but admits is explicitly romantic in its provenance. The poem chosen for these purposes is Stevens's "L'esthétique du mal," the title of course a nod to Baudelaire, another figure torn between the rhetorical rigor of the modern and the symbolic emblems of romanticisms past. But it is Badiou, rather than Stevens, who today, I think, exemplifies that anxious split, a split that given Badiou's otherwise staunch modernism, from the subtractive asceticism of his ontology of "inconsistent multiplicity" to his politics of collective discipline, assumes the form of a telling and even symptomatic contradiction.

Stevens's poem, for Badiou, exemplifies the divide between an aesthetics of positivity, what the philosopher calls "the subsistence of figural beauty,"[36] and its melancholy withdrawal. This construction should remind us of the popular reading of Stevens most recently extended by Critchley, where it is the tension between the sublime indifference of things and our need to imbue those things with meaning that makes poetry tragic both in the classical sense, and in a sense relevant to the era of repeated world wars, where the very fecundity of poetic symbol seems to ironize the drained and wan contemporary condition. For Harold Bloom, for instance, "L'esthétique du mal" is centrally a poem about the pain and perplexity of poetic language itself in such a fallen condition, "the pain and suffering inseparable from a consciousness of self in a post-Christian or Nietzschean world."[37]

The seventh part of "L'esthétique du mal" begins:

> How red the rose that is the soldier's wound
> The wounds of many soldiers, the wounds of all
> The soldiers that have fallen/red in blood
> The soldier of time grown deathless in great size.[38]

On Badiou's reading, it is the figure of the rose that, as he puts it, "formalises" the soldier's wound, serving then as a transformative symbol that brings the connective grace of life to what otherwise may be a mere pitiful scene of death. The soldier, for Badiou, "is an affirmative mediation between life and death."[39] But a closer attention to the various dissonances of Stevens's stanza may result in a very different reading. The construction "How red the rose," placed at the very beginning, is, I would claim, intended to trouble, in the very heightened rhetoricity of its phrasing, what follows.[40] One is reminded of the curdling of the Shakespearean sonnet into the truisms of the chocolate box or the greeting card, a process surely complete, ripe for parody, by the time Stevens composed the poem in 1944. And so what appears to Badiou as a transformation, as the deflation of pity giving way to the inflation of grace, of redemption, even of life itself, is rendered doubtful in advance. A further turn of the screw comes in "the wounds of many soldiers, the wounds of all."[41] From an expansionary symbolism—the lone soldier embodying in his fallenness the heroism of all the fallen, the call back here surely to Blake's images of war, to Southey's rueful view of conflict—we arrive at the wound itself as a figure of the universal, a negation of the body nonetheless shunted, with due irony, into the form of a symbol tasked with rendering the all.

Symbol, to put it another way, a device strung uneasily between conventional definitions of "form" and "content," suffers a haircut under the blade of Stevens's pen. It is unable to perform its connective function, its drawing together of the epoch or the whole, when it assumes the form of a negative image opposed, in its very negativity, to the affirmative function that it is otherwise saddled with. For Badiou, by stark contrast, "the poetic transfiguration of the soldier is also the splendid beginning of the end of this figure,"[42] splendid because, as Badiou readily concedes, the soldier as it loomed large in the historical reality of 1944 was anything but a symbol of extraworldly, resplendent promise. But the positive direction of this transfiguration for Badiou leaves open the space for a soldier to come, one that might help both incite and then embody a contemporary revolutionary upsurge that would transfigure the very historical symbols that announce its birth.

As evidence for this conscription of the soldier as a transitory symbol opening such a space, Badiou cites Stevens's observation that "his wound is good because life was."[43] But here again, one encounters an ironical negativity arranged in paralleled signifiers, that of "the good" and "life," that one might otherwise assume project only hues of recovery or regeneration. The warmth of the sun and of "summer" forms another, characteristic repeated image of apparent positivity in the poem within which Stevens finds nonetheless a kind of formative ambiguity; the sun, it is worth noting, does not "set" in "L'esthétique du mal"; rather, it "fails."[44] Badiou, importantly, riffs on what he calls a "purely affirmative"[45] reading of the season as it is pictured in the poem, although I think Stevens would rather have us see summer curdle into heat haze, into something like its internal failure: "The sun, in clownish yellow, but not a clown, / Brings the day to perfection and then fails."[46] Those anticipated hues of recovery in the line analyzed above, "his wound was good because life was," are rather beaten into submission by the figure of the "wound" itself, to say nothing of the regretful "as life was." This may well be an example of what Badiou, as I've already noted, refers to as "the powerlessness immanent to the poem's effect of power,"[47] the ways in which poetry's mobilization of syntax to trouble conventional understandings, is, in fact, what makes it efficacious. The queasy sense of mortality that issues from the transport of the past abundance of life into the present putrescence of a wound allegorizes the indirection that lies buried in poetic form more generally, the ways in which the symbol's collapse may well stand in for a kind of success. One encounters, in these clashing images, something that defines Stevens's poetics, and that I will discuss repeatedly in what follows, namely, the coming together of formal strategies and a metapoetic "commentary" on those strategies. Very often, and especially in Stevens's late verse, the argument worked out across the poems bears directly on the poems' own formal interventions, such that the very distinction between form and content is placed out of joint. But the effect of this, I argue, is to evoke that which is similarly out of kilter, unamenable to totalization, in the world.

In "L'esthétique du mal," the direct transposition of a negative valence into common signifiers of positivity is achieved, again rather ironically, by the very repetition of those images of uplift, a repetition that, the more it takes over as the principal formal device of the poem, displaces and discolors what it might otherwise have been assumed to merely celebrate. Such images appear formally here, in their canny formal placement, in a way that contradicts, I think, Badiou's wish for a temporally linear transfiguration of the abject into the affirmative at the level of content, one that would pass through a moment of fallenness before emerging, through something like a cinematic slow dissolve, into the summer sunlight. While the repeated image of the wound is, in itself, redolent of the putrefaction that life itself would seem to negate, the reader is told soon after its appearance that "No part of him was ever part of death."[48] In his choice of words, Stevens assures us again of the promise of redemption even as he achieves such a sense only through a curious negation, through the adoption of a curiously awkward syntax—"No part of him was ever part of death" instead of "Every part of him was part of life." Stevens sees fit to comment directly on the status of the negative immediately following, writing of the death of Satan as "a capital / Negation" that "destroyed him in his tenement / And, with him, many blue phenomena."[49] Even as Satan is apparently the very emblem of the negation of life, his death marks the passing of "many blue phenomena" with him, phenomena that one assumes found a paradoxical sustenance in the coexistence of a figure that would otherwise seem a mortal threat to them. This is, as Stevens puts it, an "eccentric"[50] kind of negation, one that, far from preserving what it also seems to overcome, and contra Hegel, serves as the condition of possibility of those phenomena *in toto.*

There's a sense in this poem of something always having passed—"his wound is good because life was." This, surely, is one of the defining features of Stevens's poetry, a temporal affect that somehow dislodges itself from the poetry's content and joins its formal infrastructure. If Badiou wishes to find a clenched expectation for the new, for the extraworldly emergence of an event from the constraints of presence, the reader is more often confronted with the look backward, albeit one that is formative even as it performs at the same time an ironic de-formation. If such a backward glance defines Stevens's poetic temporality as such, one would be justified in thinking this a rueful or melancholic look, occurring in a time of generalized impassivity. (Badiou himself makes repeated reference to the apparent "melancholia" of Stevens's poetry.) Yet against a frozen temporality of the eternal present, I would argue here for a cyclical logic in Stevens's verse; what is, is what will already have been, but which will be again—a temporality that, for sure, may just as likely provoke a melancholic and fatalist response, even as the constant possibility of renewal that this logic also promises may by contrast induce hope. As Stevens remarks in his "Notes toward a Supreme Fiction":

> The poem goes from the poet's gibberish to
> The gibberish of the vulgate and back again.
> Does it move to and fro or is it of both
> At once?[51]

Here the purity of the present is ruptured both by the possibility of a cycle, and by the strange suggestion that such a cycle might happen all at once: "Does it move to and fro or is it of both // At once?" The notion of a cycle of which the different stages occur all at once is only thinkable, I would argue, if one perceives such a quality to be part of the structure of poetry's paradoxical, negative and yet constructive formal ground, the "gibberish" that inheres in the apparently arbitrary marshaling of signs and metrics rather than in the inherent and incarnate power of those signs themselves.

At this juncture I'd like to contrast my position with that most powerful statement of poetic undecidability, Paul de Man's reading of Yeats's "Among School Children." That poem ends, famously, with an apparently rhetorical question: "How can we know the dancer from the dance?," the latter taken, as in for instance Frank Kermode's reading or in the account by Cleanth Brooks, to signal the final concordance between poetic expression and that which is expressed.[52] Such a fusion would, in at least one reading of Yeats's late romanticism, come to stand in for the transformative power of poetic symbol, whereby symbol, far from being a passive container of an external referent, becomes at one with, metaphysically congruent with, its objective correlate in the world. De Man, of course, finds instead a formal and material undecidability in the question, marking the structural impossibility of ever being able to definitively choose between the rhetorical reading—where the question that forms the final line of Yeats's poem is meant to remain unanswered—and the properly grammatical one, where the anguished expectation of an answer produces a temporary solution that covers over that constitutive ambiguity. The very inability to determine the boundaries that separate dancer and dance, in such a second reading, is itself a powerful example of art's determinative capacities. For de Man, there is nothing in Yeats's poem that would permit us to choose between these strictly incommensurable alternatives. But where would the generalization of this indeterminacy leave my reading of Wallace Stevens? For a certain de Man, and it will be the task of the next chapter to show another side of the critic, this aporia should be taken as the truth of poetry itself. Poetry, that is to say, comes to stage its own impossibility; it is, willingly or unwillingly, the site of its own perpetual dissolution. But the conflict between rhetoric and grammar, between emblem and allegory, that motors Stevens's poetry and that de Man finds exemplified in Yeats is as much in the service of grasping something of the world *itself* as it is resigned to performing a dance of aesthetic self-referentiality without end.

Of course, much of the initial power of de Man's defigurative criticism came from the suspicion that, far from merely rejecting the formalism of the New Critics, de Man had in fact radically reworked their attentive textualism and love for paradox from within. It's possible to find, for example, clear links between William Empson's pioneering reading of the ambiguity in Yeats's verse in his *Seven Types of Ambiguity* and de Man's later insistence on the undecidability that crowns the final stanza of "Among School Children." In a bravura reading, Empson demonstrated how what he calls the "cult of vagueness" in nineteenth-century poetry transmutes into ambiguity, in the strong, productive sense of the term that he took to be especially emblematic of poetic innovation. In his reading of Yeats, Empson worries at the back-and-forth in a pair of related poems around the notion of "brooding"; as he writes,

> the wavering and suggestive indefiniteness of nineteenth-century poetry is often merely weak. When, as here [in Yeats], it has a great deal of energy and sticks in your head, it is usually because the opposites left open are tied around a single strong idea; thus here, on the one hand, the condition of brooding is at once to be sought out and avoided; on the other, the poet, "nothing, being all," contemporaneously living all lives, may fitly be holding before him both the lives of Fergus [a brooding character in Yeats], and drawing the same moral from either of them.[53]

The ambiguity in question may be detected at the point when a poem, on the one hand, cautions against the introspection that comes with a brooding countenance—think, perhaps, of the self-serious, solitary Byronic hero—while on the other it insists that such a mood, now inflected with the promise of philosophical depth, may nonetheless allow the drawing of crucial moral consequences that transcend the isolating melancholia of its initial disposition. But it seems clear that such a construction of ambiguity is nonetheless always moved toward a kind of certainty, at least insofar as, for Empson, the polyphonic vacillation in question is the condition of an ever more fecund kind of poetic expression. Something very different seems at work in de Man, or at least in the de Man of the aporia of rhetoric and grammar; where Empson revels in ambiguity, de Man stews in the anxiety of indecision. Both thinkers, as I take leave of them here, have left unremarked the question of the movement of poetry out from its own inner voids and entanglements into the similarly perplexing densities of the world itself. As I've already hinted, the next chapter will show that de Man, in a different moment, attempted to think precisely that. It is to that movement, one that may then place in question the very inner/outer distinction that persists even after the full frontal assault of deconstruction, that "speculative formalism" must attest.

Stevens's Speculative Formalism

Back once more to Stevens, who, adopting once again a metapoetic stance to reflect on his own formal practices, writes at the opening of the fifteenth section of "L'esthétique du mal" that "The greatest poverty is not to live / In a physical world."[54] One might normally locate such a poverty in a world entirely devoid of the *extra*-physical, of the spiritual, of the numinous. And yet, immediately following, Stevens unites pastoral imagery often associated with the transmutation of materiality into something extraphysical with an insistence on just such a physicality; here even the "metaphysicals" "lie" within something palpable, hot, intransigent, their situation at ground level an intriguing rebuke to more usual estimations of metaphysical transcendence:

> The green corn gleams and the metaphysicals
> Lie sprawling in majors of the August heat,
> The rotund emotions, paradise unknown.
>
> . . . .
>
> So many selves, so many sensuous worlds,
> As if the air, the mid-day air, was swarming
> With the metaphysical changes that occur,
> Merely in living as and where we live.[55]

A number of formal features come together here to help underline this insistence on a mortal, physical—sensuous rather than numinous—vision of life. Somehow, verse that puts repetition to such productive use—notice the repeat of "air" and "living"/"live" in the second stanza quoted above—remains even-tempered and only modestly forward moving, elusive of the staccato clip that repetition often induces. The result is the tempering of any immaterial transport up and beyond both the materiality of the lines themselves, and the "sensuous worlds" that those lines evoke, such a transport being what Stevens's romantic forbears were often concerned to undertake, even if they were frequently foiled by their own poetic materials. (Indeed, earlier in the poem, even God is brought back down to earth: "The fault lies with an over-human god, / Who by sympathy has made himself a man / And is not to be distinguished.")[56]

Here again I would depart from Simon Critchley, who too often wants to claim Stevens as an existentialist for whom an anxious possibility arises simultaneously as poetic language works on the passive putty of the world, makes it meaningful again, successfully figures it anew. As Critchley characteristically writes, "Modern poetry is an act of the mind, a conscious act of creation or genius that has to find what will suffice."[57] J. Hillis Miller comes a little closer to my position when he argues that it is the "evaporation of the gods, leaving a barren man in a barren land"[58] that forms the crux of Stevens's project, although recall again the conclusion of Stevens's "The Rock": "Its barrenness becomes a thousand things," which is to say that such a material blankness is itself a kind of productivity. But it is less in the content of Stevens's verse that such a commitment to the potency of the material arises. To stay purely and *only* at the level of Stevens's content, even at the level of the metapoetic commentary I've been discussing, is to find a bewildering multiplicity of potential philosophical standpoints, especially in the late verse; some are nihilistic, some are hopeful for redemption, and so on. As Miller himself admits, "For each position and for its antithesis there are fully elaborated poems or parts of poems."[59]

Rather, the consistency that Miller believes is elusive is to be found, but at the level of the key formal features of Stevens's poetry, features that are often unexpected and in apparent contradiction to the images or figures that they encase—I've already noted how image and tense are in conflict in "L'esthétique du mal," and the matter-of-fact use of repetition just located may be added to the list. Whereas Miller emphasizes what he calls "a resolution of imagination and reality in a theory of the identity of poetry and life,"[60] I fear that this underplays the role that nonidentity and incommensurability play in opening this poetry out to its worlds. Such instances of formal nonidentity may themselves be productive of those multiple and clashing identities and forms of presence—those multiple "sensual worlds"—that jostle for precedence in so many of Stevens's stanzas. I'll develop Stevens's "speculative formalism" again in dialogue with Badiou, in the course of which I will need to distinguish Stevens's use of poetic speculation from the resonances that the latter terms have with those earlier forms of romanticism that this verse is in constant and often critical dialogue with. That earlier, romantic conception, so frequently shoehorned by critics into Stevens's own speculative universe, is best summed up by Novalis's early romantic claim that art "presents the unpresentable."[61] One should modify this slogan when reading Stevens, such that poetry enacts the presentable only on the foundations of a formal, contradictory ground, in the subterranean interstices of tense and image, meter and voice, inflection and repetition, in those moments when the poetry's commentary on itself marries with its own formal displacements and interruptions.

Within the terms of a broader commentary on the visual arts, Badiou turns once again to Stevens, and especially to his aforementioned poem "Description without Place." Stevens is marshaled here to resist what Badiou rightly associates with various philosophical perspectives on art of the past, namely the maintenance of a distinction between being and appearance; the best art, on such an older model, would be that which tears open the surface of appearance in order to allow the evanescent "being" that it dissimulates to come into view. Badiou quotes Stevens's "Description without Place" as follows in support of his rejection of this dichotomy, arguably one of the founding binaries of classical aesthetics:

> It is possible that to seem—it is to be
> As the sun is something seeming and it is.
>
> The sun is an example. What it seems
> It is and in such seeming all things are.[62]

And so the "being" of the sun, for Stevens, coincides with its appearances, or, as Badiou phrases it, "In poetry, we must name 'sun' neither the fact that the sun is, nor the fact that the sun seems, or appears, but we must name 'sun' the equivalence of seeming and being."[63] Here the philosopher seems to row back from what I've described as the more overtly romantic function ascribed to poetry in his commentary on the figure of the soldier. Whereas there Badiou argues for the incarnation of a new Idea of the soldier, qua revolutionary hero, within new kinds of artistic practice, here he describes the work of art as "a description which has no immediate relationship with a real that would be outside the description, like in the romantic conception, the absolute Idea is outside its sensible glory."[64]

Yet even as Badiou distances himself here from what he calls the "romantic conception," preferring instead an absolute equivalence between description and its object, his more frequent posture retains signal aspects of just that conception, and in particular with its eternalizing emphasis. As he writes of Mallarmé in *Being and Event,* "The extreme condensation of figures—a few objects—aims at isolating . . . a system of clues whose placement can be unified by one hypothesis alone as to what has happened, and, of which, one sole consequence authorizes the announcement of how the event, despite being abolished, will *fix* its décor in the eternity of a 'pure notion.'"[65]

Poetry is here able to both connect the particularity of an event to its pure notion, and to hold the singularity of such an event "in place" even after it has disappeared. This is a mode of appearance that, to be sure, is irreducible to what, in Badiou's commentary on Stevens, he disdains as a revelatory or, one might say, negative-theological conception of poetry's power. But it is certainly comparable to his valorization of the figure of the soldier, where, again, a figure emerges through an act of artistic affirmation that reinvents a prior aesthetic form, such an affirmation reinstalling through the back door a distinction between being and appearance (and, even, in an implicit existential register, authenticity and inauthenticity). On such a reading, the effectivity of a poetic figure is dependent on it being reinscribed in the historical present of a revolutionary break, and subsequently eternalized in the potency of an Idea. The figure of the soldier that appears within the aesthetic form of such a moment of rupture would be able to peel back its mere appearance as a romantic or classical emblem and reproduce itself as the nonmimetic truth of a new epoch.

There is, I think, a distinct tension in Badiou's thought, a cleavage between an ascetic, subtractive modernism on the one hand, where it is the form of a political action or artistic intervention rather than its contents that guarantee its evental status, and the lingering traces of an attachment to the symbol on the other, whereby an aesthetic image (or political event) produces a link between an instance and an Idea, between appearance and being, at the same time as it marks a cut between the authentic and inauthentic uses of artistic (or political) materials. No doubt Badiou's early Sartreanism plays a role in this continued wish to see in art a path toward authentic existence.[66]

But what does Badiou understand by Stevens's invocation of a "description without place"? Turning to Stevens's "The Man with a Blue

Guitar," Badiou finds once again the drawing of an equivalence between being and appearance, or as it is now termed, being and existence. Alighting on an instance of what I've already called Stevens's apparent idealism, where the word gives birth to the thing, Badiou celebrates the consequence of this flattening out of poetic reference, writing that "if a world is created before us, we have no distinction between the appearing of the thing, its existence and its being."[67] Where Badiou detects a redemptive agency in this collapse of the subtractive function of language, one should ascertain by contrast the risk of an imposed passivity, one that attaches to both the thing described by Stevens—to the guitar, apparently created by fiat through the use of poetic language—and to poetic language itself, which, in its direct association with its object (even as it is claimed that it *creates* that object), loses its disruptive, which is to say its properly creative, force. But again, Badiou risks missing what is most crucial in Stevens's verse. In a passage of "Description without Place" that Badiou himself quotes, Stevens remarks:

> It is an artificial thing that exists
> In its own seeming, plainly visible,
>
> Yet not too closely the double of our lives,
> Intenser than any actual life could be[68]

Here is reinstated at least something of the gap between word and thing, where it is word rather than the apparent effervescence of life as a separate substance or domain unto itself that embodies intensity, one that, "existing in its own seeming," excuses itself from the empirical qualities of the world at the very moment that it seems to create them. Characteristically, Stevens's ongoing metacommentary on his own formal strategies connects here with just those strategies; note, for instance, how the enjambment formally instantiates the sense of transport, of distance to be traveled, implied by "Yet not too closely the double of our lives."

It is this (in my view crucial) contradiction, namely the simultaneous appearance of presence and withdrawal, of a radical connection and apparent disconnection with the world in poetic language, that Badiou singularly fails to explain. For it is neither that the word creates the thing, nor that the thing renders inadequate the word. Instead, it is in the seeming solipsism of linguistic form itself, made all the more self-enclosed in Stevens's late style, that the asymmetric, nonmimetic intercalation of word and thing is made possible; indeed, the very metacommentary that I've been tracing could be taken to be one symptom of this airless self-referentiality. As Stevens's poetic project progressed, so did his reliance on paradox and contradiction, interruptions of any attempt to read conventionally "for content," the result an apparently hermetic poetics that refers mostly to itself. But if, for Badiou, the absolute equivalence of word and thing seems to evacuate the negativity and absence often imputed to the noncoincidence of the sign, for Stevens negativity, self-reference, subtraction are the privileged routes *to* presence, to any entrance into the worldly; even further, it is a shared negativity and noncoincidence in word and world that reveals that they are, in a way nonetheless far from Badiou's own purportedly immanent understanding, somehow of the same domain or space.

Thus, poetry is, in the words of Stevens's metacommentary on his own poetics, both "plainly visible" and "yet not too closely the double of our lives," and it is within the contradiction between the solid materiality of the word, its plain worldly visibility, and its ascetic withdrawal from any mimetic function (such that it cannot be the "double of our lives") that something like poetic reference occurs. This is, needless to say, a reference that exists far outside the logic of any correspondence theory of truth or any adherence to a transitive distinction between phenomena and the understanding, or between aesthetic sense and intellectual reason.

In "The Man with the Blue Guitar," Stevens writes:

> Poetry is the subject of the poem,
> From this the poem issues and
> To this returns.[69]

Poetic form appears here initially as a boundless interiority, albeit one that may both depart and return. Stevens continues:

> Between issue and return, there is
> An absence in reality,
> Things as they are.[70]

This internal, tautological self-reference seemingly forestalls in advance the appearance of what can, subsequently, only be absent, namely "things as they are." But crucially, Stevens goes on to ask:

> are these separate? Is it
> An absence for the poem, which acquires
>
> Its true appearances there, sun's green
> Cloud's red, earth's feeling, sky that thinks?[71]

Such a rotary movement is characterized as "the universal intercourse,"[72] Stevens's name for the topologically awkward location and dislocation of poetry within the world. Even setting aside for a moment the self-referential running commentary that is Stevens's main concern here, the formal features of this characteristic late poem already point to the strange coincidence between formal subtraction and outward poetic referentiality that marks Stevens's broader project. The relentless enjambment, in particular, introduces a judder into my attempt to piece together the metacommentary that serves, ostensibly, as the poem's content. By repeating the device with such frequency, and by mirroring its interruptive effects in the segmented tripartite clause structure of lines such as "Cloud's red, earth's feeling, sky that thinks?," poetic sense is held momentarily in suspense, such a withdrawal nonetheless pointing to the very theme of these lines, the simultaneous holding in and letting out of poetry's ambition to be more than simply itself.

Here we arrive at the crux of Stevens's speculative formalism. The circular, apparently solipsistic movements of poetic form, its coming and going in perpetuity—its "issue and return," as Stevens has it—is what allows this poetry to test, albeit in a manner quite distant from Badiou's affirmationism, the gap that might otherwise seem to inhere between the word and the thing, the sign and its referent, poetic syntax and referential object. For it is precisely in the material world, this poetry tells us, that language makes its presence felt, imposes itself, even as, in a simultaneous moment, it seems to withdraw, to persist as ascetically indifferent to the fizz and fervor of life. By making the cloud red and the earth feel, Stevens would have us appreciate this immanent interlacing of materiality and the word, of the ways in which the poetic act, in its very withdrawal from the task of verisimilitude, mimesis, or romantic transubjective union, produces an affinity with the world that is active and constructive in its very *failure* to adequately reproduce the world's empirical appearance or texture. That failure is registered in the contradictions of an earth that feels, of a green sun, and so forth, qualities that are contradictory only if one assumes that it is poetry's task to accurately and mimetically reproduce the qualities of the world.

The to-ing and fro-ing that Stevens evokes here is not the absolute transit of the word away from, and then back to, the world, but rather the registering of an internal and simultaneous absence and presence that is always to be found *in* the world, in the contradictory textures of its multiple materialities, its multiple "sensuous worlds." Importantly, Stevens will locate this internal circular movement of poetic form, previously referred to as his commitment to a cyclical temporal logic, in a register other than that of meaning, coincidence, or symmetry. Instead, such a logic inheres in the density of form per se. As he writes in his poem "An Ordinary Evening in New Haven,"

> These houses, these difficult objects, dilapidate
> Appearances of what appearances,
> Words, *lines, not meanings, not communications*
>
> Dark things without a double, after all[73]

The immediate equation here of words and lines, of difficult objects with their absence of meaning, enjoins us to think simultaneously of the sheer meaningless of material things, of the arraignments of built spaces, and the materiality of literary language itself, its construction through noncoincidence, through the very inability of the sign to make itself anything other than what Stevens calls a "dark thing without a double." Elsewhere Stevens will consciously intermix images of signification with images of nature, the better to capture their immanent if agonistic intercalation; one encounters, in the under-read "On the Adequacy of Landscape," for instance, an owl's "discursive wings."[74] Nonchalantly running two apparently incommensurable images up against one another is one of Stevens's favored modes of poetic paradox, to the extent that it becomes an integral part of this poetry's formal infrastructure.

If, for a phenomenologist such as Merleau-Ponty, poetry is especially capable of giving us access to the noncoincidence between our originary *perceptions* and our reflections on them, with metaphor identified as especially enabling of, as Jessica Wiskus phrases it, "a language capable of setting itself up within the gap between sign and signification,"[75] then for Stevens there is no originary perception to be distinguished from sign or signification in the first place; nothing, again, but those "dark things without a double," the owl with its "discursive wings." Language and materiality go all the way down as, if you like, modes of the same substance, even as they withdraw from and yet spark across to one another in unexpected ways. As Stevens captures it in "The Man with the Blue Guitar" and in "An Ordinary Evening in New Haven," both absence and continuity, formation and de-formation, must be held together in the same moment if we are to appreciate poetry's withdrawn affinity with its intercalated material other:

> Is it
> An absence for the poem, which acquires
> Its true appearances there.[76]

Is it, in other words, the absence in poetry of an ability to correlate with things that allows poetic language to invoke their density, their insistent materiality? Stevens's answer, I would argue, is yes. Even as I am tempted to evoke the romantic sublime here, that moment where it is the very failure of poetic language to capture the immensity of things that gives one notice *of* that immensity, such a move would too fully bifurcate what I think is, in Stevens, a single if topologically complex movement, that of the world simultaneously implicated in the word, and vice versa, albeit in the mode of their very apparent contradiction. That world must hold together any joy at creation or life with the negativity and contradiction that lies at its ground, a check then on any theological celebration of poetic fecundity per se, something that Harold Bloom cannot encompass in his too hasty description of the "indirection" in "An Ordinary Evening in New Haven" as "exhibit[ing] a passion for yes that could not be broken."[77] The latter is, of course, a reference taken from Stevens's himself, sourced from "L'esthétique du mal," and yet in the poem the "yes" in question issues from tragedy, from an especially aesthetic negation. There is, that is to say, just as often a passion for *no* in Stevens, a fact that does not make Stevens's verse any less of life, of the plenitude of things. It is the "no" that is expressed in his irony, in his pitting of image against tense, in his giving of his poetry over to commentary on its own formal conditions, and that prepares the soil for the growth of any subsequent "yes."

I'd like to return, in conclusion, to one of the recurrent claims made for Stevens's poetry, namely his apparent wish to recognize the creation of the world out of the effervescence of poetic language itself. Recall Stevens's evocation, in "The Idea of Order at Key West," of a "she" who "sang, the sea, / Whatever self it had, became the self / That was her song, for she was the maker."[78] If it is tempting to see in this the mark of Stevens's neo-romantic faith in the poetic symbol to convoke what it may only otherwise seem to represent, I propose instead that, both here and elsewhere, Stevens is asking us to put into question any absolute separation of the symbol and some other that it may be tasked with veiling, producing, or evoking. Rather, the symbol for Stevens "merely is," to traduce somewhat Critchley's formulation, insofar as it subsists within the world as its noncoincidental, negative and yet constructive, even definitional, inner cipher.

This idea of a world of contradictions, where contradiction is somehow the matter of word and world as they spark on and within one another, appears scattered throughout Stevens's aforementioned "An Ordinary Evening in New Haven." In that work, "metaphysical streets" exist within a "physical town," and "permanence" is "composed of impermanence," yet these point not toward an ineffable domain behind or beyond the world. Rather, it is poetic form itself that unexpectedly roots us to what Stevens's describes as "pure reality, untouched / By trope or deviation, straight to the word."[79] "Straight to the word," indeed! Suffice to register the irony here, one that remains jarring only if this book's account of noncorrelational reference is denied: it is in and on the word that the world, even if not mimetically reproduced, is nonetheless accessed in its incommensurability. Such a word might, in its very lack of a mimetic correspondence to things, point us toward the paradoxes that inhere in the great outdoors, in the way that, again in Stevens's rendering, "this faithfulness of reality, this mode / This tendance and venerable holding-in / Make gay the hallucinations in surfaces."[80]

Again, a venerable holding-in, the corseting of poetic form, is what gives us notice of the hallucinations, the tremulousness, of materiality itself. The three stanzas that follow are worth quoting at some length:

> The poem is the cry of its occasion,
> Part of the *res* itself and not about it.
> The poet speaks the poem as it is,
>
> Not as it was: part of the reverberation
> Of a windy night as it is, when the marble statues
> Are like newspapers blown by the wind. He speaks
>
> By sight and insight as they are. There is no
> Tomorrow for him. The wind will have passed by,
> The statues will have gone back to be things about.[81]

These are startling lines, somehow confident and hesitant in equal measure. The confidence comes in that unequivocal declaration of poetic intent, "The poem is the cry of its occasion / Part of the *res* itself and not about it," and in the formal equanimity with which it is presented. In two matter-of-fact, declarative lines, Stevens nimbly avoids the amplification of the paradoxes of representation that deconstruction sometimes makes its own, whereby the "*res*" is originarily lost in the ever-lengthening loops of linguistic differentiation. He is equally deft at parrying the notion one finds frequently in Badiou, whereby poetic figuration is the cipher for a kind of heroism of the extraworldly. (Stevens also successfully recalibrates his observation in "The Man with the Blue Guitar" I have already remarked on, whereby "poetry is the subject of the poem"; again, there is no intrapoetic solipsism at work here, nor simply a devilish enjoyment of tautology, the latter a persistent form to be found across Stevens's oeuvre, as has recently been shown by Andrew Goldstone.[82] Rather, poetry and thing are immanent to one another, even as they must connect nonmimetically, and thus poetry being the "subject" of the poem requires one to take the world of things as its subject, too.) Here word and world are of the same *stuff,* but this passage needs to be read in the light of the insights on temporality adduced above with reference to Stevens's "L'esthétique du mal." There, as here, the reader finds both the always-having-past and the stillness of a now, distinct temporal logics that are held in tension rather than overcome or rejected as irremediably in contradiction.

The poet, then, "speaks the poem as it is," thus participating in the world in an act beyond the distance implied by mimicry or representation; this is something like an act of spontaneity, conditioned by "sight and insight as they are," in the now (although note the apparent subject-verb disagreement here, that ambiguous move from "is" to "are"—already, perhaps, a sign that this apparent poetic success is less straightforward than it first appears). The reader will remember that I disagreed with Robert Pogue Harrison's assessment that, for Stevens, idea and thing qua nature are equivalent; are we not drawing a similar conclusion here? Precisely not: where Harrison imputes a thoroughgoing idealism to Stevens, what I have identified here is better thought of as a kind of paradoxical materialism. The act of poetic language is equivalent, not to nature (a term that brings with it connotations of holism that are foreign to Stevens's worldview), but to something like *matter,* to the blank solidity of things otherwise hymned in Stevens's "Credences of Summer":

> The rock cannot be broken. It is the truth.
> It arises from land and sea and covers them.[83]

At one and the same time, this act places the poetic subject out of joint. The time of poetic enunciation, precisely insofar as it resists incorporation into the everyday expectations of representation and of the smooth transport of the past into the future, is threatening as much as it is constitutive; it threatens the lack of a tomorrow ("There is / No tomorrow for him"), at least for the poet for whom success means a failure of mimesis, the foreclosure in advance of any successful integration into the past-present-future train of everyday representation. In that realm, one in which language and its things are in fact held strictly apart even as the illusion of mimesis takes hold, the statues, in fact *all* signs, become mere passive ciphers for interpretation, appearances that call seductively to be unveiled ("The statues will have gone back to be things about"). Poetry reaches its notion, for Stevens, when it rejects this pacifying logic of representation or mere description: the poetic sign is "part of the reverberation / Of a windy night as it is"; this could not be the case if it were tamed according to the strategies of a hermeneutic.

One has landed rather far here from Badiou's creative affirmationism. Even though Badiou, like Stevens, would have us recognize the self-sufficiency of poetic form, for the philosopher this is but an index of poetry's ability to affirm the positively, openly, generically new over the static, reactionary, and old. For Stevens, by contrast, there is no making "new," no making "gay" of the "hallucinations," without constriction and withdrawal. And as Lee Margaret Jenkins and others have noted, Paul de Man, the topic of the chapter to follow, and Stevens both share a sense of what, in his "The Rhetoric of Tropes," de Man calls "the intra-linguistic resources of figures."[84] But figurality for Stevens, even in its tendency toward decomposition, to what de Man analyzed so brilliantly as the rhetorical distanciations of allegory, opens the reader up to the world of which it is already an awkwardly interposed part. In de Manian deconstruction, by contrast, one always threatens to be tipped into the reaffirmation of an essentially Kantian division between the intellectual and the sensuous, albeit with the division transposed on to the split between the allegorical and the symbolic, the former the hero to the latter's villain.

Insofar as de Man was a formalist, and there's no doubt to me that he was, his formalism lies at the opposite, negative extreme from the kind one may associate with a representative statement by Goethe, for whom "true symbolism is where the particular represents the more general, not as a dream or a shadow, but as a living momentary revelation of the Inscrutable."[85] For de Man, by contrast, the allegorical overdetermination of art prevents the particular ever attaching to its complementary universal or, better, prevents the *singularity* of poetic form from even becoming a particular for which a universal might lurk backstage.

My position refuses this choice between a Goethian, romantic organic symbolism and a de Manian negativity as expressed, for the latter, in the absolute singularization of allegory, in what the late de Man called "allegories of unreadability,"[86] in the inability to finally settle the riddle of the dancer and the dance. There is, though, *another* de Man, a de Man that, in his readings of Kant and Hegel especially, understands the aporias of materiality to be inextricably bound up with the textual puzzles that he analyzed with unequaled power; the reader will get a sense of that other de Man in the next chapter. In any case, poetic form on my reading achieves its constructive, referential goal within the world at precisely its moments of de-completion. Deconstruction, at its worst, joins the tendency of earlier romanticisms to locate a consolatory power in the failure of a sign to signify, reproduced in a new, militant configuration in Badiou's reflections on the figure of the soldier. But what I have identified as Stevens's speculative formalism, his expansion of the structures of signification into the world and his concomitant refusal of the false choice between poetic reference or textual solipsism, may serve as a useful vehicle to move us beyond the impasse of romanticisms of the ineffable, and their deconstructive and militant progeny.

4

Paul de Man's Poetic Materialism

It is unsurprising that scholars in the humanities spend so much time talking about their apparent contemporary ills—perceived crises, changes in fashion, dispensability in the face of the corporatization of the university, and so on. Disciplines such as cultural studies, continental philosophy, and literary studies are overwhelmingly textual and linguistic in both their sources and methodologies, and a proliferation of metacommentary, the occasion for an ever-spooling series of articles, books, and lectures—an irruption of texts, to be brief—is, quite obviously, to be expected. Taking the temperature of current trends in the humanities, nonetheless, as fragmented and specialized as they've become, one reaches at least a single and paradoxical conclusion: the era of textuality, as a critical mind-set and a set of discourses defined by the slippages of the written word and its apparently endless significations, is over. Or at least, it is *pronounced* to be so, repeatedly and with high drama—almost always, of course, via texts themselves. How is it possible to speak of the ebbing of a concern for "texts" in disciplines that are founded on them? The answer may at least partially be found in the apparent eclipse of "deconstruction," a critical movement that, for many, stands in for a wider dissatisfaction with the scholastic disconnection from the world that any microscopic attention to language seems to require.

It would be hard to overstate the rhetorical severity that recent movements in the humanities have adopted with respect to their predecessor schools of deconstruction and critical theory. The germinal band of "speculative realists,"[1] a philosophical outgrowth of "actor-network theory" in the social sciences,[2] is surely guilty of an approach that tends to the "straw man," the better to sell their "turn to objects" and the real. Put briefly, such thinkers have moved to reject what they see as deconstruction's incommensurate obsession with language, preferring instead to reinstate a realist approach sensitive to "things in themselves," albeit in a fashion irreducible to the Kantian transcendental, to empiricism, or to the shackling of philosophy purely to the physical sciences. Rather, for Graham Harman and others, philosophy must recover the ambition proper to classical metaphysics, in a manner that boldly speculates as to the essential nature of objects outside human apprehension of them.

Quentin Meillassoux's text *After Finitude*[3] is the manifesto of the movement, although it is worth emphasizing the extent to which the thinkers associated with it are only substantially in agreement with what they're opposed to, namely the linguistic focus already mentioned. Meillassoux's Cartesian emphasis on those primary qualities accessible via mathematics could not have less to do with Graham Harman's speculative account of the withdrawn interiorities of medium-sized objects.

If the general trend, as identified above, is to find in a focus on language a disdain for objects, for materiality or the "great outdoors" in the sense intended by Meillassoux, one of the tasks of this chapter is to demonstrate how de Man's deconstructive literary theory was as concerned with the paradoxes of the material world as it was with the riddles of language per se, even if, in his strictly literary analyses, the linguistic tended to win the day. My aim is not primarily to defend de Man against his recent detractors, but rather to lay out the ways in which de Man's radicalization of formal methods in literary studies is crucial to any renewed formalism, and how the "speculative formalism" adduced in this book must nonetheless depart from a number of his conclusions. That critical distance will lie in our differing end points of analysis. If, for de Man, a deconstructive reading generally ends with the text in fragments, its logical or "grammatical" structure having given out under the pressure of "rhetorical reading," speculative formalism would rather trace the uncanny persistence of texts even after their apparent detotalization. I'll begin with a reading of de Man's late essays, posthumously published writings that demonstrate the critic's fullest engagement with Kantian and post-Kantian European philosophy, before turning to de Man's exemplary reading of Baudelaire as a means of demonstrating the crucial differences with my own critical method.

Rhetoric/Materiality

When Paul de Man died in 1983, he was Sterling Professor of French and Comparative Literature at Yale University. His earliest published academic work concerned the symbolist poetry of Paul Valéry, and poetics remained a central concern throughout his career. But as de Man moved from an earlier, if thoroughly agnostic, association with the New Criticism[4] to a loose (if oft overstated) affiliation with Derrida's "deconstruction," so his gaze turned more to philosophy "proper." One may say, putting it roughly, that in all of de Man's reflections on philosophy, his gaze fell on the ways philosophical reason leans on, and is inevitably betrayed by, the language it puts to use in extending its claims, a language far closer to the literary and to the unpredictable if productive resources of metaphor, metonymy, and allegory than philosophers are often wont to admit.

If Derrida radicalized the insights of transcendental *phenomenology*, such that the intentionality and self-presence of consciousness described by Husserl was both supported and undermined by a "prior" and necessary structure of linguistic difference, for de Man the paradoxes of the written word were the starting point for any subsequent investigation, philosophical or otherwise. Derrida and de Man, that is to say, traveled in opposite directions: for the former, one begins from the properly philosophical categories of consciousness and intentionality only to find language lurking beneath, while for the latter, expressly philosophical concerns were generated out of the materialities of signification as their indeterminate ground.

Many of de Man's most sustained readings of philosophy were composed in the last few years of his life, and the main essays I wish to focus on in the first half of this chapter were collected and posthumously published in a volume titled *Aesthetic Ideology*.[5] Commentators have tasked these provisional writings with representing de Man's first full foray into matters both political and historical. Such a claim has much to do with the controversy elicited by the discovery of de Man's antisemitic wartime writings and the need felt among his followers to counter the suggestion, much bandied about in the 1990s, that deconstruction inherently tended toward the apolitical at best, or the nihilistic, even fascistic, at worst.[6] Just as pertinent to the apparent political edge of the late texts, however, is the intriguing appearance of the concepts of "materiality" and "materialism," and in the readings that follow, I aim to show how such an analytical language, far from marking a full repudiation of the tropological, linguistic concerns of the "early" de Man, in fact consolidates and extends those interests in a direction that refutes those who would still wish to brand de Man a linguistic idealist or an irresponsible, textual solipsist. In the process, I hope to garner some insight into the largely unexplored connections between European philosophy and literary theory as the latter developed in primarily American universities in the mid- to late twentieth century. When we return, in the second portion of this chapter, to matters more strictly literary, I will demonstrate both how a more restrictedly literary focus sometimes compromised de Man's otherwise nuanced critical outlook and how, nonetheless, some of those most paradigmatic of his critical writings may be retrospectively enlarged when arraigned alongside the late philosophical writings, to which I'll now turn.

De Man's Materialism

In his indispensable editor's introduction to de Man's *Aesthetic Ideology*, Andrzej Warminski recounts a lecture in which de Man lamented, "We are all Schillerians, no one is Kantian anymore."[7] The quip is telling. For de Man, the radical potentiality inherent in Kantian aesthetics, a power related to the fertile ambiguity of the position of the aesthetic in Kant's system more generally, was too hastily covered over in the full-blown *aestheticism* of Jena romanticism. In Schiller perhaps even more than in those romantics who rebelled against him, the implicit and productive disjunction in Kant between the pure Ideas of reason and the domain of the sensible is too readily eclipsed in favor of the enthroning of aesthetic symbol, a resource or function that forcibly stabilizes what is, in its Kantian acceptation, an indeterminate if constructive impasse.

In a remarkable essay titled "Phenomenality and Materiality in Kant,"[8] de Man sets out to recover that repressed kernel, what he explicitly dubs Kant's materialism, understood as in opposition to the neutralization of the language of literariness, its disquieting effectivity in opening up a space for what Tom Cohen usefully describes as the "site of memory, a mnemotechnics . . . which, in advance of every hermeneutic system, marks the inevitable materiality and exteriority accorded the human apparatus."[9] For Cohen, de Man's self-consciously aberrant philosophical reappropriations, in their refusal to concede the inside/outside binary whereby language would be mapped on to the former and materiality onto the latter, are in fact closer to the properly material shock of history, when fully understood, than the New Historicisms and varieties of identity politics that followed the eclipse of deconstruction in the critical humanities.

In order to understand the idiosyncratic usage of the terms "materiality" and "materialism" as de Man, and Cohen after him, put them to use, to say nothing of "literariness" itself, one needs first to parse the distinction, raised at the very beginning of the essay on Kant, between ideology and critical philosophy. In a contemporaneous essay "The Resistance of Theory," de Man describes ideology as "the confusion of linguistic with natural reality, of reference with phenomenalism."[10] The accent should be placed here on the second clause, where ideology is understood as any conflation of reference per se—the directive, if not intentional, movement of language outward—with "phenomenalism," the word de Man used to connote something like full "presence" as Derrida was equally concerned to deconstruct it.

To be more precise, phenomenalism marks the thesis that language is symmetrically ranged in opposition to, while still in direct connection with, a substantial world of objects that is nonetheless impervious to the signs that passively come to represent it. Representation, then, as a correlational model of reference, is put radically in question throughout de Man's career. If poetic language is an especially salutary means of accessing the nonmimetic aspects of language, the late de Man would find an equally useful resource in Kant's insistence on the distinction in type between sensuous phenomenality and reason, and a convenient foil in the post-Kantian, romantic attempt to collapse that distinction through the recuperative vehicle of poetic symbol.

In "Phenomenality and Materiality in Kant," de Man takes Kant's discussion of the difference between metaphysical and transcendental principles in the third *Critique* as a means of further clarifying the distinction between what he takes to be ideology, and what he wishes to advance as a properly materialistic philosophy and poetics. For Kant, according to de Man, metaphysical concepts "imply an empirical moment that necessarily remains external to the concept,"[11] in much the same way as they would in a referential theory of language, where language and object transmit to one another in an easily commutative dance. Metaphysics, in this sense, is akin to ideology, insofar as both assume the establishment of a sharp distinction between interiority and exteriority, between a thing and its external cause, even as the two traffic with supposed ease. Transcendental claims, by contrast, burrow into the conditions of knowledge, and are thus on the side of the kind of ideology critique that it is de Man's task to elaborate. But far from being merely opposed, what de Man calls ideology or metaphysics on the one hand and critical philosophy on the other are causally linked, with transcendental critique serving to destabilize and so put in motion the ideological presuppositions that it sets out to investigate.

As de Man explains, "Critical philosophy and metaphysics (including ideologies) are causally linked to one another . . . [They] become each other's motion: if an ideology is considered to be a stable entity (body, corpus, or canon), the critical discourse it generates will be that of a transcendental motion, of a motion whose cause resides, so to speak, within itself."[12] Ideology, then, far from being a mere appearance to be stripped away, is irreducible, somewhat akin to what Derrida considered to be the inevitability of the ghostly return of the metaphysics of presence, no matter what deconstructive armory is ranged against it. I should also note the echo with Louis Althusser's influential rethinking of ideology in its Marxian acceptation, whereby ideology is a material set of relations and practices rather than a mere illusion to be dispelled.[13]

One of the tasks of Kant's third *Critique*, of course, was to find a way of mediating between the claims of pure and practical reason, or between the realm of the transcendental conditions of possible knowledge and the direct, self-sustaining determinations of free action. As is well known, Kant never fully accounted for the articulation of theoretical (which is to say transcendental) and practical reason (the distinction a repetition at a more general level of that between transcendental and metaphysical principles already discussed), but de Man's interest falls on the question precisely because it is the *aesthetic* that the third *Critique* would task with bringing the two into conversation. By investigating the paradoxes of language as themselves a kind of quasi-transcendental condition of meaning, de Man finds a way to re-pose the already seemingly asymmetric relation between the transcendental and metaphysical and Kant's more specific distinction between theoretical and practical instances of reason. Language, one might say, occupies "transcendental," "theoretical," *and* "practical" levels, although I should caution against the collapse of de Man's position into a kind of pragmatics of linguistic paradox; such a reduction would efface what is, already in Kant, the status of practice as itself a manifestation of reason. I'll return to the complex and unexpected resonance of de Manian theory and pragmatics at the end of this section.

What Kant needs to find, then, is a "phenomenalized, empirically manifest principle of cognition on whose existence the possibility of such an articulation [between theoretical and practical reason] depends. This phenomenalized principle is what Kant calls the aesthetic."[14] For de Man, to speak of something as "phenomenalized," as he does here of Kant's attempted concept of the aesthetic, is to immediately place it under suspicion; a fully "phenomenal" entity would be one that, in the manner of ideology, tries to cover over the materiality of language that must necessarily serve as its paradoxical ground. As will be seen, even if Kant had wished to find such a positive, substantial logic of recuperation, such that the two fundamental aspects (theoretical and practical) of his philosophy could be reconciled, it is his failure to do so, and the disruptive and constructive materiality exposed as a result, that so fascinates de Man. The latter turns to Kant's discussion of the sublime in order to trace the productive failure in question, productive precisely in the sense that it may well be within and through such a failure that access to the "great outdoors," to the internal inconsistencies of materiality and history, may be best found.

De Man and the Kantian Sublime

It is telling that, in his discussion of the Kantian sublime, de Man should counterpose the philosopher's account with that of Wordsworth, one of the high romantics whose seeming investment in the power of poetic symbol to reconcile language, mind, and the world served as a frequent foil to de Man's own investment in allegory. The latter device, in its stretching out of language beyond any ostensibly referential function, stages the material, irreconcilable finitude proper to temporally situated human existence. The romantics, for de Man, were capable in their better moments of using allegory precisely to insist on the irreducible, but nonetheless *constitutive,* gap between subject and object, self and other that symbol, or ideology as it was phrased above, would wish to deny.[15] Apparent in de Man's discussion of Wordsworth in "Phenomenality and Materiality in Kant" is his belief that poetics and philosophy are different openings on to the same, radical finitude proper to the human experience. What the reader is presented with, at any rate, is very far from a "philosophy of literature," were that term tacitly to ensure the predominance of philosophy as the master key to the mysteries of literary language. Rather, poetics as a critical literary intervention or "inscription" produces its own negative philosophical insights immanently, according to the torsions and indirections of the language that both poetry and its critical commentary must inhabit.

De Man introduces Wordsworth's famous poem "Lines Composed a Few Miles above Tintern Abbey" at a crucial moment in his reflections on Kant, when he has established that, far from being the mere feeling of reason's superiority over nature or the imagination, the sublime rather names a more profound failure, one that emerges at the fateful point when the imagination attempts, on behalf of reason, to encompass a totality. As de Man writes, "[The] ability of the imagination to achieve syntheses is a boon to the understanding, which is hardly conceivable without it, but this gain is countered by a corresponding loss. The comprehension discovers its own limitation, beyond which it cannot reach."[16] Such an argument is relatively standard fare in Kant commentary. Immediately following, however, and through an analogy with the process of *reading* whereby the mind's synthesis of what has come before meets a limit, de Man situates this experience of sublime failure within the remit of language; as he bluntly phrases it, "It describes not a faculty of the mind . . . but a potentiality inherent in language. For such a system of substitution, set up along a paradigmatic and a syntagmatic axis, generat[es] partial totalizations within an economy of profit and loss."[17]

The imagination's capacity to synthesize the sensible manifold meets limits that it must subsequently attempt to overcome. It does so by passing back and forth from the part to the whole and back again, the process beginning to resemble the dense arraignments of language *tout court,* the displacement of signifier to signifier and the compression and displacement of signifiers into metaphor and metonymy, respectively, so famously described by the linguist Roman Jakobson.[18] The intertwining of the (cognitive) sublimity of imaginative failure found in Kant's third *Critique* with the movement of signification, whereby it is in the inability of linguistic devices to capture a sense of the whole or of a totality that drives them on to nonetheless induce the spark of sense, confirms that, for de Man, language is very far from being a mere passive representational tool or transparent system of appropriation, one that might supervene in a time somehow "after" the material objects that it may come to appropriate or represent. As noted above, the very logic of representation is contested by de Man, for whom language is a stubborn materiality, interleaved in complex ways with the object-world that it otherwise is assumed only to mimic.

If de Man finds an unlikely ally in Kant for such a view, the vision of the Wordsworthian sublime proffered in the poet's famous "Tintern Abbey" forms something of an opposite take, picturing a sublimity of plenitude and harmony in stark contrast to the materialist asceticism that de Man distills from his readings of German philosophy; the poet famously wrote of "a sense sublime / Of something far more deeply interfused."[19] For Wordsworth, the sublime is "an instance of the constant exchange between mind and nature, of the chiasmic transfer of properties between the sensory and the intellectual world."[20] Of course, a standard reading of Kant would emphasize the transport between the intuition and the understanding in terms similar to de Man's characterization of Wordsworth above. As Kant is generally taught, the interaction of the two fundamental facets of mind is constitutive of knowledge as it is submitted to the necessary limits proper to human cognition. Instead, de Man finds in Kant a seam of contradiction that gains its full symptomatic expression in his reflections on the aesthetic, that category so frequently appealed to in philosophical history as a bridge over an impasse. De Man, far from being the linguistic idealist of legend, seeks to find in Kant the ontological limits of the aesthetic as a kind of materiality (insofar as it must be expressed through the more general texture of language as itself a material thing, at least of a kind); as something, at any rate, that is not simply a passive, ideal vehicle of correlational sense.

Perhaps most strikingly, it is the very lack of a mind eager to lace the world with meaning in Kant's invocation of the sublime, let alone one seeking connection or stable knowledge of its exterior, that most detains de Man. Kant writes in *The Critique of Judgment* that to view the ocean, for example, as sublime enjoins one to view it as poets do, "merely by what the eye reveals [*was der Augenschein zeigt*]—if it is at rest, as a clear mirror of water only bounded by the heavens; if it is stormy, as an abyss threatening to overwhelm everything."[21] Of course, one might be forgiven for expecting the "poets" to view the sea as something pregnant with multiple symbolic possibilities. But instead, Kant would have us imagine the sea in its very sublimity *as it is*, in its "mereness." De Man immediately seeks to distinguish this materialist vision of the sublime—materialist insofar as it is focuses on the physical insistence and actual consequence of worldly features over their ideal meaningfulness—from that later, romantic attempt to arrest natural features in the creative potency of symbolic language. As he writes, distinguishing Kant again from Wordsworth, "Kant's passage is *not* [like Wordsworth's] because the sky does not appear in it as associated in any way with shelter. It is not the construct under which, in Heidegger's terms, we can dwell (*wohnen*)."[22] The sky and sea simply *are*, and it is this which grants them their sublime potential—their very capacity to slip loose of the all-too-human need to neutralize the world under the idealist pretenses of symbolization.

For De Man, the final power of Kant's vision is to be located in its affinities with what is a necessary correction of our understanding of language more generally, both in its specific aesthetic manifestations and in its wider usage as a means of gaining knowledge of the world. By "affinity," I don't mean to suggest any symmetrical correspondence between the word and the thing; for de Man, such an assumption would deny the material power of language to disrupt the surety of our knowledge, to unexpectedly reorient its priorities. Rather, I refer to the manner in which both the physical world and language itself for de Man behave in uncannily similar ways, even as they otherwise elude one another. Language, like Kant's sublime ocean, *insists* in a way that ultimately escapes any attempt to make of it a passive means of mimesis. De Man underlines this strange, noncorrelational affinity toward the end of his essay by reference to the recurring language of the corporeal to be found in Kant's first *Critique*. This repeated reference to the unity of the body is also, for de Man, a sign that, for all the materialist potential in Kant's architectonics, the latter is as tempted as any romantic to at least attempt to reinstate the organic completion of nature that would be the necessary ground of symbolic language's connective function.

By contrast, the vision of nature that underlies the concept of the sublime articulated in the third *Critique* and as discussed above is "entirely material, emphatically not tropological, entirely distinct from the substitutions and exchanges between faculties or between mind and nature."[23] Yet aspects of the discussion of the architectonic in the first *Critique*—"architectonic" being the term that Kant reserves for the constitutive divisions of transcendental philosophy that, for de Man, are directly impacted by the former's thinking of the sublime—tend toward a vision of organic unity, what de Man refers to as "the recurring metaphor of the body, as a totality of limbs and parts."[24] By the time Kant writes the third *Critique*, this insistence on unity and articulation comes implicitly into question, insofar as, in the passage on the ocean as sublime discussed above, "sea and heaven, as the poets see them, are more than ever buildings. But it is no longer certain that they are at all *articulated*."[25]

Here the metaphor of the body reappears, albeit in a different register than in the insistence on unity evinced in the first *Critique*. Instead, Kant writes of "the sublime and the beautiful in the human body. We must not regard as the determining grounds of our judgment the concepts of the purposes which all our limbs serve . . . and we must not allow this unity of purpose to influence our aesthetic judgment."[26] Insofar as, for de Man, the aesthetic figures both a projected unity for Kant's philosophy and, more pressingly, the sign of the necessary failure of that unity, this resistance in Kant to viewing the corporeal as a unity while it is under the aesthetic gaze helps us underline the importance of that constitutive disunity for Kant's system more generally. Kant, that is to say, explicitly links the body as disunified with the aesthetic point of view that might otherwise have served as the broader system's unifying cement. As de Man phrases it, "If the architectonic . . . appears, very near the end of the analytics of the aesthetic, at the conclusion of the section on the sublime, as the material disarticulation not only of nature but of the body, then this moment marks the undoing of the aesthetic as a valid category."[27]

We may, of course, question the surety with which de Man reaches this conclusion, based as it is on an isolated portion of Kant's discussion of the sublime that otherwise tends rather close to the romantic (*avant la lettre*, so to speak) than de Man might wish us to acknowledge. And the vision of the corporeal offered here is different enough, too, from Ponge's invocation of the body as it queasily interacts with comparably intransigent properties of the poetic, and as analyzed in chapter 2. But an acknowledgment of the seeming partiality of de Man's reading of Kant's sublime would not necessarily invalidate de Man's claim, at least to the extent that the critic is interested both here and at least in portions of his broader literary-critical output in capturing those moments in a text or in a philosophical system where formation and de-formation coincide; where, to echo Derrida's appropriation of Kantian terminology, a condition of impossibility persists simultaneously as a condition of *possibility*. While it is frequently claimed of de Man that his concern for disarticulation makes him a nihilist, I think his close reading of Kant here places as much, if not more, emphasis on the *constructive* potential of such impasses than on their defigurative consequences. This will, alas, not be in the case in some of the literary readings discussed in the second half of this chapter, where, instead, de Man's intricate tracing of the dissolving of textual architecture threatens to lapse into something approaching a negative theology, a reveling in the points of incompletion that I would rather theorize as necessary to any relatively successful project of formalization.

In an essay on Hegel's aesthetics, de Man writes of the "necessity, which is also an impossibility, to connect the subject with its predicates or the sign with its symbolic significations."[28] One may note here, in conclusion of this section, the strange echo of de Man's materialist literary theory, one that I would not especially wish to amplify, with the concerns of American pragmatism. For Richard Rorty and others, the failure to relate linguistically to any absolute is not in itself a reason to stop trying; indeed, the very inner motor of linguistic reason is compelled by its failures. De Man remains, I think, a more vital thinker than his pragmatist contemporaries precisely in his refusal to disconnect pragmatics, taken here as the practical consequences of language's failures, from the philosophical heritage that the latter is too often taken to place in the shade. (In this sense, de Man's "practice" has, on the whole, more to do with Kant than it does with William James.) From within the very canon of transcendental philosophy, de Man finds a logic of constructive paradox to be located not just in the now-familiar slippages of the signifier, but also in the world itself, in its very sublime, material insistence. Such a project would have us place under suspicion any clean, symmetrical opposition of word to world, just as it would have us demur from finding in the inevitable aporias of reason an easy nihilism of nonmeaning, of blank cognitive despair. Rather, de Man, at least in these final essays, highlights those points at which the most material, intransigent dimensions of both language and the world find a noncorrelational resonance, such that we find ourselves within the folds of materiality at the very moment when we seem most removed, most caught within the imposing landscapes of the linguistic.

De Man's Baudelaire

At this juncture, I should begin to contrast my "speculative formalism" with de Man's invigorating critical project, one as concerned, as shown above at least in the context of the later philosophical writings, with the impasses of the world, of the density of things, as it is with the unpredictable circuits of the word. To begin, I'd like to investigate de Man's startling essay "Anthropomorphism and Trope in the Lyric,"[29] an essay that offers pathbreaking remarks on belonging and nonbelonging, particularity and collectivity, as they pertain to the lyric form. Taking as his source two sonnets by Baudelaire, "Correspondances" and "Obsession," de Man initially reads the latter as the fulfillment of the former, a fulfillment that tells us more about the revelation of the former's internal aporia than it announces any completion or resolution of the former's structural deficits; as de Man writes, "We read '*Obsession*' thematically as an interiorization of '*Correspondances*,' and as a negation of the positivity of an outside reality."[30] Yet it is just as plausible to read "'*Correspondances*' [as] the negation of '*Obsession*': the figural stability of '*Obsessions*' is denied in '*Correspondances*.'"[31] The two poems are thus chiasmatically related, each undoing the other's differing claims to inviolability. De Man's reading of "Correspondances" is, for sure, the more paradigmatic of his method, and for that reason it will form my initial focus. I will then propose my own reading of "Obsession" in contrast to that offered by de Man; to preview, "Obsession" may be both more *and* less stable than de Man imagined.

At first glance, "Correspondances" seems concerned to elaborate "obscure and profound" unities, a series of relations between humanity and nature that read as almost parodic of the (supposed) romantic desire for the harmony of spirit and nature. As Barbara Johnson comments, in an essay quite as brilliant as de Man's, "A traditional reading of the poem would say that the lateral analogies among the senses (perfumes fresh as a baby's skin, mellow as oboes, green as prairies) are signs that there exists an analogy between man and nature, and man and the spiritual realm."[32] Here I should quote "Correspondances" in full:

> La nature est un temple où de vivants piliers
> Laissent parfois sortir de confuses paroles;
> L'homme y passe à travers des forêts de symbols
> Qui l'observent avec des regards familiers.
>
> Comme de longs échos qui de loin se confondent
> Dans une ténébreuse et profonde unité,
> Vaste comme la nuit et comme la clarté
> Les parfums, les couleurs et le sons se répondent.
>
> Il est des parfums frais comme des chairs d'enfants,
> Doux commes les hautbois, verts comme les prairies,
> Et d'autres, corrompus, riches et triomphants,
>
> Ayants l'expansion des choses infinies,
> Commes l'ambre, le musc, le benjoin et l'encens,
> Qui chantent les transport de l'esprit et des sens.[33]

> The pillars of Nature's temple are live
> And sometimes yield perplexing messages;

forests of symbols between us and the shrine
remark our passage with accustomed eyes.

Like long-held echoes, blending somewhere else
into one deep and shadowy unison
as limitless as darkness and as day,
the sounds, scents, the colors correspond.

There are odors succulent as young flesh,
sweet as flutes, and green as any grass
while others—rich, corrupt and masterful,

possess the power of such infinite things,
as incense, amber, benjamin and musk,
to praise the senses' raptures and the mind's.[34]

De Man focuses his analysis on the placing of "comme" in the poem, a usage that, at least until the final stanza, seems to produce its usual effect, proposing resemblances and drawing together the heteronomous images of the poem into a unity, what de Man refers to as the poem's "totalizing expansion."[35] But if the effect of "comme" is analogical in the first three stanzas, the effect is rather different in the last, where instead of the connective function of analogy, de Man finds a list of isolated particulars: "Instead of analogy, we have enumeration, and an enumeration which never moves beyond the confines of a set of particulars: 'forêt' synthesizes but not does not enumerate a set of trees, but 'ambre,' 'musc,' 'benjoin,' and 'encens,' whatever differences or gradations one wishes to establish between them, are reframed by 'comme' ever to lead beyond themselves."[36] That list of scents, far from rhyming with the other natural or symbolical elements of the poem, persists instead as an open-ended sequence set apart from the poem's wider tropic texture, one that serves to disturb the totalizing ambitions of the poem's previously implied figural ambition. As de Man explains, "What could be more perverse or corruptive for a metaphor aspiring to transcendental totality than remaining stuck in an enumeration that never goes anywhere? . . . Enumerative repetition disrupts the chain of tropological substitution at the crucial moment when the poem promises, by way of these very substitutions, to reconcile the pleasures of the mind with those of the senses."[37]

De Man establishes an opposition here, as brutal as it is inventive, between the unifying effects of metaphor and analogy and the disunity of repetition. Repetition merely permits the replacement of the one with another, word with word, absent of any *telos.* This local opposition is a metonym of de Man's more general pitting of the artificial unities of grammar against the disassembling impetuses of rhetoric, with the latter, as I've already intimated, gaining the upper hand in the majority of de Man's readings. But as I've also mentioned, this privileging of the deformative over the formative may well be a blind spot in de Man's otherwise meticulous critical gaze, a lapse into something approaching negative theology; parenthetically, in the conclusion I will discuss how Paul Livingston has explained any such attempt to hold to the necessity of the whole, even if in the demonstration of its impossibility, as an essentially theological ruse, one that must cover over the necessary impasses that any movement of totalization generates. Why, after all, should an apparently contradictory moment of disassembly cancel out the constructive forms that otherwise populate a verse? Might it rather be that the "transcendental totality" that I think de Man rightly identifies in Baudelaire's postromantic sonnet is both grounded *and* threatened by the repetitive enumeration that closes out the verse? This tense standoff between formation and deformation is at the heart of the speculative formalism outlined in this book, and it is sustained by the success *in* failure that de Man too often mistook for the failure in success; it is conditioned, that is to say, by the modes of incompletion or inconsistency that de Man, at least here, confuses for the impossibility of any kind of poetic stability per se.

It may even be that the enumeration that closes "Correspondances," whereby the unifying function of "*comme*" is negated by its placement at the beginning of the line, reveals something central about the success of poetic form. To this end, the repetitive logic that ends the poem may be taken as a poetic logic in its own right, one that interacts with but is autonomous of the analogical and relational texture established over the first three stanzas. As will be seen in chapter 5, the connective function of repetition is most obviously to be demonstrated in experimental verse; there I'll trace how the negation of classical meter in the verse of Ron Silliman, Bruce Andrews, and others, far from resulting in formlessness, in fact serves as its own principle of coherence, one ratified by the strategic use of repetition. In Baudelaire, the logic of enumeration and repetition is as much a recognition of the priority of formal, structural, even asemantic elements as it is a failure of any postromantic tendency toward the transcendental; it this crucial insight that de Man's reading risks missing. By emphasizing enumeration as a negation of a prior symbolic plenitude, de Man remains inside the romantic ideology—one challenged, lest we forget, most often from within romanticism itself—that he otherwise wishes to contest, insofar as he understands as merely limiting what is, in fact, one of the positive conditions for poetic sense in Baudelaire.

But what of de Man's parallel ambition to seed his radicalized formalism within a new philosophical approach to materiality, as read above? Here an implicit aspect of that ambition not yet fully discussed in this chapter should be addressed, namely the glancing connection made in those late essays between materiality and the vexations of historical time. As already mentioned, de Man was wont to associate his vision of materiality as disruptive excess with history, the latter rethought against all teleological temptations as a force irreducible to linear or narrative plotting. To articulate the heights of literary undecidability with the problem of historical time was no doubt partly strategic. De Man was often criticized for neglecting, in a manner said to be not dissimilar to his formalistic New Critical forebears, the question of literary historical context, a charge he threw back at his critics with the accusation, expressed in one of the epigraphs to this book, that they had not nearly been formalistic enough.[38] And yet the power of de Man's method is, at least if one traces its consequences, the refusal of any sharp distinction between text and context; at its most persuasive, de Manian deconstruction is concerned to trace the asymmetric intercalation of literature and its spatial and temporal environments in such a way that no one variable gains the upper hand. At one and the same time, history (context) and text may both be the sites of asemantic force, of the nonmimetic movements of signification beyond stable sense. All of this makes de Man's neglect of the specifically historical and temporal dimensions of "Correspondances," an analysis after all contemporaneous with his reflections on the dislocations of historical time collected in *Aesthetic Ideology*, all the more striking.

Where, then, do time and history enter the frame of Baudelaire's sonnet? Perhaps unsurprisingly, it is in the transition from the logic of analogy to that of enumeration announced by the final stanza that such an irruption of history into form is to be found. This intervention of history into form—or better, the intervention of history *as* form—will be most extensively analyzed in the final chapter, but I'd like to lay the ground for that fuller analysis here. Of course, the dichotomy maintained by de Man between reparative analogy and the solvent of enumeration, one nonetheless read as chiasmatically distributed across and within both "Correspondances" and "Obsession," is one version of a binary that has a long critical history. Most obviously, one hears the echo of those interminable battles between the countryside and the city, between the social collective and the starkly individual, between the mechanistic and the organic, that are frequently mobilized in explaining, say, the reaction of romanticism against classicism, or modernism against naturalism. Consider the eloquence of Edmond Wilson's verdict on the (retrospectively codified) battle between naturalist mechanism and symbolist ephemeral-ity: "All that vaporous, confused and grandiose world of Romanticism had been resolutely ordered and compressed; but now the objective point of view of Naturalism, the machine-like technique which went with it, begins to cramp the poet's imagination . . . The reader begins to chafe at the strain, and the artist begins to betray it."[39] Such a dialectic, when translated into the rubric of shifts in historical production and political organization, becomes something like the cultural back-and-forth between countryside and city so impressively documented in the terms of its aesthetic consequences by Raymond Williams.[40]

Where such binaries as listed above tend to be resolved one into the other, de Man's wars between analogy and enumeration, or more generally between grammar and rhetoric, more often end only in icy détente. Such is the case in "Anthropomorphism and Trope in the Lyric," where "Correspondances" and "Obsession" trade irreconcilable literary structures and designs, only to conclude more or less where they began. The dynamism that I identified above in de Man's late philosophical reflections on materiality seems weaker here, less effective, and yet the portion of "Correspondances" most in question is, far to the contrary, the site of a most characteristic and fecund intervention of historical time on the rival logics of poetic form. For what are the items listed at the culmination of "Correspondances"—"*l'ambre, le musc, le benjoin et l'encens*"—if not covetable *commodities*, markers of a trade in "exotic" goods whose simultaneously high-religious and pagan resonance covers, and then only superficially, an emergent and staunchly utilitarian ethic of exchange? Perhaps the seemingly organic movements of analogy instituted by those earlier uses of "*comme*" are not stout enough to resist the brutality of such *arriviste* imperatives, shattering as they are of earlier forms of organic, perhaps especially agrarian forms of collectivity allegorized by the unifying logic of the first three stanzas. (Parenthetically, one should note here in passing the importance of Walter Benjamin's rather different reflections on Baudelaire and the logic of the commodity.)[41]

Such, at any rate, would be the payoff of a more or less conventional historical reading of the sonnet, one especially colored by the concerns of Marxist criticism, these latter very much of interest to me too. But if my speculative formalism is to update, rather than simply reproduce, earlier attempts to read literature within the terms of time and history, I must take due consideration of how poetic form itself may reproduce, resist, and remain impervious to, all at the same time, the historical pressures just mentioned; form, on my reading, is liable, at the least, to both endorse and undermine its contents, such a seeming paradox persisting nonetheless as the very condition of poetic sense. The first thing to note in this connection is obvious, but no less crucial for all that: by encoding the ruses of commodification within what now appear to be exaggerated encomia to the "expansiveness of infinite things," a starkly utilitarian imperative is ironized, distanced, held at a reserve, blunted by what precedes it. Indeed, one senses throughout the sonnet a kind of winking knowingness, the sense that its romantic pleas have grown rhetorically stale, that its worship of nature and its apparent attempt to harmoniously fuse word and world have been undertaken with the deflating knowledge that such a project is, more likely than not, doomed to fail. I've already had cause to note the ambivalence of the spiritual significance of the items arraigned in Baudelaire's list; here, I would only add that the liturgical voice that apparently incants those objects is itself laced with an insincere portentousness, one that creeps into every corner of the verse once one has initially registered its booming presence.

When reframed in these broadly parodic terms, then, the final enumeration of objects cut off from that prior vaulting symbolic ambition seems to mark the point at which the mask slips, when the poem's underlying structure, its own true commitment to an unmasking of romantic illusion, becomes most clear to the eye. "Moment" is perhaps especially apposite, for the list in question is as bound up with the poem's particular temporal rhythm as it is with its resistance to, and solicitation of, history, figured here as the individualizing imperatives of commodification as they eclipse the prior authorities of religious ritual. That individualizing drive is, to be sure, underlined by the single-syllable beat of each object, no two terms collapsible into the other and yet each identical in metric weight, but just as important is the interruption of the earlier rhythm of the poem that such a list effects. Where otherwise "Correspondances" behaves more or less in accordance with the rules of the sonnet and with the strictures of the French alexandrine, here one finds little of the singsong musicality of the previous stanzas. On the replacement of analogy with repetition, the poem stutters, gives itself over to the logic of interruption, betraying as it does so its earlier commitment to temporal fluidity and spatial contiguity.

If such a temporal interruption could, at first glance, be read as formal confirmation of the bald, ineluctable, stark historical truth of the commodity-world introduced in its wake, another reading may justifiably hear in the highlighting of this discrepancy, one further achieved through the pointedly clumsy rhyme of "*l'encens*" with "*des sens*," an intensification of the poem's bid for artificiality: one superficially static historical picture—romantic, spiritual, organic solidarity—merely replaced with another, the equally one-note reduction of social life to the indifferent movements of a newly capitalist economic base. On this second reading, the apparent intervention of history at the end of the third stanza is no occasion for critique, for the triumphant unveiling of archaic illusions, for the breathless victory of the New over the Old. To the contrary, the very poeticization of history and time, the cloaking of historical change in the smirk of parody, in the disingenuousness that seems to issue from the very heightened *ingenuousness* of Baudelaire's style, has negated in advance the possibility for poetry to even attempt such a politically responsible task of critique. Instead, all that is left is a kind of impassive presentation, the mere reading of a list, the New shrugging itself into existence and appearing for all that to be just as paper-thin as the Old. To oversimplify, one could say that the first reading, that of the overtaking of a prior sensuous organicism by the mechanical rhythms of modernity, the latter exposing itself to the detriment of the former's illusions, is suggested most strongly by a political context supervening from well outside the bounds of the poem itself: namely, by the supersession of a lingering feudalism by capitalist modernity, one already, of course, substantially under way, if not completed altogether, at the time of the poem's publication in 1857.[42]

The second reading, whereby the artificiality of romantic yearning is met by the equivalently synthetic, and already-ironized logic of repetition that announces the poem's end, each instance of artificiality facing the other without any supersession—such a reading is induced only by the poem's form itself, in opposition to any redemptive "contextualization" intervening from outside. But for all that I am concerned to grant poetic language its speculative possibility, no poem is so turned in on itself as to be utterly indifferent to the rhythms of its multiple temporal and spatial outsides. At one and the same time, there is no way of cleanly wrenching poem from "context," word from world, outside from inside. Rather, as I've been suggesting throughout this book, word and world awkwardly intercalate in a manner irreducible to any priority of context over text, text over context. But to deny this kind of causative priority is not for all that to denude poetry of its formativeness: even as historical time may pressure the poem from within, it does so only at the risk of being refigured by the poem's own speculative resources.

Baudelaire's sonnet, then, denies us the resources to finally and absolutely adjudicate these two readings, but in both instances the agnosticism of the poem's form is constructive rather than merely deconstructive. The poem enables rather than disables the possibility that history, whether received under the sign of parody or not, is complexly imbricated in what otherwise appears as a rippleless aesthetic surface. But in either case, historicization is not reducible to "context," if one were to take the latter as any more or less transparent social or biographical intentionality. Rather, it is poetic form itself that both announces and defers its articulation with historical time, even as historical time in turn bears its own formal influence on the poetic form that enables and threatens to negate its appearance; the roiling dialectic that results is, I would venture, a threat to any attempt to fully extricate the one, poetry, from the other, history, just as much as it makes impossible the subordination of text to context, or context to text.

Rather, both subsist as forms that find a curious amenability at the moment of their apparent incommensurability, at the point at which the one takes up battle with the other. I'll have much more to say about this rocky relation of poetry and historical time in the final chapter, but suffice at present to note how what, for de Man, seemed to announce the trouncing of grammar by rhetoric is rather, on my reading, the contingent foundation for the very multiplication of historical and semantic possibilities alike; an enlargement of the poem's creative capacity much more than a reduction of the verse to a mere allegory of disappointment. It is precisely this more hopeful tenor of form that de Man found outside literature and in the more dour province of philosophy proper in his final writings, in the perversely fecund blankness of materiality itself, and in the rerouting of sublimity away from the promise of unification and toward the possibilities of things as they "merely are."

What, though, of Baudelaire's "Obsession"? For de Man, recall, the second poem sits, by virtue of its tropic consistency, at an oblique angle to "Correspondances"; not as its opposite, exactly, but as an assertion of poetic closure over the apparent direction outward suggested by "Correspondance"'s broken form, its hymning of the "transports of spirit and sense." "Obsession" reads as follows:

> Grands bois, vous m'effrayez comme des cathédrales;
> Vous hurlez comme l'orgue; et dans nos coeurs maudits,
> Chambres d'éternel dueil où vibrent de vieux râles,
> Répondent les échos de vos "De profundis."
>
> Je te hais, Océan! tes bonds et tes tumultes
> Mon esprit les retrouve en lui; ce rire amer
> De l'homme vaincu, plein de sanglots et d'insultes,
> Je l'entends dans le rire énorme de la mer
>
> Comme tu me plairais, ô nuit! sans ces étoiles
> Dont la lumière parle un langage connu!
> Car je cherche le vide, et le noir, et le nu!

Mais les ténèbres sont elles-mêmes des toiles
Où vivent, jaillissant de mon oeil par milliers,
Des êtres disparus aux regards familiers.[43]

Great woods, you frighten me like cathedrals;
You roar like the organ; and in our cursed hearts,
Rooms of endless mourning where old death-rattles sound,
Respond the echoes of your "De profundis."

I hate you, Ocean! your bounding and your tumult,
My mind finds them within itself; that bitter laugh
Of the vanquished man, full of sobs and insults,
I hear it in the immense laughter of the sea.

How I would like you, Night! without those stars
Whose light speaks a language I know!
For I seek emptiness, darkness, and nudity!

But the darkness is itself a canvas
Upon which live, springing from my eyes by thousands,
Beings with understanding looks, who have vanished.[44]

As de Man notes, where the first lines of "Correspondances" are defined by an uncertain anthropomorphism or de-naturalization—"Nature is a temple . . ."—the beginning of "Obsession" moves in an opposite figural direction, serving instead to naturalize that which is unnatural: "Great woods, you frighten me like cathedrals." The cohesion that de Man sees as operational across the poem is secured at its opening, so we are told, by a harmony of imagistic elements, ensured by the conventional usage of "*comme*" (in contrast to the use found at the denouement of "Correspondances") and in the neatness by which the central images in question—wood, wind, fear, cathedral, organ—affirm one another. "Everything," de Man writes, "can be substituted by everything else,"[45] the whole poem then becoming a chiasmus, airtight in its interlocking conventionality. Moreover, both poems in question map one onto the other, such that the temple in the first becomes a cathedral, albeit with one key difference: there is no equivalent disruption of grammar by rhetoric in "Obsession" that de Man locates as central to the overall discontinuity of "Correspondances," and this precisely because "Obsession" is a *reading* of "Correspondances," one that seeks to heal the latter's wounds. And yet in its very exemplarity, in its formal self-closure, "Obsession" holds its patient's wounds open as much as it attempts to stitch them shut. Such blemishes—in sum, the ruinous tussle between transcendental aspiration and rhetorical disarticulation revealed in "Correspondance"'s final stanza—can then be said to produce the unstable ground on which all lyric poetry grows, and which it tries thereafter to conceal. As de Man writes, "Whenever we encounter a text such as 'Obsession'—that is, whenever we read—there is always an infra-text, a hypogram like 'Correspondances' underneath."[46] Any apparent poetic impermeability as represented here by "Obsession," that is to say, is always only an attempted reparation of a breach that dwells ineluctably at its root. And thus de Man's reading of the two poems in question becomes allegorical of the more general disruption of grammar by rhetoric, of symbolic purity by figural excess.

It's a highly accomplished reading, surely one of the most impressive in the history of twentieth-century literary criticism, and yet its own flaws are as difficult to conceal as the structural rifts that scar "Correspondances." Even taking into account the pedagogical power of de Man's allegory, one must ask whether the establishment of an antinomy between a self-enclosed grammar on the one side and a disparate rhetoric on the other, mapped onto two separate ballads by Baudelaire, is not, in its form, of the very order of contiguity and symmetry that de Man otherwise seems minded to challenge. De Man's reading of literary-historical periodization as a kind of "resistance" and "nostalgia," one that he relates to the equally reparative drive toward holism sought by literary-critical tradition, is certainly salutary from the vantage of our contemporary valorization of all things empirical and historical. Nonetheless, and as I have demonstrated with respect to "Correspondances," there are other means of reading history into and against a text, methods that may locate poetic figurality itself as the meridian for a constructive battle between opposed forces, poetry in one corner, historical time in another. On closer inspection, such apparently reified agents are revealed to be always partial mixes of the one and the other; purified distillates of each only tend to be produced when a critic, very much like de Man, seeks to dramatically range antagonists against one another who may, in fact, be mutually polluting, much like the subject in its routing through the other in psychoanalytic theories of identification or, at an earlier moment, in Hegel's account of the fight between lord and bondsman.[47] This interreliance of the two is what moves them both to war, motivating them in turn to try and wrench free from the other's clasp and gain a measure of autonomy. Where de Man *ends* his reading with such starkly opposed forces, I will conclude mine with the no less antiholistic scene of a clashing set of logics nonetheless molecularly intertwined, logics whose incommensurability would prove an opening out onto poetic possibility rather more than its cancellation.

In this light, "Obsession" can be read a little differently. Instead of finding in the poem a reparative obverse to "Correspondance"'s broken structure, one would, based on the above, expect to find instances of both construction *and* deconstruction played out across the text's surface, points at which the overall structure coheres and others where it defiantly pulls itself apart. Such instances would be as difficult to fully extricate one from the other as they would be concerned to project just such an illusory separation. Consider those first two instances of "*comme*" in the poem, the woods "like" a cathedral, the roar "like" the organ. Is the figural architecture here as water-tight as de Man seems to think it is? The organ is a metonym for the cathedral itself, and yet we find it immediately separated from its father image, pressed into service instead as metaphor for the wind, the cathedral already having been conscripted for the representation of the woods themselves; that said, the "roar" in question is never explicitly specified as the wind, never formally compared as through the conventional use of the French "*comme*" that so otherwise exercises de Man and that apparently stands in for the formal congruity of "Obsession" as against the jumble of "Correspondances." It was the irregular usage of "*comme*" in the latter, recall, that permitted the establishment of de Man's dichotomy in the first place. And so metaphor and metonymy, two tropes whose separate and seamless operation in "Obsession" would seem necessary to bear out de Man's antinomy, fall into a certain indistinction, begin to fuse and intertwine. Of course, it could well be that the "roar" of the woods is in no need of any explicit formalization of its metaphoric status, is in no need of that emphatic "*comme*" otherwise so prominent in the poem; perhaps one simply *knows* that any woods that roar do so because of the wind coursing through their trees. But are there not other reasons why woods may roar, not least the fearful presence of animals whose characteristics have, after all, been used here through the figure of the roar to deepen one's sense of the fright felt by the poem's lyric voice?

For de Man, of course, "Obsession" is a poem defined by naturalization, by the moving of human traits into a natural tropic context; as he writes, "The benefits of naturalization—as we can call the reversal of anthropomorphism—are at once apparent. None of the uncertainties that obscure . . . '*Correspondances*' are maintained [in "Obsession"] . . . The analogism is so perfect that the implied anthropomorphism becomes fully motivated." But is the usage of "roar" here exactly an instance of naturalization, and just how perfect is that analogism if so? What should one call the imposition of animal but nonhuman traits on inanimate nature? (Humans shriek, roar, or bellow, it's true, but my sense is that the setting and the indeterminacy of the French *hurlez* ("howl" is also suggested) pass us to something that edges into the nonhuman; indeed, we say that humans roar or shriek precisely in order to animalize them.) It's not anthropomorphism, of course, the trope that de Man takes to sharpen the confusion that issues from "Correspondances," although the otherwise unelaborated replacement of "naturalization" by "anthropomorphism" in the third sentence quoted above seems, curiously, to claim otherwise. But neither is it quite "naturalization," at least if one takes the latter to signal the casting of inanimate traits on animate things, this being, at least, de Man's definition. The distinction between anthropomorphism and naturalization is as crucial an antinomy for de Man as that between grammar and rhetoric; the former is metonymic for the latter insofar as the casting of human traits on the inhuman sows confusion that is otherwise made stable by the absorption of changeable features into the fixity of nature. Equally, the more local distinction is the effect that can be said to retrospectively "prove" the general breach of grammar and rhetoric as cause. It is key for the wider integrity of de Man's argument, then, that a firm separation between these differing devices holds water.

That it *doesn't* do this, and that "Obsession" itself puts into question the purity of a distinction that is meant, paradoxically, to demonstrate an otherwise overriding *im*purity between grammar and rhetoric, is not to deny the local insights of de Man's reading, and neither is it to ignore the multiple instances in "Obsession" where trope echoes successfully with trope, fulfilling the principle of unity that defines the poem overall for de Man. But what the intervention of that apparently innocuous word *hurler* demonstrates is the potential of a third term, something like an inevitable and formative impurity, here at least pseudo-animalistic, that knocks out of kilter the otherwise seamless matchup of figural logics that de Man would need "Obsession" to embody as such. That seamlessness, recall, is read by de Man in contrast to the relative dissymmetry of "Correspondances," and in a manner explicitly dramatized by the arrangement of the two poems along what is referred to as a "positive/negative axis." No longer, on this reading, can "nature" and the "human" (the "anthropomorphic") face one another in a relation of absolute negation. But my intention is not merely to find disorder where de Man finds order; or, at least, it is to disturb the antinomic impulse that would so firmly separate the two. This third term, one that could provisionally be stabilized as the "animal," far from fitting "between" nature and the human, comes to put any stable identification of the natural and the human into question. This would be the impure admixture that I predicted above in contrast to de Man's monumental ranging of opposites. In the very establishment of such an impurity, one should trace a new route of semantic possibility otherwise denied in de Man's rhetorical reading.

One encounters, after all, a rather firmer instance of anthropomorphism, otherwise said by de Man to define "Correspondances," in the third stanza of "Obsession," where, in a high romantic style, the stars in the night sky are the subject of an apostrophic address: "How I would like you, Night! without those stars / whose light speaks a language I know! / For I seek emptiness, darkness, and nudity!" The subject, whose lyric voice is certainly more pronounced here than in "Correspondances," is dismayed by the very predictability of a natural feature, the light disappointing his or her melancholic demand for darkness and for the unadorned and dark truths of the flesh. If, in the poem's muddying of the distinction between anthropomorphism and naturalization, I noted the production of a third term, the animal, that rendered indistinct features taken by de Man to be uniquely legible, here one finds the lyric voice decrying the legibility and certainty of starlight by use of the very device, anthropomorphism, that, for de Man, is the avatar of *un*certainty; and thus, anthropomorphism is employed here precisely to highlight a certainty where one is so keenly not wanted.

The lyric voice of "Obsession" that so shrinks from the clarity of an anthropomorphized starlight and its "language" would, one conjectures, be rather happier with the stars, in Kant's terms, "as the poets see them," as naturally sublime in their dark indifference or mereness, the latter of course being their status for de Man in his "Phenomenality and Materiality in Kant" and discussed at length in the first half of this chapter. Perhaps "naturalization" and "anthropomorphism" are not so easily distinguished according to axes of certainty and uncertainty, of stability and instability, just as the human/animal and human/nature binaries can be said to slip out of sequence in Baudelaire. Such slipping and sliding is, nonetheless, rather more inclusive, more constructive, than de Man would wish us to believe, encompassing as it does a fertile nonplace between metaphor and metonymy, between anthropomorphism and naturalization, one that is perhaps especially conducive to the agonized cries of the newly libidonized lyric voice as it roars through "Obsession."

How to relate the critical reading of "Anthropomorphism and the Lyric" and my own analysis of Baudelaire to the more celebratory account of de Man's late philosophical essays that opened this chapter? Normally, one would expect two such apparently different readings of the possibilities of an aesthetic opening on to the world to have been composed at different times in an author's intellectual development; indeed, those who would wish to impose a telos from linguistic solipsism to philosophical maturity onto de Man's career require precisely this periodic difference. This isn't the case, however; both "Phenomenality and Materiality in Kant" and "Anthropomorphism and Trope in the Lyric" were delivered as part of the same set of lectures at Cornell University in 1983. There are, of course, shared themes across both sets of texts, not least the ways in which literary and philosophical thinking have similarly struggled to sharply maintain nature as against the human, language and meaning as against the brute facticity of the natural world.

The de Man of the late essays produces, one could say, a formalist account of the presence in both nature and language alike of asemantic elements, zones of non-sense that exist in implicit repudiation of the more familiar, romantic poetic conscription of nature and language as sources for human-centered meaning making. This de Manian perspective will then serve us as a broader, more general take on the intimate approach to constitutive non-sense as pioneered by Ponge and as discussed in chapter 2. There I demonstrated how Ponge, far from being a poet of objects-in-themselves—a purview that is the mere flipside of the subsumption of objects under the totalizing imperatives of romantic anthropomorphism—is in fact the prophet of a nonmimetic poetic reference, one that would respect the autonomy of word and world both while demonstrating the asymmetric intermingling of each. What Ponge demonstrates for individual objects, de Man shows for nature as such.

Insofar as I have maintained a distinction here between the de Man concerned principally with the self-deconstructing ruses of poetic structure and the de Man of a speculative philosophical attention to materiality, the reader may be tempted to conclude that I surreptitiously concur with the idea dismissed more than once above, namely that only the "late" philosophical de Man is truly worthy of recuperation. To reiterate however, the two main examples adduced in this chapter—"Phenomenality and Materiality in Kant" and "Anthropomorphism and Trope in the Lyric"—*date from the same year.* The division seems less stark, nonetheless, when one considers how, in both essays, imperatives to tame the outdoors by way of symbolic incorporation—think, again, of Wordsworth's symbolic sublime as implicitly countered by Kant's attention to the sublimity of things as they are—are resisted, not in the name of an abstract valorization of the "object" (a move that, once again, would only inflate the "subject" as its occluded background), but rather through a negation of the very dominant terms of text and context, signifier and signified. What results is not, one should emphasize, a mere textual solipsism, but rather a critical-theoretical formalism of interpenetrating domains of sense and non-sense, one not unrelated, if not identical, to that pursued through the course of this book. While de Man frequently fell back from the more radical consequences of his pioneering critical project, it needn't take too much of a shift in perspective for the novelty and power of his writings to come back into view. And while speculative formalism would put much more of an emphasis on the formative force of the linguistic and philosophical binds that de Man took pleasure in exposing, my outlook must build on his foundations. As I intimated above, de Man was inconsistent in thinking the temporality and historicity of literary form, and it is to those questions, pressing for any formalism, that I'll turn in the next and final chapter.

5

Language Poetry, Psychoanalysis, and the Formal Negotiation of History and Time

What to make of the so-called "language poets," thirty-five-odd years since the height of their influence? Most poetic movements, it should be noted at the outset, resist their incorporation into movements at all, if such an attempt is even made during the lifetimes of the poets in question. Symbolism, the decadents, the spasmodics, to say nothing of the most contested of such categories, the romantics and the moderns—these, among many others, were groups formed largely in hindsight. When contemporary attempts were made to codify their divergent poetic projects, such attempts were frequently resisted, even as such moves were not infrequently to come from within the ranks of the poets themselves.[1] "Language poetry" is a rare exception: Bruce Andrews, Ron Silliman, Charles Bernstein, Lyn Hejinian, Susan Howe, and their disparate comrades fully conspired in their own canonization, not least through the production of the journal *L-A-N-G-U-A-G-E,* which housed some of their most important works, works often distributed ambiguously between prose and verse, between poetry and criticism.

As such, any consideration of language poetry must inevitably raise the question of *self-nomination,* or how the installation of a group name by the collective, and the subsequent challenges to that name that inevitably emerge, must subsequently inflect our understanding of the verse. This problem of self-nomination will also, in a slightly different light, be shown to be part of the problem of history as it appears within and without poetic form more generally. Verse as self-anointed as that produced by the language poets seems to be ghosted by a metacommentary announcing its belonging to or resistance to the collective, even as such poetry is so often also accompanied by an insistence on individuality or singularity, on semantic and syntactical irreducibility. This, I will argue, is something rather different from the emphasis on self-reflexivity and knowingness that has been said to characterize postmodern narrative fiction, the roots of which are traceable to Swiftian irony and to many other and varied precursors.[2] Rather, language poetry, insofar as it can be taken as a delineable phenomenon of its own, is identifiable by a simultaneous unity and disunity, a dynamic push and pull toward and away from a sense of collective belonging. The posing of the problem of collective nomination is not simply a metatheoretical indulgence of this experimental verse, that is to say, but is rather the particular way in which it raises the questions of time and history, an approach that may open out onto a thinking of the poetic articulation of time and history more generally.

The qualifying clause in the penultimate sentence of the last paragraph—"insofar as it [language poetry] can be taken as a delineable phenomenon of its own"—takes on an especial resonance with this most legacy-conscious of movements. It is a standard critical maneuver to posit the unity of one's object, only to then demonstrate its internal heterogeneity; this isn't my concern here. Instead, I hope to be able to demonstrate the attraction to and repulsion from history even within individual poems associated with language verse. Terms like "collective" and "collectivity" are nonetheless immediately shadowed by irony when one considers the time and place within which language poetry rose to eminence. The United States of the late 1970s, 1980s, and much of the 1990s held notions of collectivity in suspicion, such ideas said to be definitional of the outside—the Soviet Union, most pressingly—as they were inimical to the interior polity and its economy.[3] More than this, the question of history itself, of posterity and the fear of obsolescence as they may pertain to, say, the race to technological hyperadvancement, were especially charged, caught up in angry tides of oppositional political rhetoric. At the same time, history *tout court* was increasingly said to be *over*, at least for those on both sides of the mainstream political spectrum, Democrat and Republican, for whom liberal capitalism represented the apotheosis of historical political development.[4]

History and temporality, it must be said, are, at least explicitly, often absent from the self-consciously fractured and experimental verses that occupy the pages of *L-A-N-G-U-A-G-E* and its related journals; the kinds of disjunctive logics of time and succession that I found so pressing in my reading of Wallace Stevens in chapter 3 seem, as a result, missing, surplus to requirements. Yet one of the lessons of literary form that I've traced in this book is the constructive power of absence, its ability, under certain conditions, to leave its traces even where only blank space seems to pertain. It is for that reason that I've chosen to make explicit the theses on time and history that speculative formalism must presuppose with a reading of verse that seems, at first blush, to erect something like an eternal present, a synchronic, absolute "now" not unrelated to the diachronic stasis so frequently, if inaccurately, imputed to structuralist theory.

This is why one should be suspicious of any attempt to reduce language verse to a mere variant of antireferentialism. On the publication of a book collecting the first three volumes of *L-A-N-G-U-A-G-E*, Charles Bernstein and Bruce Andrews confronted this misapprehension head-on:

> The idea that writing should (or could) be stripped of reference is as bothersome and confusing as the assumption that the primary function of words is to refer, one-on-one, to an already constructed world of "things." Rather, reference, like the body itself, is one of the horizons of language, whose value is to be found in the writing (the world) before which we find ourselves at any moment.[5]

It's a curious quote, one that both succinctly repudiates a false hypothesis—that language should or can be stripped of all referentiality, such a falsehood presumably imputed to the language poets themselves—and that offers an intriguingly ambiguous proposal in its stead. Andrews's and Bernstein's gesture is far from merely defensive; the reduction of language poetry to the thesis that language is all there is has been a commonplace in the critical literature, a position eloquently recommended by Henry Sussman: "The world [for language poets], such as it is, is already language, and poetry is the index, the culmination of this linguistic dynamics."[6] To take such a position would be to read Andrews's and Bernstein's phrase above, "language . . . whose value is to be found in the writing (the world) before which we find ourselves," as proposing an exhaustive *equivalence* between writing and its referents. It is, by contrast, the moments of formative disequilibrium within and between language, poetry, referentiality, and history that concerns language verse, not the collapse of all into one. But how to parse the claim, also advanced above, that reference serves as "one of the horizons of language"? Does the term "horizon" suggest that reference comes *before* language as its condition of possibility, rather as the world of observable objects is so often assumed to precede language, the latter then coming to represent it? What would it mean to think of a referential process preceding the means—language itself—by which words are able to "refer" at all? Or perhaps "horizon" has a more general meaning here, making of reference merely one of many things that language is capable of doing. Where do history and time fit in?

The gesture toward the body is intriguing too, said to be another horizon of language alongside reference. One thinks back to Francis Ponge who, as was demonstrated in chapter 2, saw poetry as giving access to the queasy, ambivalent intimacy between words and flesh; the analysis of such an interchange founds its apogee, of course, in Sigmund Freud's theory of the erogenous zones, those mucous membranes, detachable in fantasy, that both announce and conceal the body's fleshly reliance on its various others, including the other of the Symbolic itself.[7] I'll have cause to reflect on psychoanalysis at the end of this chapter, a discussion that will serve as the culmination of my search for a model with which to understand the complex relation of poetic reference and history. The work of the French psychoanalyst Jean Laplanche will prove useful in that search. Laplanche takes from both Freud and Lacan the sense that psychoanalysis must admit of its own temporal rhythms, intimately connected to the interweaving of language, desire, and the objects of both. But insofar as the subject of the unconscious is never entirely transparent, never merely the passive province of its prior histories (no matter what vulgar reductions of Freudianism might suggest), that subject and its temporal entanglements may well prove a useful corollary for my investigations of poetry in its agonistic dealings with history and time—the subject of the unconscious and poetry alike, that is to say, are equally the products of, and resistant to, the *imperium* of language, the "enigmatic signifiers" that Laplanche describes with such analytical verve.

Might history itself, then, be one of language's horizons, perhaps its most crucial? The notion hides as many pitfalls as it does possibilities. If the account of "speculative formalism" developed in the preceding chapters is novel in even a minimal sense, it cannot, at this late hour, fall back into a historicism of the kind so ably criticized by Althusser and Macherey and as discussed with reference to its alliance with the "digital humanities" in chapter 1. Such a theory would install history as both poetry's ultimate condition and its final referent, stripping poetic form in the process of its very formativeness, its ability to gain an at least partial autonomy from its conditions and to reconfigure them in turn. There are other possible ways of thinking history as horizon, ways that would, for instance, take seriously the formative and formal absence of history at the level of the line as one of history's most efficacious modes, and that would incorporate the centrality of retrospection, the *après coup*, or the way poetic figures may serve to revise after the fact that which they otherwise seem tasked only to represent.

If it is indeed the case that poetry is impacted, and impacts on, history at every turn—and this, as the reader will see, is an unavoidable consequence of the speculative formalism already adduced in this book—then, as this chapter will also demonstrate, history will do so in a manner irreducible to both radical historicisms, whereby history entirely overruns the resources of poetic speculation, and radical constructivisms, where anything other than the agglomeration of words drops out of the picture. This is, of course, a relation of the dichotomy that Andrews and Bernstein's comments on referentiality above are intended to contest, but the labor of this chapter will lie in specifying what the alternative is, a process that will take us through the paradoxical formal imperatives of one of the most inspiring if sometimes frustrating avant-garde poetic movements of recent times. Those imperatives will be shown, finally, to be surprisingly exemplary of poetic form's more general articulation of time and history. It is worth beginning with a reading of one of the most complex prose poems published by the group, one that is simultaneously explicit and coy in its engagement with the tropes of recent American historical memory. The ethic of close reading demonstrated in all that follows hews closely to the consequences of an observation aptly made, once again, by Henry Sussman: "The theory of language poetry does not dwell somehow apart from the poems themselves. It is inscribed, imbricated, within the poems."[8] Language poetry's theories of history and time are equally immanent to the poems themselves.

Albany

Ron Silliman published his first poetry while a student at Berkeley in the 1960s, and much of his verse seems indelibly imprinted by his experiences in the Bay Area over a period of some forty years. In its formal experimentation and refusal of transcendence, Silliman's verse distinguishes itself from the lingering Beat heritage that clung to San Francisco's poetry scene for many of the decades following the Second World War. Silliman first became associated with language poetry in the 1970s after an initial association with a movement that Silliman himself named the "School of Quietude," a grouping that, interestingly enough for my broader argument, may well be a retrospective construction of the poet, both a loose categorization with movable boundaries and an ironical commentary on the very urge to draw such boundaries. "Albany," the object of my concern here, was first published in 1981 and was collected in the author's book *ABC* in 1983.[9]

Presented as one long paragraph of prose, it is defined by its declarative sentences, various in length. As Marjorie Perloff has observed, the poem is striking initially for its apparent lack of a voice, personal, collective, or otherwise; it is, of course, the presence of an implied first-person voice that has traditionally defined lyric poetry (although the exceptions to the rule are too numerous to list), and language poetry is generally associated with its subversion of this generic expectation. Silliman himself, it should be noted, made much of the critique of any unified poetic ego in his bracing work of criticism, *The New Sentence*, to be discussed later.[10] But as Perloff perspicaciously notes, the apparent lack of a voice in "Albany" does not preclude the poem's having a shape and a sense of place. As she writes, "Indeterminacy of agent and referent does not preclude an obsessive attention to particular 'realistic' detail. Despite repeated time and space shifts, the world of Albany, CA, is wholly recognizable."[11] Here I should introduce the poem; my reading will focus on the first thirty sentences, paradigmatic of the poem as a whole:

> If the function of writing is to "express the world." My father withheld child support, forcing my mother to live with her parents, my brother and I to be raised together in a small room. Grandfather called them niggers. I can't afford an automobile. Far across the calm bay stood a complex of long yellow buildings, a prison. A line is the distance between. They circled the seafood restaurant, singing "We shall not be moved." My turn to cook. It was hard to adjust my sleeping to those hours when the sun was up. The event was nothing like their report of it. How concerned was I over her failure to have orgasms? Mondale's speech was drowned by jeers. Ye wretched. She introduces herself as a rape survivor. Yet his best friend was Hispanic. I decided not to escape to Canada. Revenue enhancement. Competition and spectacle. kinds of drugs. If it demonstrates form some people won't read it. Television unifies conversation. Died in action. If a man is a player, he will have no job. Becoming prepared to live with less space. Live ammunition. Secondary boycott. My crime is parole violation. Now that the piecards have control. Rubin feared McClure would read Ghost Tantras at the teach-in. This form is the study group. The sparts are impeccable though filled with deceit.[12]

The first line acts as the frame for everything that comes in its wake. This would be a critical banality if the line did not both announce and challenge the ghost-poem, the metacommentary, that will thread throughout the rest of the poem—that virtual text concerned, less with the declarative intent of the sentences actually on the page, but with the "function of writing" *tout court*: "If the function of writing is to 'express the world' . . ." One finds, at one and the same time, both the announcement of a critical project over and above the poem itself, one intended to register the uses of writing per se, and recognition of that project's inability to assume the function of a master-narrative or key to the actual poem's various inscrutabilities; this ghost-narrative would be the particular instance of that more general feature of language verse already identified, the shadow frame that comments on, even if only in an oblique way, the fealty or otherwise of the text to the broader movement in question. The impossibility of the poem's completion, and therefore the impossibility of its full incorporation into a "movement," is foreshadowed by the lack of any concluding clause to accompany the conditional clause that forms the totality of the first sentence. The effect, however, isn't to hoist spectral quotation marks over the apparently sincere composition that follows, a tactic often imputed to postmodern narrative fiction. Rather, Silliman establishes both the necessity and impossibility of any extrapoetic metalanguage, one that might establish once and for all the paratextual truth of the text-in-itself. Perloff, incidentally, notices this intriguing use of ellipsis, but leaves unremarked its status as both the truth of the rest of the poem's form, and the striking manner in which that truth is crossed over on its very irruption. Where, then, might one locate the "then" that should, by rights, follow the "If" that forms the very first word of the poem?

The obvious answer would seem to be "nowhere," at least if such a "then" would lead inexorably to an expressive account of the text's "function." For what Silliman's poem establishes is irreducible either to such an empiricist accounting, whereby the poetic sign passively radiates its meaning to the reader, or a radical constructivist one, where the disruption of poetic structure embodied by the ambivalence of Silliman's choice of form—is this poetry or prose, is it prose poetry?—would lead inexorably to a freeplay of signification, one that would take advantage of the absence of usual poetic constrictions, most obviously meter and the creative arbitrations of the line break. It makes no real difference, I would argue, whether such a play of the signifier were to be sought in the text itself (it becoming thereby something like a textbook instantiation of Derridean *différance*) or in the reader (as in variants of reader-response criticism) or somewhere in between, for Silliman's verse embodies something rather different, something not unrelated to the uncanny formal hinterland between poetry and prose, between self-sufficient aestheticism and the determined move outward from text, that I located in the poetry of Francis Ponge in chapter 2.

Even if Silliman's verse can't be slotted into regular metrical patterns, neither is "Albany" untainted by what I characterized in earlier chapters as poetry's disciplining of prose, its formative dis-figuring of language's rhythms. The sentence form itself takes on a role in "Albany" not unlike the clipping of rhythm otherwise performed by metrical arrangement. Instead of the line break enforcing its contrapuntal movement from line to line, the period at the end of each sentence thuds with particular force here, sometimes remarking on the sentence's semantic inadequacy, its inability to convey any locatable sense of place or agent—"My turn to cook" or, more poignantly, "Died in action." Even more regularly, that punctual break invokes the sense of a resumption, of a kind of semantic and temporal refreshing that serves to partly erase, in a retrospective movement that will become crucial to my argument as it develops, what has gone before: "She introduces herself as a rape survivor. Yet his best friend was Hispanic."

The first period in the quoted sentence above is a kind of all-purpose hinge, one that both exacerbates the quiet sense of horror announced by the crime in the sentence it concludes, and that prepares the ground for the resetting established in the sentence that follows, one consolidated by the change of gender from "she" to "he": "Yet his best friend was Hispanic." One may speculate that the force and horror of the first sentence's event, one nonetheless "survived" by the subject of that sentence, has forced the poem itself to repress it, to even switch subjects in a swerve of avoidance, both through the pronominal shift already mentioned, but also in the move of theme from sexual violence to the ethnic designation of the second sentence, hanging abstract in the air.

But that reference, "Yet his best friend was Hispanic," as bald and impersonal as it is, rather fails as a tactic of repression, insofar as a registering of explicit sexual violence gives out only on to a more implicit, but nonetheless still somehow troubling, invocation of ethnic classification, the subject's specificity erased at the point of its inclusion in an official rubric. Of course, the ethnic tag is supercharged in advance by the much more explicit use of a racial epithet toward the beginning of the poem, the rank force field of which can be said then to invade the rest of the poem without rest. Nonetheless, there is a retrospective movement of erasure at work here too, the scrubbing clean of identities serving as the first appearance of the logic of *après coup* or retrospection that will become central to my arguments below. The blankness of the ethnic designator is, at any rate, a rather different kind of anonymity than that celebrated in Hart Crane's "A Name for All," as discussed in chapter 2. There, the reader will recall, the flight from individual names ends in an act of collective, divine nomination, "Struck free and holy in one Name always," one nonetheless less positive, less "freeing" than the poem initially seems to suggest. Here one is dealing rather more with the anonymity of bureaucracy and punishment, evoked elsewhere in the poem by the reference to juridical parole, to those "long yellow buildings," strikingly surreal in their first impact (yellow buildings?), although finally revealed to make up a prison—and no less surreal for that.

This creeping sense of a punitive (and, finally, penitentiary) history, of containment and the reaping of consequences, is surely heightened by the use of the third person, such a distance serving to exacerbate the leaden bureaucratic tinge of the descriptor. This sentence, it's worth remarking too, is a companion fragment to the very first sentence of the piece. Where that first sentence is, as I've noted, a conditional clause without any accompanying result clause, "Yet his best friend was Hispanic" is a result without a conditional—an answer without a question, if you like. Here the minimally identified subject of the sentence is given an empty sign of historical/ethnic identity without the complex backstory that any such designation may otherwise both recall and threaten to obscure.

One is already, needless to say, firmly on the terrain of history, the poem both inciting and deferring our wish to know the criminal and ethnic histories only incompletely evoked before being swallowed back into the declamatory structure of the paragraph. Such histories are both individual—proper to the incompletely identified subjects of the alternating sentences—and irrevocably *collective,* marked with the imprint of political contestation, and thus with something like history proper as the poem would seem to understand it. (The protestors chanting "We shall not be moved" mark the point in the poem where that political-historical shading comes fullest into view.) If Crane's poem moves toward an inevitable collectivity, that "name for all," one is left in "Albany" with only the ghostly remnants of such a collective possibility, its wisp or husk barely detectable on its forgetting; and where Crane moves ambiguously from the natural to the theological ("Struck free and holy . . ."), Silliman's verse leaves us without the possibility that either nature or religion could fill the now absent place of historical force and rupture—at which point the plaintive cry of "We shall not be moved" takes on an even more tragic valence, the "we" no longer even *accessible* as a vehicle of historical legibility. All that remains are the violent experiences imprinted on one's past and on one's present, as in the rape survivor, or as with the abstract generality of bureaucratic ethnic tags that otherwise mute one's singularity as much as they block avenues for collective solidarity with others.

If the example of the rape survivor and the "Hispanic" dramatizes a particular kind of poetic forgetting—the rape itself erased by the finality of the period that ends the one-clause sentence that announces it, the complex history of ethnic identification covered over by the objectifying "His friend" and "Hispanic"—a kind of remembrance by repetition is to be located nonetheless in the poem's frequent rhyming of themes from line to line. One of the most striking of these repetitions is to be found in references to the failed mediations of speech, of doomed attempts to maintain a kind of energetic collective presence through resistance to any dilution for broader consumption. I'll have cause to discuss below the critical invocation of "television" in "Albany," but an equally important instance comes in the line "If it demonstrates form some people won't read it," surely an example of the specific anxiety of the poet—why write experimental verse that only a small number will ever read?—that dovetails here with the poem's broader concern for the prismatic reflection of voices across time and space, and for the ways in which the efficacy of those voices may be blunted.

Before addressing the most overt references to collective historical memory in the poem (instances, one should underline, that exist only on ever-shifting temporal sands), it is worth briefly summarizing what has been found so far. Silliman's poem, at least, seems to stage a more general transformation of poetic temporality into history proper. What I've been tracing, that is, are a series of partially hidden formal strategies that crisscross "Albany" and implicate it in a broader logic of poetic form in its relation to history and time. The most basic of those strategies lies in the very choice of the single sentence, often only one clause in length, as the primary temporal building block of the paragraph—by no means an obvious choice for a language poet, as will be seen presently in my reading of Bruce Andrews. As I've noted, each period both divides and links the content contained in the sentences that precede and succeed it, marking our attention or linking up with notably charged aspects of the imagistic content—even if by re-marking the incompleteness of that content, its refusal to alight on a firm referent.

History appears here as another formal logic, at the moment at which an agent, whether linked to collective political action, to sexual violence, to ethnic classification, both appears and is effaced by the temporal movement of the verse's underlying structure, by the inevitability of the end of one sentence and the beginning of another; temporality, that is, gives out onto signs of historical events, only for history to succumb to the temporal once more, in a movement of repetition that is also defined by the power of retrospective assimilation, neutralization, and erasure. The simultaneity of appearance and disappearance, of success and failure, is inscribed into the very equanimity of "Albany"'s structure, where each claim, each sentence, is arraigned alongside the other with no concern for their relative thematic weighting. The reader won't have failed to notice the reappearance here of the process that, I've been arguing, is central to poetic structure more generally, where the coimplication of figuration and disfiguration, formation and de-formation, here historical appearance and disappearance, far from leading to any kind of poetic solipsism, results rather in the only kind of reference that poetry is capable of, and one that is capacious at that. I've defined such a reference as a nonmimetic production of sense mortgaged to a promised correlation of sign and object, here sign and historical event, that can never be fully honored; as one of Silliman's collaborators put it in a crucial essay addressing *L-A-N-G-U-A-G-E* poetics, "How does (some of) the forest go together with the trees. How might it, anyway. Forest of possibilities (in language anyway)—ways in and ways out."[13] For language to make anything of the forest of historical memory, one at least as complex as that evoked by Baudelaire in his reference to a poetic "forest of symbols" and as discussed in the previous chapter, it must get lost as often as it makes it out safely—and there is no "all" of poetic reference that might complete that "some of," such completion being only the dream of the mimetic fallacy. This is another way of saying that poetic remembrance and memory, so often held up by a basic temporal structuration, must find their ground on the equal necessity of absence and loss, of those moments at which temporal solidity—the brutal but sturdy cuts of Silliman's full stops, say—gives way to the conflicting tides of memorialization and forgetting that must also find their footing on that precariously liquid foundation.

Remembrance, forgetting, and repetition, and their complex articulation, have been addressed with particular force in the work of Jean Laplanche, and I will recast some of my conclusions within his terms at the culmination of this chapter. But it is worth flagging at this early stage that such movements, especially those by which an apparently synchronic temporal instant acts simultaneously as the recasting, even deletion, of what had gone before it, are never simply individual nor utterly collective or historical for Laplanche, and it seems clear that there is an equal refusal to concede this forced choice in Silliman's verse. It may well be that the very anxious inability of poetic language to settle on either of these poles is one of the key symptoms of the poetic conscription of history, of the dissonance produced by the clash of properly temporal and properly historical logics in verse. The most pressing instantiation of this uncanny logic of an appearing and disappearing history occurs in "Albany" by way of its insistent reference to politics and to the apparent failure of any collective historical imagination, and it is to those themes that I'll now more concretely turn.

Failed Collectivities

The most obvious picturing of historical memory in the poem, one that is both specific to its location, the Bay Area of California, and that echoes ironically with the year in which the poem was first published, is signaled by the images of protest, of collective action, that thread through the paragraph. Such images are dramatized in turn by quieter, indecisive moments, the effect achieved through a kind of negative amplification. Notice, for instance, the movement, only half ironical although surely funny, from "They circled the seafood restaurant, singing 'We shall not be moved'" to "My turn to cook." Explicit here is the function hinted at above, whereby a collective "we" dissolves into a muted "my." The dissolve is only *half* ironical because one senses genuine sadness in Silliman's lines, the melancholy notion that what had been a place and time of collective endeavor has lapsed into an atomized domain of mere private responsibility, of domestic calm concealing a pronounced loss of possibilities. Perloff, as useful as her reading is, elides the sharp break between the two historical scenes of the poem—one collective and historical, the other defined by atomization—by risking the conclusion that the poem is an unbroken temporal and semantic field: "The poet is a political activist: he participates in demonstrations and teach-ins, is briefly jailed, avoids the draft and so on. There are many explanations of everyday things the activist must deal with."[14] But the everyday in "Albany" is what is left after the potential for collective political action has been diffused.

Those smaller, private images that settle in history's wake are rarely domestic, however. More often, they stage the decay of collective potentiality in moments of a kind of privatized punishment, or of the urge to run—whether acted on or not: "I decided not to flee to Canada." Without providing us with any sense of certainty, the poem heavily implies that the agents of change have become, in an unspecified future, the subjects of a controlling state, of something like the "society of control" powerfully described by Gilles Deleuze in his "Postscript on the Societies of Control."[15] Where at one time one reads that "Mondale's speech was drowned by jeers"—Mondale here referring to Walter Mondale, vice president under Jimmy Carter—at others one sees the resistance of the crowd collapsing into instances of anxious private confession: "My crime is parole violation." Where a lesser poet may have chosen to differentiate such scenes either through the use of a linear narrative frame or through the isolation and foregrounding of a particular voice, Silliman pictures the degradations of historical possibility precisely through his determined staging of the *absence* of plottable narrative unfolding, in the very instability of the (barely hinted at) subject-positions from which the poem's particles of sense can be thought to emanate.

This is an instance of what I've identified above as Silliman's staging of the move from temporality to history—history insofar as it appears poetically subsists as *another formal logic*, one that by necessity must take its place alongside the other figural logics at play across the surface of the text. What I'm tracing here is, I would argue, a very particular employment of constitutive absence, the absence in question being that of historical action, for Silliman something necessarily overlaid with the frisson of political contestation. The absence is marked in the poem by the withering of history to a state of solitary resignation. Earlier chapters have demonstrated how absence reverberates in literary form in determinate and even definitional ways. The loud, irradiating absence of Ponge's objects was shown in chapter 2 to be crucial to the success of his poetic project, dramatizing the nonmimetic success of his language even as it highlighted the failure of any correlative connection of word to world. At a time and space closer to Silliman, one might invoke the poetry of Robert Creeley, whose sparse late verse is something of an object lesson in absence as heavy, melancholic presence:

> They say a
> woman passes at
> the edge of the
> house, turning
>
> the corner, leaves
> a very vivid sense,
> after her,
> of having been there.[16]

But where in Creeley the reader is left to face *only* absence and its traces, situated here in a poem defined by an icy intimacy apparently outside history in its collective guise, in Silliman the disappearance of history and the more mundane reality that accrues in its wake are arranged symmetrically, with a formal equanimity that appears determined to avoid the pathos that hangs over Creeley's verse. (And notice, incidentally, Creeley's supercharging of Stevens's commitment to enjambment, commented on in chapter 3.) The result is that the formative absence that, in very different ways, operates in both Silliman *and* Creeley is made clearest in the former's apparently more affectless formalism. Parenthetically, I find myself at a certain distance here from the equation of history with absence to be found in Jameson's deservedly influential *The Political Unconscious*;[17] if, for Jameson, narrative emerges as the symptom of which history is the massive, absent cause, history in Silliman's verse appears as just one more logic populating its surface, albeit one that appears only as it is fading melancholically from view.

One reads signs of contestation and signs of defeat in "Albany," then, rendered formally equivalent. Notice, for instance, how a sentiment implicitly ranged against the media appropriation of grassroots activism and articulated through an expressly oppositional frame—"The event was nothing like their report of it"—is neutrally counterposed with "Television unifies conversation." Between the two proclamations, between the event and its lapse into mediatic "conversation," a set of values has been exchanged, one set of historical assumptions lost and another, more private set of values gained; in the first sentence, a critical voice prevails, one unlikely to take an official narrative of events at face value. In the second, "conversation" becomes the occasion for consensus rather than for an agonistic plurality of voices, and the mass media the site of that diffusion of contestatory energy.

"Albany," it is worth now underlining, was first published in 1981, the year that Ronald Reagan took office. For many on the political Left, this year and the presidential tenure that it inaugurated marked the end of decades of oppositional political creativity that began in the middle to late 1960s. But even as one may detect notes of loss in the poem, it would be a mistake to task it entirely with the indulgence of nostalgia. Even as collective power is exercised, it is undercut, dissipated by, the tones of defeat that harmonize on the same stave as those moments of clenched political potentiality. And it's worth emphasizing that there is no clear-cut "workerist" thematic at work in "Albany" either, despite the lamentation of lost labor power already mentioned. One is as likely to meet barriers to historical change from within movements against the ruling classes as in the agents of those movements' historical defeat: "Now that the piecards have control." ("Piecards" was the term given by members of the International Workers of the World, or "Wobblies," to the conservative leadership of the American Federation of Labor in the early years of the twentieth century.)[18] Silliman's poem generalizes a kind of constitutive failure, signaled by the placing side by side of the urge to join the train of history through collective action and the moment at which that action converts into a kind of atomized accommodation with the state of things—"Becoming prepared to live with less space." The coimplication of formation and dissolution produced at the level of thematic content here is, as I've suggested, grounded at the level of the poem's form, where a striking image, a glimmer even, is as likely to be undermined as it is to be amplified by the predictable cut of the period ending the sentence in which it is offered up.

The inevitable beat of those periods forms, as I've already had cause to remark, the basic temporal underpinning of "Albany," the stark foundation on which the minimal historical logic located above gains its footing. Language poetry would more often seem only to offer the temporal structure as such, the bare bones of which seem unable to sustain any kind of historical reflection, no matter how indeterminate or subject to the vicissitudes of memory and its failures. The poetry of Bruce Andrews will serve as a useful reminder of this broader assumed characteristic of language verse, one that, nonetheless, I'll see fit to challenge. Take Andrews's extraordinary "Blueier Blue," nine chunks of continuous prose that interpolate sections of an earlier poem, "Blue Horizon," the full, undated version published online by the 2nd Avenue Poetry collective.[19] Despite the poetic appropriation of prose proper to both poems, "Blueier Blue" produces an almost opposite effect to "Albany," at least as far as its obvious formal characteristics are concerned. Where "Albany"'s division into punctual sentences induces the rhythm of historical remembrance and foreclosure, the Andrews poem initially seems free of any such basic temporal plotting; or, better, its gusts of nouns and neologisms form *nothing but* a blowsy temporal grid, albeit one powerfully distinct from the austerity of Silliman's. Here is the opening of the first of "Blueier Blue"'s nine sections; again, my selection is paradigmatic of the poem as a whole:

> ink including knowbotic knife-marked paten polyp symbiosis pronounced as if thievery corporation there were no "xyz" "y" americanizados azul know fociality full well iota i aim where ick is she dire hightime high direct—liminal hex limewashed lexa time-jump jig time actuarial ace talk to the rabbit one peppercorn per year of one peppercorn appealing peepul alpha pearl alleged presaucer rule precessor real, chafing night cielo crucis . . . . instruments gone crazy radar i chemo- can humptydumpty hum up and close upper curtseying curve debelligerent determined by ease eye smuggled small cocoonery cooperage spin the globe! starshine &—maché mcblobbing making am-ness a belfry-tree—match me if you can shrew dee trees sherwood forest factitis factotum kenglo kinda muddier creationism medium cool big siren bigger issues . . . . leira detlluav-kciht, eetsorf yddon noddy frostee, thick-vaulted ariel fluffier first grade piratical pirate's bounty radar reder layercake lookytat lump lurid lump bode bash broad brush hodge podge hope for my budget in the always to hand absence of jaws to rendezvous rig bull's-eye bullseye blares out booms outon your silencers on the jib—confectionary icing cow poly polly paw-paw pandowdy czarina czar, quash kinda quiz kid white pox whitewashed bathysphere prefab protobathysphere dahn [de roun d curve] dwns fabulosity flame havoc hippo star caza catic prop byes prep breeze, hashed hatoof kaput kel tween tot upside-down unmistaken inter-spec inky gaia george medietrieval medieval, slinkier sky well aloft impurists at heart illustyrian bursa bubo bumblebee biolage jo-lor-ris juleightee moongate moonglow lopes of the lupin[20]

The poem is not, it should be noted immediately, free of punctuation or indeed rhythm, perhaps the first hint that what may initially present itself as verse entirely untroubled by the defining constrictions of nonexperimental poetry may, at a second glance, be said to be entirely *of* them. The claim that the poem is, despite initial appearances, nothing but a temporal grid of a particular kind, and the notion that it is concerned primarily with the constrictions it rather loudly announces itself free of, links this most contemporary of poems with Mallarmé who, as noted earlier in the book, saw in the "crisis" that free verse threatened to rain on traditional meter the chance for the amplification and reenergization of poetics per se. Mallarmé commented that "recollection of strict verses haunts these approximations [of new verse forms], and . . . they benefit from it";[21] so-called "free verse," that is, is ghosted by the disciplinarian imprecations of prior verse forms (most obviously the Racinean alexandrine for Mallarmé's time), taking sustenance from that which it apparently opposes—the law is its own transgression, to coin a phrase. When Andrews's "Blueier Blue" is placed up against "Albany," one notes the seeming forward motion of the writing in the former, albeit a motion interrupted at crucial moments, with sudden seasick jolts. That first double dash after "hightime high direct," nonetheless, instead of subsisting as a temporal marker on its own, serves instead to direct our gaze backward to the word-string that precedes it. (Where Silliman's periods act like well-oiled hinges, often re-marking events in the text both before and after their position, the punctuation in "Blueier Blue" seems more determinately retrospective, inducing a firm twist of the neck backward.) The word-string one is directed to can be said to begin with "dire," proceeding then as "dire hightime high direct." The close repetition of consonants in "hightime high" is to be found across the poem as a whole, and its effect is heightened by the hardly softer assonance that is implicated in the "i" sound of each word. But that long "i" sound is further framed by the short repeated "i" of "ick is" that just precedes it, and what we have in sum are hard consonants and equally tough vowels made durable through their repetition, a repetition that can be said to replace the structural function of the period in Silliman.

This move, whereby the rhythmic function that meter traditionally performs in the spaces between the words of a poem is transposed onto repeated fragments of the words themselves, has a venerable history. If it was the partial intent of language verse to trouble the romantic vestiges that clung even to high poetic modernisms, such an ambition would surely be troubled to find, in Coleridge's notebooks of all places and at the very apex of the romantic cause, the following: "'Thing': id est, thinking or think'd. Think, Thank, Tank—Reservoir of what has been thinged-Denken, Danken—I forget the German for Tank/The, Them, This, These, Thence, Thick, Thing, Thong, Thou."[22] There is, for sure, a movement around a semantic center here set in motion by that initial

"Thing," an inquisitive and careful exploration, where in Andrews one instead finds a kind of relentless drive outward to newer and ever thicker semantic and asemantic tangles. But notice the punctual use of alliteration, not so different from that found in "The Blueier Blue," and how, the half-rhyme in Coleridge aside, both rely on phonemic similarity for their overall sense of congruence. Coleridge's musing, one must concede, halfway as it is between poetic sketch and note-to-self, is in its essence preliminary; one expects it to be the foundation of some fuller formed verse to come. For Andrews, by contrast, the preliminary is all we have, but the structural and temporal regularities made in its name are no less solid for all that.

What kind of temporal logic is at work in Andrews's poem, then, and how does it differ from Silliman's? In the final analysis, the two differ only subtly, no matter the initial gulf that may seem to separate them. Both poems depart from traditional meter insofar as they reject the arbitrations of the regular line break, the one feature that has historically differentiated poetry definitively from prose. Both are equally loath to accommodate to prose per se, with its relatively stable flows, its broadly linear currents. Instead, the temporal ground of each is constructed through the seemingly senseless repetition of linguistic units more frequently used, in prose at least, for the communication of semantic meaning.

In "Blueier Blue," as I've already noted, time is pushed forward by the agglomeration of words, that rush onward marked most often by a kind of alliterative mania—"lump lurid lump bode bash broad brush"—arrested only by moments of shared assonance that briefly reverse the temporal flow, sending one back to the word where the vowel sound originated, an act of retrieval that often feels made just in the nick of time, just before that word definitively disappears in the next glut of neologisms and free associations. It is tempting, in the face of this avalanche of semantic particles, to locate Andrews's verse in a kind of eternal present, albeit one occasionally ruffled by the shift backward already indicated. (Here one thinks of Barthes's contention that "there is no other time than that of the enunciation and every text is eternally written *here and now*,"[23] a claim that I challenged in the introduction, and that would be inadequate in characterizing Andrews, despite the apparent effect of smooth atemporality performed in "Blueier Blue.") History, at least as conceived of as a dialectic of collective remembrance and forgetting, one structurally mandated and politically infused in "Albany," certainly seems to be absent in Andrews's poem, although it may be more accurate to say that the process of forgetting is rather more advanced in "Blueier Blue" than it is in Silliman's poem.

If "Blueier Blue" can be read as a testament to the repression of historical depth, one only ever incompletely achieved in "Albany," this is not to say that history has no bearing at all. Consider the reappearance of monetary terms in a poem that otherwise strains to keep up its commitment to a nonrepetitive semantic novelty—"actuarial," "budget," those two terms then underscored by one of the longest chunks of complete prose in the poem, "match me if you can." Might the poem be asking us to match its own relentless innovation, its textual entrepreneurialism, with a financial value? Of course, "Blueier Blue" is the kind of poem that encodes resistance to interpretation in its very form, and my own reading can only be as provisional as the poem's ever-provisional temporal ground, one that never quite settles into a predictable pattern; the poem's regularities are largely found in those complex rhythmical structures already evoked rather than in the self-consciously irreducible thematic content. But one further hermeneutical leap may be risked here, for the poem when viewed from a distance, when taken as a whole, all of a sudden begins to resemble the ever-streaming signs on a stock-market ticker—on the apparently impermeable consolidation of capitalist interests, what more appropriate poetic mode?

By embodying aspects of the formal infrastructure of financial capitalism—if, indeed, that's what the poem does—the poem acts neither as a critique of that most tenacious of ideologies or as a celebration of it. Silliman, in his guise as critic, captures this ambivalent status of the poem in high capitalism[24] rather well: "Poems both are and are not commodities."[25] The poem, that is, is no longer able to assume the role of a rallying cry; indeed, it is hard from our contemporary vantage to imagine such a thing was ever possible, although literary history tells us otherwise.[26] But neither is the poem merely the passive vessel of social and political pressures. Precisely in this sense, through its only having been minimally marked by political imperatives, the poem assumes its political voice, testifying to the final outcome of the weakening of collective power evoked with some power in Silliman's own "Albany."

Silliman the critic focuses on the contextual rather than simply textual aspects of poetry's political resonance, commenting that "poetry in America reflects struggle carried out, unfortunately, in an unorganized and often individualist manner. This struggle is as much one between audiences as it is between poets (or, to be precise, it is one between social formations, including, but never limited to, economic classes, from which audiences are composed around individual authors). It is class war."[27] It's a salutary reminder that poetic form never coalesces in a vacuum. Nonetheless, if there's a lesson of Silliman's poem, it is that class war, at least in recent decades, has been rather ruthlessly repressed. Such suppression is allegorized in "Albany" through the blockage that prevents the poem's temporal logic fully acceding to history as such, with the dialectical richness of the latter present only in the mode of its retrospective memorialization. Silliman, that is to say, bears witness in "Albany" to the dissolving of collective action into private penitence, with the latter still haunted by the former with the superegoic reminder of its own impotence: "My crime is parole violation." In "Blueier Blue," by contrast, one is faced largely with the triumph of ego-speak over the potentially constructive admonitions of any political superego voiced from the past; those concatenations of words, while superficially reminiscent of the structural permutations of the unconscious or, indeed, of the stream of free association unleashed by the analysand in the clinic, present rather more as defensive strategies against historical truths, ostensibly creative constructions better suited to *preventing* the irruption of the truth proper of the poem. That truth is surely found in the wiping out of popular power in the (final?) victory of oligarchic takeover, and in the cleaving of even textual form to the meaningful meaninglessness of stock prices on a screen. Far, then, from verse being unable, in its rigidity or abstraction, to bear the weight of history, history itself becomes in "Blueier Blue" too thin to be properly embodied at all.

As unlikely as my political (and, now, psychoanalytic) reading here may sound—and to reiterate, "Blueier Blue" is such that *any* reading, when impacted by the poem's formal resistance to interpretation, will appear both audacious and presumptuous—it returns us once again to the problem of political history and its articulation in verse. One may say that the symptomatic resistance just mentioned, symptomatic insofar as Andrews's compulsive lists of particles seems to conceal a drive to ever-*more*-meaning rather than any attempt to resist meaning entirely, is as much a push back against collectivity, to the possibilities of collective history-making hymned and lamented in "Albany," as it is a refusal of any readerly desire for order. (Indeed, such a push back may well have been rendered unnecessary in advance, given the thinness of history mentioned above, although it is quite characteristic for resistances to shadowbox illusory enemies . . .)[28] The very difference in the primary formal units of "Albany" and "The Blueier Blue" should alert us to their differing perspectives on the possibilities of collective potentiality. For all their stop-start motion, Silliman's sentences group words *together*, inscribing a most basic kind of collectivity into the formal ground of the verse. Andrews's isolated words, by contrast, ward off their conscription into sets, an avoided moment of group nomination that is nonetheless teased by the shared assonance analyzed above.

The New Sentence

I have landed back at the question of nomination raised at the very beginning of this chapter. There I insisted that any contemporary reading of language poetry must raise the question of self-nomination, of how the conscription of a poem within a wider movement may then haunt the poetry for the contemporary reader, imposing a metacommentary announcing its belonging to the collective, testifying, even if only in a ghostly fashion, to its fealty to the group. Nonetheless, as my readings of Silliman and Andrews have demonstrated, this is an *anxious* process that is as much, in fact surely more, about the problem of history and collectivity generally in an age of enforced atomism. I might revise my initial claim, then, with the proviso that collective nomination must also be shown to *fail,* a failure that haunts, I think, Silliman's most sustained effort to argue for the novelty and importance of his and his peers' poetry.

In the brief reading of his influential essay "The New Sentence" that follows here, I'd like to propose along the way that my theory as to the necessary failure of collective nomination, the latter understood as one of the symptoms of history in its fullest sense, while especially acute in the language poets, may also be a condition for poetic form per se. Poetry, that is, seems ineluctably caught between the individual and the collective, or between the particular and the universal, and it is at the level of poetic form that these formative contradictions are best accessed. What I am tracing here is related to, but nonetheless distinct from, what Jonathan Culler has identified as the tendency of lyric poets to utilize performative address, the apostrophe in particular, as part of a wider attempt to summon into being that which may otherwise only be represented: "In locating lyric value in a certain performativity, I have essentially treated it as an active form of naming, which performatively seeks to create what it names, and may fail or succeed in this extraordinarily arrogant ambition."[29] The problem of naming reappears once again here, but in what follows poetic nomination will be less about the poetic attempt to conjure reality into being, and more about the fraught negotiation of poetic form with history as that which somehow both conditions and eludes the movements of versification. The conjunction of naming and historical time, that is to say, will be progressively shown to be central to how poetic form negotiates the currents of time and history.

Silliman's essay surveys the difficulties faced by linguists, philosophers, and literary critics alike when they attempt to provide a stable definition of the sentence as such. Nonetheless, Silliman risks the thesis that contemporary American verse, especially that which both engages and subverts the now canonical form of the "prose poem," has produced a new form identifiable nonetheless as that of the "sentence." What are the characteristics of this "new sentence," and the poetry within which it appears? Silliman helpfully lists them, and I'd like to attend to just a few of those apparent features. The first, one that Silliman spends some time on, is as follows: "The paragraph organizes the sentences."[30] But crucially, this organization is not linked to any especial amplification, diminution, or alteration of the semantic content of the poem; rather, it is a mere quantitative apportioning, a gathering that has no meaning in and of itself. As Silliman writes, "There are roughly the same number of sentences in each paragraph and the number is low enough to establish a clear sentence:paragraph ratio. Why is this not simply a matter of the way sentences are normally organized into paragraphs? Because there is no specific referential focus. The paragraph here is a unit of measure."[31] This surely holds true for Silliman's "Albany," but also for Andrews's "Blueier Blue" in its arrangement in paragraphs of isolated particles, which leads one to suspect that it may not be the *sentence* per se that is uniquely suited to the paragraph form. For Andrews, that is, it is individual words themselves that are marshaled by their arrangement into nine paragraphs of roughly equal length.

Another crucial characteristic of the "new sentence" for Silliman relates to what he calls "the limiting of syllogistic movement," a move that is said to "keep . . . the reader's attention at or very close to the level of language."[32] This form of creative limitation is best illustrated through Silliman's own use of truncated sentences, sentences that are only the conditional or result portion of a sentence—recall, most potently, Silliman's "Yet his best friend was Hispanic." But just how novel are these aspects of language verse? Might not the line break or the unexpected ending of a stanza train the eye on the minutiae of language in a fashion similar to the cutting off of the conditional-result syllogism highlighted by Silliman? Consider the first stanza of "A Crazed Girl" (1938) by W. B. Yeats:

> That crazed girl improvising her music.
> Her poetry, dancing upon the shore,
> Her soul in division from itself
> Climbing, falling She knew not where,
> Hiding amid the cargo of a steamship,
> Her knee-cap broken, that girl I declare
> A beautiful lofty thing, or a thing
> Heroically lost, heroically found.[33]

Notice how the line break functions here to both incite and frustrate our desire for knowledge. The first line introduces us, literally enough, to a crazed girl playing music; the immediate question is whether the derangement in question is best understood as an artistic passion or something darker, more dysfunctional. The second line points us toward the first, consoling conclusion; one learns of the potency of her music, now ennobled under the sign of poetry and granted agency and autonomy of its own. The third line introduces doubt once more, dividing the girl's soul from itself, this new insight serving, in a manner not dissimilar to a key characteristic detected above in "Albany," to reset and retrospectively ironize the previous line's note of uplift. Were this movement from uplift to subjective fracture to be contained within one line, the effect would take on the appearance of a logical progression, would bear some of the fluidity and continuity that one more often associates with prose. The transmutation of this spiritual fracture into a physical one a couple of lines later—"Her knee-cap broken, that girl I declare"—is inscribed materially into the very structure of the poem by being given its own line, a line that again retrospectively ironizes the rather dry description of the line that precedes it, "Hiding amid the cargo of a steamship." Consider how the former line itself, "Her knee-cap broken, that girl I declare," may be said to function independently, that second clause when considered only in the context of its line becoming almost a gasp of exasperation—"That girl, I declare!" The latter clause, nonetheless, is simultaneously of a part with the line that succeeds it. One finds embodied in the poetic unit both an individual autonomy—the potential semantic self-containment that allows the phrase to cohere without support from the verse that surrounds it—and the ineluctable collectivity that follows from the travel of sense from the latter clause of the line to the first clause of the phrase that follows it.

The reader will provide his or her own favorite examples of this most elementary effect of the poetic line break. My claim is that this basic formal tool bears within itself the division of poetry between the personal and the collective, between the part and the whole. Here I'd like to refocus our attention on the problem of history, although I have been, even in my discussion of Yeats above, discussing history all along. For it is precisely at the level of the division of a poem into its most basic segments, a division that occurs at the level of the paragraph and the sentence in Silliman, at the level of the paragraph and the word in Andrews, and at the level of the line and the stanza in Yeats and in much of the Western lyric tradition, where the strain of poetry's ambiguous situation between the individual and the collective, between an eternalized present and the ruptures of time, is felt with the utmost clarity. In Andrews, the paragraph form represents, not merely an arbitrary quantitative measure as claimed by Silliman in "The New Sentence," but rather the sign of an inevitable if most basic kind of collectivity, the collocation of particles standing in for a kind of radically minimal historical logic. As much as the poem insists on the particular, even the singular, as its fundamental form, a kind of baggy togetherness nonetheless emerges. It is an arbitrary one, admittedly, and it falls far short of the unification of purpose that characterizes the force of history in its fragile persistence in "Albany," but it nonetheless haunts the poem's staging of atomization as collective history's back-projected other, absolutely inadmissible as such history is within the broad terms of the poem's expressive function. In traditional lyric form, the line break may be said, perhaps surprisingly, to perform a similar, paradoxical role; the singularity and starkness that poetic figures so frequently perform is heightened, made tense, by the cut of the line, but without those cuts the poem could not cohere, could not accrete into an identifiable unit, distinct from other textual instances.

Consider, in the Yeats above, how the isolation of that broken kneecap in its own line, indeed within in its own *clause*, amplifies and exacerbates its violence—the poem almost seems to crack at one with the bone—and yet its foregrounding ensures its connection to the more spiritual forms of dislocation staged by the lines surrounding it. And thus one finds allegorized at the most basic level of poetic form that indeterminate placing of poetry inside, outside, and between ahistorical particularity on the one hand (a bone breaking as its own event, its own self-sufficient moment outside history) and the charge of historical belonging on the other (that bone now of a piece, so to speak, with the more general violence of and inflicted on the artistic soul as it is immersed in the unstable currents of the world).

Lyn Hejinian and the Everyday

When I found a double-logic of particularity and universality, of aggregation and disaggregation, in the interaction of the word and the paragraph in Andrews, or between the line as isolating imperative and the line as vehicle for a kind of minimal sense in Yeats, I located in each instance a ground where Paul de Man, say, would more often have traced an inevitable dissolution, the canceling out of poetic possibilities. At this juncture I'd like to formalize those different conditions for a simultaneous individuality and collectivity, aggregation and disaggregation, conditions located in Andrews, Silliman, and Yeats, the better then to identify what is useful in Jean Laplanche's thinking of language and time, to be introduced toward the end of the chapter. To do so, I'll ask what happens when a poem mixes those three elementary forms of segmentation and arrangement, found at the level of the paragraph and the sentence in Silliman, at the level of the paragraph and the word in Andrews, and at the level of the line and the stanza in Yeats. Fortuitously enough, one finds a fascinating example from within the language movement itself. Lyn Hejinian, a professor of poetics at Berkeley, is often cited as a founding member of the group and has, like Silliman, balanced the roles of poet and critic. There are both striking similarities and telling differences in her compelling verse when compared with that of Silliman and Andrews; her poetry is some of the most powerful and innovative to have been written in the latter decades of the twentieth century and the first decades of the twenty-first. I'd like to concentrate on an extract from "The Guard," a long poem published in 1984:

> Yesterday the sun went West and sucked
> the sea from books. My witness
> is an exoskeleton. Altruism suggestively fits.
> It's true. I like to go to the hardware store
> and browse on detail. So sociable the influence
>
> of Vuillard, so undying in disorder is order.
> Windows closed on wind in rows,
> Night lights, unrumorlike, the reserve
> for events. All day our postures were the same.
> Next day the gentleman was very depressed
> and had a headache; so much laughing
>
> had upset him he thought.[34]

"The Guard" as formal structure, one might say, sits somewhere in between "Albany" and "Blueier Blue," while also flirting with traditional lyric form. Where "Albany" mobilizes the sentence as its constitutive form, and where "Blueier Blue" makes much of the isolated word as the vehicle of atomization, "The Guard" is divided into recognizable stanzas and finds a use for enjambment and for the creative manipulation of the line break. But like "Albany," "The Guard" is a poem of *sentences*, generally short in length, and it finds its particular energy, as well as its humor, in this uneasy counterposition of traditional and experimental forms.[35] The poem surprises the reader looking for the spiky thrills of experimental verse through its interpolation of self-consciously "poetic" phrases, aperçus that carry with them in condensed form the essence of a kind of anthologized romanticism, a romanticism already filtered and distilled for posthumous consumption: "So sociable the influence // of Vuillard, so undying in disorder is order." That latter clause, in its chiasmic portentousness, threatens parody, but doesn't quite get there, hovering instead between prophecy and resignation. The reference to the painter should work metonymically, as a kind of shorthand or key to the poem's overriding aesthetic, but it doesn't; rather, it stubbornly sticks out, askew to the rest of the piece.

In a manner not dissimilar to Silliman's "Albany," the poem begins with a moment of metacommentary, with the establishment of that ghost narrative that concerned us toward the beginning of this chapter. Such narratives, as I've since established, often serve to comment implicitly on the verse that follows, hinting at the theory of textuality that the poem implicitly follows. Hejinian's striking image of the sun sucking the sea from books can, of course, be read in multiple ways, but two slightly different readings seem most apt. First, the trope appears to establish an antinomy between nature and literature, between natural phenomena and the artifices of the symbol. The sea would suck the sun from books as nature more generally would override the human caprice embodied in language, the frivolous manipulation of symbols as nothing compared to the crashing movements of the sun and the seas. Read in such a fashion, the poem indicts its own significance even before it has properly begun. But why would the sea be found in books in the first place, such that it could be "sucked" away, if nature and language were truly antithetical? An alternative notion suggests itself, namely that the antinomy between the awesome power of natural phenomena and the limp abstractions of writing and reading must be produced, must *occur.*

The difference may seem slight, but the second reading holds open the prospect that nature and the symbol might once again commingle, only for the poem's inaugurating event—that sucking separation of nature and the word—to threaten once again. The second reading, in other words, introduces a measure of *time* into the poem, a before and after that threatens to revolve and repeat, temporality produced here as epic in both scale and consequence. That epic effect is retroactively and negatively confirmed by the appearance three sentences later of the deflating and funny—and decidedly *non*-epic—"I like to go to the hardware store and browse on detail." And so time takes on a monumental quality in "The Guard," in part through the interposition of an exaggeratedly everyday observation, making the poem both metaphysical and prosaic, the increasingly capacious ghost narrative now as much about the establishment of an overriding temporal logic as it is concerned with the poem's implied theory of text. I should emphasize too the intervention of the "I" here, another sign that Hejinian is more concerned than either Andrews or Silliman in flirting with the conventions of the lyric, only to jilt those conventions through the creative employment of the isolated sentence already mentioned.

One of the most striking formal features of the extract is the slippage it stages between different subjective positions, from subjectless impersonal sentence, to the emergence of the "I," and culminating in the massified subject that is implicated by the line "All day our postures were the same." Hejinian has written of her desire to maintain an "open" text, one that "is open to the world and particularly to the reader . . . [It] invites participation, rejects the authority of the writer over the reader and thus, by analogy, the authority implicit in other (social, economic, cultural) hierarchies."[36] It's an admirable ambition, but it's not quite what's at work in "The Guard," a text that, for all Hejinian's departure from certain language conventions, draws her close to Andrews and Silliman, at least in this meticulous concern for the mutability of the "I" and the "we," of the individual and the collective, of individual instances and their collation into a readable archive. The openness that Hejinian seeks is, as I've shown throughout this book, only ever the effect of various kinds of formal *constraint.* And it is with reference to this feature of language poetry that the psychoanalytic reflections on subjective time to be found in the work of Jean Laplanche will prove especially useful, insofar as the time of the subject, rather like that of the poem, is as structured and contained as it is open and fluid.

Laplanche and the Incitements of Time

Up to now, I've been concerned with outlining a theory of poetic temporality and its accretion into something like history, where the latter is understood as naming the promise of dynamic collective possibilities, buffeted by their potential always to be erased, misremembered, or artificially and nostalgically commemorated. There's something of that irksome nostalgia in Silliman's recollections of Bay Area activism, but there's also genuine mourning at work, and the weight of these terms and their associations—remembrance, remembrance then implying memory, memory as a species of mourning, forgetting as a kind of repression—inevitably raises the specter of psychoanalysis. I have made sure not to simply impose on the literary texts discussed in this chapter, indeed in all of the chapters of this book, a priori forms of philosophical or psychoanalytic interpretation, and that's certainly not my aim here. But there are questions left hanging in the foregoing, questions that may well have begun to gnaw away at the reader.

Not the least of these, appositely enough, is the question of the role of the reader herself. To what extent, the question would go, is the theory of poetic time and history sketched above a consequence of the reader's experience of the poem, and if indeed the effects discussed are the product of reception, how does the reader's own situation in time and history affect my conclusions? Of course, the question of the reader has been pointedly aimed with some frequency at formalist accounts of literature. Not only, so the story goes, do such theories neglect the mediations of history with respect to the text, but the reader, and their own situation in history, go equally unaccounted for. In the reader's place one finds an inflation of the text as such, the *ur*-text becoming a kind of writer, reader, text, and context all in one, the apparently closed folds of which were memorably and critically invoked by Fredric Jameson in his reference to "the windless closure of the formalisms," with their reliance on a "mechanical causality."[37]

One can begin to answer these concerns by noting that the most impressive formalisms are as concerned to trouble the very self-sufficiency of these categories—text, context, reader, author, history—as they are to pick out and generalize only one of them. When such terms *are* used, a formalism concerned to mobilize language's speculative resources should wish to revise their very meaning from the ground up, a revision that is only possible when the boundaries between these putative analytical objects (reader, text, context . . .) is considered, not only as porous, but as radically undecidable, such an undecidability opening out onto, rather than blocking, a relationship to the world. Ponge's poetry of objects, picturing at one and the same time the impossibility of a mimetic correlation between word and world and the possibility of a more complex, asymmetrical kind of reference, as was seen in chapter 2, is an exemplary source for such a revised formalism; Wallace Stevens's dismantling of the romantic faith in symbol explored in chapter 3 is surely another.

If such an outlook does, indeed, propose a more capacious definition of what can count *as* text, and I'm not averse to the notion, it is only in the sense that the movements of formation and deformation, figuration and disfiguration, temporality and atemporality that I've traced thus far are as constitutive for the spaces and times at which a text is "received" as they are for any internal formal machinations within the text itself, the very applicability of "reception" as an isolatable instance then falling, perhaps fatally, into question. The "time" of the text is a time that persists, in all its heteroclite evasiveness, after and beyond the idealistically frozen meeting point of subject and object implied in the dogma of readerly inventiveness so crucial to aspects of, say, Barthes's early project, indeed to anyone concerned to foreground the reader over anything and anyone else.[38] The danger is that the inflation of the reader becomes the mere mirror image of the inflation of the text that has been imputed so often to formalism. Such a danger obtains equally for the inflation of history into the ideology of historicism, a danger addressed at length in chapter 1, and to be posed somewhat differently again in the conclusion.

The theory of poetic time as retrospection, where what comes afterward may reconstitute what comes before, already poses considerable problems for both the notion of the self-contained text as uniquely causative, and its mirror image of the reader as sovereign creator of literary sense. It is true, to be sure, that one tends to read a poem from beginning to end, and this would seem to suggest that the retroactive effect is only to be located squarely in the consciousness of whoever is doing the reading, but consider that, at the "time" of such a moment of (apparent) comprehension, the logics that I've identified as at work in the formal mechanisms of the poem are likely to cloud the transmission of meaning, inducing the effect of the eternal present already discussed. Alternately, they may force on the reader a kind of semantic erasure, precluding any sense of that reader as a semantic innovator, revising and reconstruing the sense that she receives from a text. Such a negative outcome is surely as likely as any predictable transport through the steady grooves of teleology, or as any preordained gathering of readerly insight. The difference I'm identifying here may well be that between retrospection proper, as unpredictable and as distributed across and beyond text, context and reader, and retrospection as a readerly *telos*, to be found nowhere in the messy and always erasable articulations of what has in the past, and inadequately, been stabilized as text and context, writer and reader. And all of the caveats listed above as applying to the fantasy of the all-powerful reader must also apply to the notion of an equivalently self-contained text, imparting its message to a reader construed as passive receptacle.

The distinction between *telos* and contingency is crucial to the work of Jean Laplanche, whose insights I am finally in a position to introduce. Such dilemmas are relevant also to the characteristic pronominal shift that I've shown to be at work in language poetry, whereby the temporal and historical pressures of the verse have been shown to induce the repression of one subject position, only to announce another—"she" to "he," "I" to "we." Such movements, given the often desperately affirmative novelty of what appears after the moment of repression, are not quite reducible to the familiar Freudian logic of the "return of the repressed," insofar as what "returns" is markedly different from the object initially repressed. It is necessary, then, in the reading of Laplanche that forms this chapter's conclusion, to trace how his reflections on time and language may help us better frame these disturbances of history and the subject within the folds of verse.

Jean Laplanche, who passed away in 2012, studied philosophy at the École normale supérieure before being introduced to psychoanalysis at, of all places, Harvard, where he visited for a year (1946–47). On receiving his doctorate in medicine, Laplanche remained distant from the creeping cultishness that scarred Lacan's legacy, while nonetheless appropriating much from the latter's teaching.[39] Like Lacan, he was a great thinker of language and its effects on the subject, and perhaps his most crucial insight lay in his thinking of psychoanalytic temporality as it interacts complexly with the logic of the signifier.

In an essay titled "Time and the Other," Laplanche skillfully tesselates specific reflections on the temporality proper to the psychoanalytic clinic with an assessment of the relevance of such insights for broader questions in historical and social analysis. In particular, Laplanche insists on "translation" and "loss" as key functions in mediating between the competing temporal forms constitutive of the subject and of broader forms of social history. Four distinct levels of time are distinguished: cosmological time, "the time of the world"; perceptual time, "that of immediate consciousness"; the time of memory and the individual project, "the temporalisation of the human being"; and the time of history, "the time of human societies, or even humanity conceived as a whole."[40] Freud, for Laplanche, was concerned most explicitly with the second level, with the theory of perceptual time, but implicitly, and most importantly, one may reconstruct a Freudian account of level three, that of the "temporalisation of the human being." After an illuminating discussion of what is referred to as Freud's "nonpsychoanalytic" theory of perceptual temporality, one that Laplanche judges to be overly defined by a linear, progressive model of temporal unfolding, he concentrates instead on level three, a level explicitly bound up with the subject in its entanglements with language.

The third level, the level proper to human existence as exposed to the effects of the unconscious, is structured by loss. As Laplanche remarks, "The dimension of loss is probably co-extensive with temporalisation itself."[41] The loss in question, that of the primordial unity with the mother, is mourned, a process characterized as "work" that occurs over a particular duration. While Freud tended to situate such labor at the level of the individual, Laplanche notices that, in the second chapter of Freud's *Totem and Taboo*, a number of psychic phenomena related to mourning are discussed with reference to early forms of collective social living, located at the juncture of prehistory and history proper.

Such forms, most obviously that of the "primal horde," are said to emerge from the sacrifice of the primal father, whose death eventuates in the system of totems and taboos that establishes the normative framework of the clan. One such taboo discussed by Freud is the taboo of the dead, an interdiction on touching the deceased that applies for a certain amount of time, dependent on the person in question. "The time of the taboo," Laplanche writes, "evokes . . . irresistibly the time of mourning." He continues: "Besides, mourning itself, even quite recently, was ritualised: one 'wore mourning' for a certain precise period, longer or shorter according to one's closeness to the person one was mourning."[42]

In my reading of Silliman's "Albany" above, I noticed how events both personal and collective—the rape suffered by the nameless rape victim, the rise of political activism in the Bay Area—were simultaneously marked and elided by the poem's temporal and historical logics. The sentence form inscribes such events into the archive of the verse before the accretion of periods allows them to dwindle into the individualized form of the present, such a present permitting only the registration of particular repetitive actions in the now. One could argue that history itself becomes a kind of taboo in "Albany," the term allowing us to include the ways in which history haunts the seemingly imperturbable present that its suppression produces. Nonetheless, it is with the introduction of the problem of language that Laplanche's exposition may truly benefit my investigation of poetic temporality. Intriguingly, Freud includes in his discussion of taboo a "taboo on names." As Laplanche explains, "Among the things that cannot be touched, there is the name of the dead person, which can no longer be pronounced. The best way to avoid the temptation of uttering the dead person's name is to change his name."[43] Eventually, the names of any number of things associated with the deceased—objects dear to him or her, even associated persons—are similarly altered. The effect, Laplanche argues, is "an obstacle to writing history,"[44] one encountered most dramatically by missionaries and anthropologists who wished to reconstruct family histories over generations.

It is anxiety around the proper name that motivates Freud's discussion, an anxiety that I've argued is definitional to "Albany," and that has a privileged place in poetic history; one thinks of Mallarmé's complaint that "to name an object is to do away with the three-quarters of the enjoyment of the poem which is derived from the satisfaction of guessing little by little."[45] The frequent lack of even an impersonal subject in "Albany"'s sentences is only apparently mitigated by the inclusion of a handful of proper names—"Rubin feared McClure would read Ghost Tantras at the teach-in." But the stark isolation of those names, their facelessness, in fact serves only to underline both the collectivity of history as it irrupts—

think, once again, of those massed protestors chanting "We shall not be moved"—and the loss of individual autonomy that attends its withering away; this, it is fair to say, is a general characteristic of language verse, where syntactical impersonality prevails over the more usual subject-voice of the lyric. One thinks once again of the rape survivor and the nameless Hispanic, acephalous subjects introduced by a pronominal shift (from "she" to "he") that may well be motivated by an inability, within the logic of time and history opened up by the poem, to process the complex interweaving of personal and collective histories that the poem is nonetheless forced up against, and that are often to be found concentrated in the proper name. Such an inadequacy is precisely that which Freud and Laplanche are concerned with in their interrogation of the forgetting of names, of their stubborn refusal to translate across temporal borders. The question, Laplanche confirms, is that of the "proper name, of its translatability, or even of the right to pronounce it."[46] In Freud's example of the "primitive" society, "all the attributes of the dead person can be reworked: but his name is untouchable, impossible to *metabolise*."[47] It is, I think, this impossibility of metabolization that animates the poetic approach to history and identity analyzed above.

For Laplanche, Freud's example is generalizable to what he calls the "enigmatic signifiers" that primary caregivers implant in infants' unconscious, the opaque words and gestures that children sense are laden with significance but that they are unable to decode. The proper name is surely the paradigmatic case of such signifiers, the name usually predating the very birth of the subject in question. Laplanche refers to the "swamping [of] the child's capacity for apprehension and mastery" that results from "messages . . . offered on all sides." Laplanche continues: "By messages I do not necessarily nor chiefly mean verbal messages. Any gesture, any mimicry functions as a signifier. These originary, traumatic signifiers I propose to call 'enigmatic signifiers.'"[48] Such signifiers are traumatic to the infant not simply because, as already mentioned, they are unable to be understood. More than this, "*adults themselves* do not have the code";[49] the unconscious significations and feints that overdetermine any primary caregiver's orientation to their child are part of the broader, opaque texture of desirous investments and hidden communications that discursively structure human life. Such signifiers must be translated, but such a process is never complete; such attempts must fail. As Laplanche has it, "It is these signifiers, received passively, that are the object of the first active attempts at translation, residues of which are primally repressed."[50] Here, just as in my reading of the formal tactics embedded in poetic structure, acts of disappearance (for Laplanche corresponding to the repression of enigmatic signifiers unable to be metabolized) are always attended by the formal establishment of that which is apparently being disposed of; I've shown in this chapter how history and time, and the proper name may now be considered as an especially overdetermined cipher for both, operate poetically according to this paradoxical logic, where the apparent absence of one seems to foretell its subsequent re-emergence, while the apparent presence of another is only the premonition of its vanishing.

For psychoanalysis, the repression of enigmatic signifiers is formative to the extent that, once repressed, such messages serve as the opaque foundation for the subject-in-formation, that creature then ever to be haunted and sculpted by those ciphers from their position in the unconscious. Think of how Bruce Andrews's "Blueier Blue," a poem that seems determined to flatten time and history in the onrush of its semantic fragments and in its refusal of any determinable organization, is nonetheless structured despite itself, history entering through the back door via allusions to economic imperatives, the latter nothing but the endgame of the privatization of history staged by Silliman's "Albany." Nonetheless, an objection may at this point present itself, for are we not simply drawing an analogical relation between two irreducible domains, poetry and psychoanalysis, the theoretical resources of which fail at the point of any attempted translation? Yet analogy is only one of many formal logics that, as they tessellate and pull apart, seem to encompass both verse *and* analysis, domains defined by their immersion in and partial resistance to the broader imperatives of language and the vicissitudes of the subject. John Kucich captures this well when, in the course of a remark on Paul Ricoeur, he writes that "subjectivity—including critical subjectivity—occupies the same discursive plane as textuality. Because both are constituted in language, they are equally given . . . to an ineluctable tension between what can be spoken and what remains hidden in every utterance."[51] Equally, history and time are, for poetry as much as for the subject, what both can and can't be spoken, at one and the same instance. If there is a legacy of Lacan's reinvention of Freudian theory, and of Laplanche's sophisticated extension and displacement of that legacy, it is surely this insight: that word, world, and subject alike, in all their complex and asymmetrical entanglements, make contact at moments of apparent untranslatability; that is the broader thesis of this book with respect to literary form in particular.[52]

The reader attuned to the recent history of literary theory may notice a parallel of sorts, here, with Harold Bloom's contention that lyric form, in particular, is defined by that form's self-breaking; Bloom has, of course, made ample use of psychoanalysis in furthering this view. And yet Bloom's central concern, at least during the 1970s and 1980s, might be summarized in his own words as the "connect[ion] of trope and psychic defense."[53] Such a position links defense and repression not to the broad and explicitly political vision of collective history (and its poetic repression) envisioned here, but to a rather insular "history" of struggle between poetic successor and precursor. As thrillingly nonreductive as Bloom's use of psychoanalysis is, my aim is different: to detect in poetic form logics that, rather than being confined to a retrospectively constructed agonistic dialogue, overspill poetic, psychic, and historical bounds alike, placing in question, in turn, the strictness of the boundaries between them.

There are, to be sure, numerous poems that round their proper names out with backstory, and that struggle by the same movement to capture the nuances and depths of time and history. Nonetheless, such acts of inclusion can never be equivalent to a full digestion of the complex history and density that the singularity of a name or the density of a history may otherwise convoke. The proper name, even in its absence, may stand in for those incompletely glimpsed histories, caught between the individual and the collective. As Laplanche puts it, "The proper name . . . is *untranslatable*: it could only be exchanged, in a rigorous sense, for the person himself."[54] History and time find themselves in a similar dilemma, although I would need to add that this apparent impossibility of translation is just as much a condition of *possibility* for their poetic articulation. Poetic form itself seems to both legislate for and try to block the development of an archive, the feasibility of which is simultaneously teased and denied by, say, the ambivalent shortening effects of Silliman's sentences, or by the establishment of the open-ended list of particulars that ends Baudelaire's "Correspondances" and that overdetermine Andrews's "Blueier Blue."

This conflictual character of poetic time and history is shown most plainly, for sure, in the experimental forms discussed in this chapter, but it is also demonstrated by the mutabilities of the more conventional lyric structure explored in my reading of Yeats, and in the Baudelaire sonnets that preoccupied us in chapter 4. Even as the "conventional" lyric may seem defined by the unification of its voice, one would do better to notice the synchronous push and pull of such voices as they are buffeted by the formal pressures adduced in this book; such voices are subject to the vacillations of history as the latter archives them one moment, and silences them the next. It is worth emphasizing once more that the formalistic approach to literature, far from excluding the pressures of history and time, can, when speculatively enlarged, find no shelter from their complexities.

Conclusion

From one angle, this book has concerned itself with the pact between literary, and especially poetic, form, and the meaning we assume it produces. Wordsworth, in his "Preface to the *Lyrical Ballads*," comments on his own setting up, and then breaking, of such a pact or contract:

> It is supposed, that by the act of writing in verse an Author makes a formal engagement that he will gratify certain known habits of association . . . I will not take upon me to determine the exact import of the promise which by the act of writing in verse an Author, in the present day, makes to his reader; but I am certain, it will appear to many persons that I have not fulfilled the terms of an engagement thus voluntarily contracted.[1]

"Contract" bears within it multiple meanings in its Wordsworthian[2] usage, but I use it here to capture something of this historical moment, reducible from one angle to the romantic as it passes almost imperceptibly into the modern, on which an individualizing set of economic promises, capitalism itself, is solidified and reproduced quite apart from the needs and capacities of the individual as such. Poetry here seems to evoke equivalent promises made to an individualized and pacified reader, promises that must, nonetheless, be simultaneously broken if that putative contract is to be fully discharged. Without, that is to say, the frustration of expectation that Wordsworth laments above, form would remain immobile, would be unable to assume the speculative and productive capacities that I have insisted throughout this book are its foremost characteristics.

The lesson of the previous chapter, of course, is that such promises, contracts, or pacts between history and literature are never easily exchanged, never smoothly or entirely successfully sold one to the other, poetic form never merely passively reproductive of the complex machinations of the historical, or vice versa; indeed, their becoming equivalent would merely cancel the effect of each. And it might be worth insisting too, at this stage, that the inflation of a new category between history and text—"power" or "affect" would be two prevalent recent examples[3]—is not in itself enough to mitigate these dangers, no matter how striated or decentered we might imagine such mediatory elements to be. Indeed, it may be that mediation itself as a figure proves inadequate to the processes in question; I'll soon have cause to question such a usage as it appears within what has come to be known, once again, as "world literature."

Language poetry, in chapter 5, became a concrete particular, one that nonetheless offered a lens onto the more general characteristics proper to literary form in its agonistic interactions with history. The verse of Bruce Andrews, Ron Silliman, and others, on my account, became an optic through which a more abstract formal movement, the palpable if elusive presence of history within poetic form, took shape, albeit at the moment at which poetic form seemed to rid itself of the burdens of history, and at a historical juncture (the conservative 1980s) at which it was the supposed absence of history that proved the surest symptom of its presence. Yet any absolute universalization of that logic, any complete and always successful translation of the seeming absence of historical form into the proof of its textual abundance, could never fully encompass a connected but opposite turn that also caught my attention, whereby the pregnant and constitutive absence of history—think, once more, of the traces of collective autonomy threaded through Ron Silliman's account of the privatization of such a political potential—becomes, instead of a charged presence-in-absence on the page, a new kind of nostalgia, one especially symptomatic of a historical moment where history as such was frequently said to have ended.

Such acts of passive memorialization can also be read as a shrinking away from the difficult task of giving history a *name*. Nomination becomes a taboo as a consequence of the very power of the name, its potential to concentrate within itself both past and future transformative historical possibilities. If psychoanalysis offered one resource in chapter 5 to theorize this taboo of the name in its complex interactions with history, Roland Barthes may offer another: "To read (to perceive the *readerly* aspect of the text) is to proceed from name to name, from fold to fold; it is to fold the text according to one name and then to unfold it along the folds of the new name. This is proairetism: an artifice . . . of reading that seeks out names, that tends toward them."[4]

Barthes skillfully keeps in balance here two concurrent but different phenomena. First, he registers a kind of narrative flow that supersedes any attempt to fix it in time and space (this flow for Barthes to be accessed only on the intervention of a reader), and second, he records the temporarily fixed names that are dissolved in circulations of the aforementioned flux, fixity and flow thus changing places in an unending movement of aggregation and disaggregation. Such movements seem to reserve a special place for the name even as that which is to be overcome, and which nonetheless may always come to settle back into place. But there are other ways of figuring the name, not least through the inflation of the Author itself as a kind of insurance against the dissolving of nomination that Barthes was otherwise keen to track; Wordsworth above, in his reference to a capitalized "Author," himself, would seem to wish to put his own authorship up as collateral for the broken contract that he confesses to his reader, while Barthes's own and famous concern for the "death" of the author would leave in place the name as it is deformed and reformed in his theory of "proairetism."

In any case, Wordsworth's having "not fulfilled the terms" of his engagement would seem to involve rather more than the (false) modesty of a poet humbly addressing his public. Rather, what may seem a resolutely interpersonal question in the quote from Wordsworth above, is, instead, thoroughly a question of history and politics as they announce themselves in and against the literary line. In this conclusion, I will recall the twists and turns of my preceding argument while further insisting on this concrete texture of my position, one that aspires to a kind of materialism not unrelated to that found in nascent form in the posthumously published essays of Paul de Man as analyzed in chapter 4. It is not enough, I would wager, to evoke historical anecdotes or details in order to claim the name of this "materialism," for to do so is only to quiet that which one would otherwise seek to amplify—literature, on such a reading, denied its own material productivity. It would be equally disadvantageous to forgo the ambient associations of materialism ("historical-materialist" and otherwise) through any strategic choice of a phrase such as "absolute realism," as in the following from Augusto de Campos: "Far from attempting to evade reality or deceive it, concrete poetry is against self-debilitating introspection and simpleton simplistic realism. It intends to place itself before things, open, in a position of absolute realism."[5]

The latter position would seem to confuse an initial speculative moment whereby poetic form tries to latch itself onto things, a first moment thoroughly ironized and then superseded in Ponge's poetics as explored in chapter 2, as the resting point of form per se. This initial move, one that has much in common with Hegel's starting point in the *Phenomenology of Spirit* of "sense certainty," would adopt the posture of a uniquely receptive phenomenological openness, one reproductive in a putatively secular register of the theological position of absolute submission to and reception of divine illumination. The power of Ponge's poetics, to say nothing of Hegel's own productive negation of sense certainty, is in its demonstration of the creative annulment of this posture in its very coming into being. Just as poetic language is apparently submitted to the dense, heavy exteriority of things-in-themselves, so it is violently thrown back on itself, the very same solidity of things then seeming to infect poetic language in its apparent self-closure. But Ponge's irony also points to a route beyond such an impasse, an impasse that Ponge nonetheless enjoyed with lip-smacking relish.

For just at the point at which poetic language seems unable to convey the densities of its referent, a shared incompletion across the world of language and the world of things comes into view, one to be understood as the necessary *incompletion* that is produced whenever a form overextends itself, contracts itself to a vision of wholeness or totality without contradiction. Formalization, on such a reading, is the name for the aspiration to totality that must nonetheless result in various different kinds of incompletion, through the gaps of which one might nonetheless glimpse the speculative capacities of form that have been the principal topic of this book. And so even as I gladly acquiesce in the association of my position with a kind of materialism, the choice of the phrase "speculative formalism" for the broad theoretical outlook of the book remains apt: materialism left to its own devices would threaten to confer materiality only on those determinants—economics, nature, commodity exchange—that have historically been explained under its rubrics. Here, by stark contrast, I have sought to push recent "high" theory beyond the recognition of the "materiality of the signifier" that distinguished the best of French philosophy of the 1960s. In the engagement with the recent work of Paul Livingston that will conclude this conclusion, I'll show both the potential and limits of this storied "logic of the signifier" or of "signifierness," limits that may still prove productive for the theory of totality and totalization, of globality as a planetary instance of the formalization of forms, that can only be inadequately sketched here.

But to what extent is my attempt at a formalization of form itself, this book's attempt at a determination of determination to provide its Marxist inflection, itself already historical, which is to say material in the more limited sense just alluded to? Should any attempt to generalize this striking kind of formalization beyond its immediate historical horizon be condemned as a mere reifying attempt to deny that very historical specificity? In a passing comment on modernism that is filtered through Adorno, Jameson writes:

> But reification . . . is a tendential social law which has ultimate effects on and implications for aesthetics and the work of art . . . Adorno is only the foremost among those who have tried to define aesthetic modernism itself in terms of reification, and that in a twofold way: for reification defines the situation and the element the work wishes to resist, but it also defines the logic of that resistance, as a kind of homeopathic remedy which fights a general logic of objectification by way of the objectification of its own forms.[6]

Is not what Jameson describes here as proper to modernism, a self-defeating self-objectification conducted in the name of the critique of just such objectifications, perilously close to the more general formal logic I've been tracing throughout, a logic that tries and no doubt fails to stay true to its own promise of universality? A number of solutions pose themselves, none of them immediately definitive. The first would claim that what appeared with especial force on the irruption of the various modernisms is, in fact, to be traced, in comparable if not equivalent ways, in significantly different literary periods. Thus, one might search within both canonical and forgotten texts of romanticism alike for a similar logic, whereby, say, the very romantic attempt to upset the strictly marshaled verse of a Pope or Dryden becomes its own kind of objectification. The transgression of such earlier limits through the enlivening resources of the symbol could be shown, that is, to produce the category of the symbol as itself an empty and reified object, one voided of its energy after so many attempts to trade it in for the connection of body and spirit, nature and subject. Nonetheless, one could well be accused in turn of simply reading back an especially modern logic, that of reification and its necessary tethering to an already globalizing capitalist economy, to earlier times and places. And yet perhaps one is always fated, in mobilizing already indeterminate and problematically capacious categories such as the romantic and the modern, to place in motion a certain dialectic of reification and de-reification, autonomy and dependence, one that inevitably creeps in at the level of methodology where previously one had been concerned to track its traces at the level of literary texts themselves. This is nothing to be regretted within the terms of this book's speculative formalism, of course, in that it reveals at a metatheoretical level—Paul Livingston will refer to it as a metaformal level[7]—what I have been concerned to show all along, namely that the sliding of theory into method, history into its objects, is always the *beginning* of the generation of sense out of form, of history out of temporality, never its end.

A second solution would seek to deny any parity of the logic described by Jameson with that proposed in this book. After all, Jameson's process ends in two static fields, the first literary form as fixed object and the second the object-world as equally frozen in space and time, whereas the insistence here on formal conscription as enabling of movements beyond itself would rather take this apparent end as, again, only a beginning, an incitement to change rather than a confirmation of the impossibility of that change. If Lukács saw fit to question certain literary forms for their historical stasis and immovability—most crucially modernism itself, of course[8]—I would rather find in these varying modes of stasis an opening, a provocation that may well be indicative of features of literary form as irreducible to any absolute historical "context" as they are elusive of any metaphysical attempt at absolute universalization, totalization or, which is the same thing, eternalization.

My recruitment of aspects of both of these "solutions," while rejecting others, will, I hope, be both demonstrated and justified in the remainder of this conclusion, where I will translate my concern for the noncorrelative interaction of form and history, stasis and productivity, into the terms of a debate that has recently crystallized around the category of "world literature." It may be useful, to begin, to rethink at least one facet of that category in the terms of constitutive incompletion summarized above, at least to meet the terms of the pact announced at the conclusion of chapter 1. There I quoted Peter Osborne's recent diagnosis of a contemporary globalism, one that "exhibit[s] the structure of a subject (the unity of an activity) only objectively, in [its] product, separated from individual subjects and particular collectivities of labor."[9] I announced, in turn, my intention to reflect speculative formalism through such a prism at the conclusion of the book.[10] How, then, might one begin to imagine a theory of the global interaction of forms that avoids, even as it trains its gaze precisely onto such reified structures, reproducing at the level of method the sense of such an abstract stasis as something immovable, natural, or impervious to analytic disruption?

Such a method would need to encompass the impasses and interregnums that, I've been arguing, operate always at the noncorrelative point of connection between relatively autonomous processes of formalization. As I sketch those details, one may need to find a place for the very point of reification or movementless aridity that Lukács, Jameson, and Osborne lament. I will then trace its at least partial overcoming, and yet its simultaneous and persistent threat of return, in something like a move from "form" to "formalization," or from the fantasy of a complete totality to that of a necessarily incomplete movement of *totalization*. Finally, I will seek resources for thinking such incomplete and yet productive totalities, close enough as they may be to the kinds of forms-in-becoming analyzed in this book. What follows will be of necessity provisional and incomplete; a full articulation of speculative formalism with questions of the global and globalization, with the perplexities of so-called world literature, and with the wide panoply of problems that more generally intersect literature, politics, and institutional critique, must be deferred for another time. But one might, at least, shine a new light on the arguments already made in the preceding chapters, while opening a tentative path beyond some of the aporia that define current debates in comparative literature and the literary humanities, broadly conceived, especially as they have broached a move beyond extant models of form and content toward a vision of the planetary or global per se.

World Literature?

The storied notion of "world literature" has become something of a rallying point in contemporary literary studies, with the widening of the canon that it presupposes proving especially attractive to comparatists as they negotiate a disciplinary identity after the waning of high theory.[11] While the move to broaden the geographical horizon under which literary study occurs has been fulsomely welcomed in some quarters, others have questioned the haste with which scholars have been enjoined to engage literatures written in languages they do not master and ensconced within cultures of which they know little. An even more pertinent criticism has recently been advanced by Emily Apter, for whom the category of world literature tends toward "reflexive endorsement of cultural equivalence and substitutability, or toward the celebration of nationally and ethnically branded 'differences.'"[12] Such criticism rests on an allied and more explicitly political fear that the call for ever more inclusion is, in fact, the mere extension of a commodifying and neutralizing drive attached to the omnipresence of the world market. Such literatures as may now be admitted to the canon begin to resemble, according to such a critique, tastefully exotic baubles to be collected by scholars, the better to embellish their claims to cosmopolitanism.[13] One is left, so this story goes, roughly in the position Peter Osborne diagnoses above, with the various opacities and stubbornnesses of cultural objects reduced to avatars of accessibility, such a picture coming close to the latter's vision of a globalized subjectivity ironed out and "separated from individual subjects and collectivities of labour."

At base, and conceding the vastly different approaches that have already been marshaled under the sign of world literature, the predominant criticism as essayed above pertains to the model of totalization that world literature as a new disciplinary configuration would seem to require. It is not, that is, the desire to approach the limits of what is knowable in literature that is to be rejected; it is certainly not, even more, the desire in and of itself to totalize that is at issue. Rather, it is the particular vision of totality that apparently underpins the comprehensiveness of the "world" in "world literature" that seems, on my reading, contradicted by what I've repeatedly referred to as the "formativeness of form." The celebrants of world literature, it should quickly be noted, have taken some care to avoid precisely such overgeneralizing or reductive temptations. The following from David Damrosch is exemplary:

> A central argument of this book will be that, properly understood, world literature is not at all fated to disintegrate into the conflicting multiplicity of separate national traditions; nor, on the other hand,

> need it be swallowed up in the white noise that Janet Abu-Lughod has called "global babble." My claim is that world literature is not an infinite, ungraspable canon of works but rather a mode of circulation and of reading, a mode that is as applicable to individual works as to bodies of material, available for reading established classics and new discoveries alike.[14]

The image of "circulation" is used to offset any impression that world literature may only be capable of an extreme cultural particularism on the one hand, or a bland homogenization on the other, the latter dichotomy a more general version of that between rigidly national literatures at one end of the spectrum, the dissolving of the national into the worldly on the other. Indeed, the trope of circulation, subtly displaced here from its more usual habitat in Marxist criticism, is now an identifying motif for the field of world literature per se; Franco Moretti is surely the pioneer here.[15] To induce a sense of circulation is to suggest the puncturing of any airless totality, any static vision of a world whose boundaries would be easily and unproblematically delineable. The flip side of this airless totality would be the single, particular text containing multitudes, this latter dichotomy now one more stand-in for the nation/world dyad just invoked. As Moretti would have it, using Wallerstein's world-systems writings as a model, world literature proper would reject both sides of this self-confirming duo: "The text which is strictly Wallerstein's . . . occupies one third of a page . . . the rest are quotations . . . Now, if we take this model seriously, the study of world literature will somehow have to reproduce this 'page' . . . Literary history will quickly become very different from what it is now: it will become 'second hand': a patchwork of other people's research, *without a single direct textual reading.*"[16]

The "other people's research" in question would be the spatially and temporally broad-range content analysis enabled by computation and interrogated in chapter 1. Cultural objects, on such a vision, could be seen to circulate, to intermingle, to distance themselves, thus to never settle into anything approaching a rigid "world," just as much as their particular content—the self-enclosed modulations of the individual book—would fade from relevance. Two totalities are rejected here, or so it seems: the world as a finally delimitable totality, and the individual book as lure to the rabbit holes of close reading. But just as important to detect in such a rejection is the exclusion of the nation/world antinomy itself, Moretti wishing to avoid the mere obverse of what has, in disciplinary terms, been parceled out as so many nationally specific literatures and languages.

Damrosch's and Moretti's visions are far from being equivalent, of course; Damrosch, for instance, seems more at ease with the full semantic weight of the term "world," its indication of a provisional planetary fixity, where Moretti would rather wish to perpetually reset such a putative boundary according to the particular digital-historical analysis in question. Moretti, characteristically, would want to rely on methodological innovation in order to upset theoretical rigidity. Nonetheless, Moretti and Damrosch rely on the trope of circulation, as already mentioned, and one surely can only come to understand such a notion, such a suspiciously graceful ballet of perpetual literary movement, according to an implied border or limit as its necessary other, a limit within which, even against which, such entangled movements may become visible in the first place. To foreground circulation per se risks positing movement as its own justification against any more critical questioning of the arena within which such movements are tacitly assumed to take place, or the model of totality that this valorization of motion otherwise presupposes. Refocusing our attention onto the implied totality inherent in the worlding of the "world," to abuse Heidegger, may then lead to the proposal of alternative models of totality or totalization, models attentive to the zones of incompletion and opacity that the search for the "all" must always produce.

Form and the Global / The Global as Form

The fate that Osborne cautions against in that now familiar quote above, the seeming intransigence of the abstract subject and object of planetary capital, has found related expression in any number of critical, literary, and theoretical traditions. To pick almost at random, one thinks of Brecht's admonitions in his dramaturgical writings against "integration" as a kind of "soup": "As long as the arts are supposed to be fused together, the various elements will equally be degraded, and each will act as a mere 'cue' to the rest."[17] The dissolving of all particularity in an undifferentiated vision of integration, that is, can only degrade the particulars that make it up, deny them their sliver of speculative possibility, what I've been insisting on as the indirect but nonetheless powerful means by which literature accesses and potentially reroutes its objects. Translating this insight back into the debate over "world literature," one may conclude that the "world" is the whole under which all particular cultural objects, and infra- and intercultural differences alike, are negated.

Such negations have, for Brecht, a properly subjective effect too that he sketches through the experience of the spectator: "The process of fusion extends to the spectator, who also gets thrown into the melting pot and becomes a passive (suffering) part of the total work of art."[18]

Substitute "total work of art" for "world" in the latter and one encounters something of the inadequacy of the vision of totality that "world literature" as a field threatens, despite itself, to advance. Brecht's insight, versions of which are to be found in Adorno no less than in, say, Mallarmé's reflections on the "crisis of verse," equally alerts us to the different scales at which this denial of autonomy may take place: while in my account, it is both the literary object as such and its historical "outsides" that threaten to be fixed by the "worlding" of the "world," for Brecht such a process is detectable even at the level of a subject's interaction with a singular work of art, at least when that subject or self is construed as an entirely passive and congruent part of that work of art's ensemble of effects.

In the reading of Ponge's poetry in chapter 2, the "work" itself was shown to perform its own self-objectification, only to then overcome such an initial stage through its ironical deflation. Such an initial stance, that of sitting passively in wait of the truth of external objects, erecting as a consequence an artificially rigid distinction between subject (qua poem) and object such that one can swap places easily with the other, is only the foil by which a fuller, nonmimetic, and asymmetrical intercalation of subject and object may then be enacted. One encounters, here, different *scales* at which objectification or reification may occur, and according to notably different ends: for Brecht, objectification—itself a kind of inadequately abstract movement of totalization—occurs principally when the spectator of a work of art is rendered passive by the lure of realism-effects that such works, when insufficiently self-critical, produce.

But at the level of the line in Ponge, such processes are necessary only insofar as they can be overcome; this not unlike Brecht's own strategic deployment of theatrical reification ("alienation," in his own terms) as one crucial moment in a critical dialectic. Of course, the dialectical quality of Ponge's poetics, leaving aside now Brecht's theatrical vision, lies in its presupposition that such a moment of reification may well come round again, this time induced by a different element of the poem's form or through the pressure of a different object or referent. This shifting back and forth between motionless and kinetic accounts of a form in its encounters with its outsides is given further expression in Wallace Stevens's jar in Tennessee, as discussed in chapter 2. There the characteristics of the alien object implanted in an equally alien landscape begin to bleed into those surrounds, the landscape in turn inflating the object according to its own proportions—and without, for all that, either becoming merely indistinguishable from the other and without the relative autonomy of each being breached in the name of a suffocating whole. For some, autonomy in any cultural sphere must be construed as a fiction, even if an enabling one; this is often no doubt a defensible claim. It may nonetheless be possible to trace how the fictive self-staging of autonomy performed by literary works is only one formal means by which a truer kind of formal quasi-freedom may be accessed, a possibility left tantalizingly open by Ponge's poetics, where the smirk of an ironical image or figure often transforms into the grimace of an arduous, nonmimetic, and unpredictable mode of reference.

But it is surely possible that any flat-out denial of autonomy, at least when imagined as the end point of a process rather than its initial moment to be rejected, may harm the very aspiration toward totality itself, an aspiration that is as necessary to the analytic of form and formalization that I've traced in this book as it is to those critical Marxisms, Brecht's included, that have wished to complicate any unilinear understanding of the movement from the specific to the total, from the particular to the universal. The language alighted on in this conclusion—totality, totalization, particularity, universality, and so on—cannot but invoke Hegel, and it is through a specific reconfiguration of a speculative Hegelian dialectic that Peter Osborne seeks to account for the freezing of both subject and object under conditions of what he calls "high capitalism." Such polar conditions deny any truly global horizon except for that projected and then endlessly enlarged by capital itself, capital then becoming the historically specific name for that indistinct "world" that, in a different guise, threatens to blunt the critical potential of the newly interred rubric of "world literature": "Only capital," Osborne writes, "manifests a subject-structure at the level of the global."[19] One might replace "global" with "world" here, but Osborne's indictment broadly coincides with my own suspicions as to the mode of totality that underpins world literature as a category. Such a reduction of totality's possibilities must always, at base, build itself on three key elements, two opposing poles with a mediatory element in between. Damrosch relies on this logic in the following:

> A given work can enter into world literature and then fall out of it again if it shifts beyond a threshold point along either axis, the literary or the worldly. Over the centuries, an unusually shifty work can come in and out of the sphere of world literature several different times; and at any given point, a work may function as world literature for some readers but not others.[20]

There is, I think, an implicit clash, if not outright contradiction, between the two sentences quoted above. The first sets up the three-part structure just mentioned: two opposed poles—literature and world—with the "work" as a mediatory element in between. Such an element loses its mediating function, one gathers, if it cleaves too closely to either of the two antipodes. The second sentence, rowing back a little from the apparently austere conceptual architecture of the first, attempts to demonstrate the variety that may subsist within such an architecture's walls; thus, an especially "shifty" work and its unpredictable trajectory appears to render appealingly ambivalent, if not to alter completely, the stark three-part structure that the analysis nonetheless continues to lean on. Perhaps it would be churlish to point out that, for all the emphasis here on shifts and movements "in" and "out," the "work" apparently remains the work—isolatable, delineable—even when it is properly, which is to say for Damrosch *symmetrically*, distributed between the category of literature and the "world" as its arena; such a distribution is the requirement, for Damrosch, that it be counted among the members of the set "world literature" at all. Too much "world" or too much "literature" and such an analytic poise would be unceremoniously toppled.

Of course, for Osborne and other Marxist critics, it is only on the assumption that there is *always* too much of one thing—too much, that is, of capital in its totalizing and exploitative drive—that the contemporary may be readable at all. The contemporary itself would then need to be understood as, broadly speaking, the name, fictional as it may be, for what has superseded the modern. This holds so long as one presumes, as Osborne at least does, that the "postmodern" as a periodizing name was always insufficient to capture the seeming futurelessness of the present, the inability of our current conjuncture to permit a genuine, nonfictional supersession—a "post," that is—of its own temporal and spatial imaginaries. Osborne phrases it as follows: "The idea of the contemporary poses the problem of the disjunctive unity of space-time, or the *geopolitically historical.* The temporal dialectic of the new, which gives qualitative definition to the historical present . . . but which the notion of the contemporary cuts off from the future, must be mediated with the complex global dialectic of spaces."[21]

I'm unsure that the spatializing figure of mediation is sufficient to capture the process that Osborne characterizes here, not least because of the temptations detected in Damrosch's appeal to the "work" as mediator, such temptations threatening to naturalize, or at least place at too far a remove from analysis, the reifying frame in question—here named "capital," in Damrosch named "world." The mediating figure or object in such a logic would, at worst, provide an alibi for the fixity of the opposed terms that it relies on for its consistency. But Osborne's, needless to say, is a rather different appeal to mediation than that made by Damrosch. Here we encounter the suggestive notion of a "disjunctive synthesis," a Deleuzian coinage that greets, if rather awkwardly, the updated Hegelianism implied in Osborne's articulation of a spatial and temporal dialectic.

There is no neat supersession to be had: if anything, space colludes in the blockage of the new implied by the category of the "contemporary," the expanding immensity of the present under the reign of capital taking on spatial form in the complex aggregation under the law of the market of ever more remote corners of the globe.

It may now be of use to recall the discussion of the clashing temporal and historical logics in language verse in the previous chapter. There I noted how, in Bruce Andrews's disconnected particles of sense especially, a strikingly brutal temporal logic, one imposed on the verse by the regular cut of the period and the dash, served to refuse the translation of time into history that is found more fully in progress across Ron Silliman's poetry. The addition of the category of space complicates things somewhat; those stark cuts of the period in Andrews are surely as much a spatial phenomenon as a temporal one. Nonetheless, the type of space at issue for Osborne is very different indeed, a necessary reminder that, for all the complex intercalations of literary, historical, political, and temporal forms explored over the course of this book, the instantiation at one level of a particular formal logic—here, space—can never with any accuracy be treated as entirely congruent with its instantiation at another. Such a vision of infinite and easy translatability is exactly what is threatened, I've argued, by the category of "world literature" itself.

In his assessment of planetary capital, Osborne is at pains to distinguish what he calls capital's status as "form" from "collectivity," a rather different figure for the coming together of different kinds of practice: "Capitalist sociality (the grounding of societies in relations of exchange) is essentially abstract; it is a matter of *form*, rather than 'collectivity.' Collectivity is produced by the interconnectedness of practices."[22] It is at this point in his argument that the quote I've deployed now more than once appears: "But the universal interconnectedness and dependencies that capital produces exhibit the structure of a subject (the unity of an activity) only objectively, in their product."[23] That "but" speaks volumes: where collectivity, ideally, would seem to embody a kind of practice usefully distinct from the standardizing imperatives of capital, even "collectivity" as a putatively utopian image of practice is here recognized as a fiction, is forced back into the impoverished version of "interconnectedness" that capital itself produces across its ever more capaciously drawn territories. Collectivity, even *as* a fiction, takes on something of the promise of ideality here, one that by definition can now never be actualized, and I wonder whether we need sacrifice the figure so easily.

Instead, and as explored in the previous chapter, collective historical action, what may now be rechristened as processes of collective *historicization*, can be seen to persist—virtually, abstractly, as a promise—

even in moments of their apparent failure. To produce an analytic of collectivity that holds true to this seeming paradox, to the persistence of a collective structure in history that finds sustenance in its never quite achieving its goals, one would need to bring back together what Osborne wishes to keep apart, namely form and the collective, the collective always being a kind of form in motion. Form in motion would be another name for what I've been calling formalization, and the latter preserves the measure of historical possibility that Osborne's "form," the latter understood as entirely overrun by the reified logics of high capitalism, would definitively evacuate. Ron Silliman's "Albany," for all its lamentations for past political effectivity, would still, in its very open-endedness, seem to hold the space open for positive action anew, action that may eventuate from the very fictive globality that is otherwise the ideological skin of globalization.

Toward the end of the poem, in a section I neglected to discuss in chapter 5, Silliman writes: "There were bayonets on campus, cows in India, people shoplifting books."[24] This is no pristine utopia of planetary reinvention, for sure; collectivity here re-emerges, but it does so as enmeshed in practices other than the international labor movement that the earlier sections of the poem seem to hymn—such new practices including, here, religion (cows in India, a figure not far from a religious fetish), but also individualized attempts at sabotage (shoplifted books). Where a privatized diminution of historical possibility had seemed to prevail, though, now history reinvigorates itself in an explicitly global register, the forms in question traveling beyond the elite confines of the Bay Area to terrains that had seemed foreclosed in the first twenty lines. One glimpses, at least, an alternative vision of global collectivity than the deflated fiction crisply analyzed by Osborne and the too-neat vision promised by "world literature." To firm up a theoretical understanding of what such a form may look like, and to conclude this book, I'll turn to a recent attempt by Paul Livingston to reimagine what he writes of as "totality." Livingston's bracingly rigorous writings on different kinds of totality, totalization, and formalization may, when reinscribed in a literary register, hold out powerful models for an alternative picturing of the contemporary as a theater of constitutively incomplete global forms.

Globality and Constitutive Incompletion

In his essay "How Do We Recognize Strong Critique?"[25] Paul Livingston rehearses various ways of thinking formal wholes and their limits. He does so in order to redynamize our understanding of formalism, especially as it has operated in the domains of formal logic and mathematical theory. The latter have, for Livingston, promising things to say to spheres of action and critique otherwise apparently severed from them, most notably radical political theory. In this, he follows the lead of Alain Badiou among others,[26] although his conclusions are sufficiently different from the latter to make him a powerfully original thinker in his own right. I will be unable to do full justice to his philosophical originality in this short concluding reflection; instead, I will reappropriate and reconfigure the conceptual resources he offers in the light of this book's overriding concern, namely the production of a literary-critical formalism that is capable of thinking the possibility of literature's touching its referents, history and politics included, without recourse to strong historicisms, mimetic fallacies, or pseudo-deconstructive nihilisms.

What does Livingston mean by "strong critique"? "To indicate," Livingston writes, "the formal structure of strong critique," "it suffices . . . to discern the *fundamental orientations of thought* which unfold the formal ideas of completeness, consistency and reflexivity as they structure the configurations in which the real of being gives itself to thought."[27] "The real of being": there's no shortage of ambition here, Livingston's intention being to signal how a focus on different kinds of formal limitation—broadly and in my terms, those instances when the process of formalization meets a limit that, when viewed from a certain angle, is appreciable as its constitutive ground—may give us access to a form of ontological truth. For my purposes, however, it is Livingston's innovative insistence that a focus on the symbolic, on what Lacan called the "logic of the signifier," far from foreclosing questions of reference and reality, is in fact a prerequisite for their proper investigation. The same holds true, I've been arguing, in the register of literary theory: it is by no means a concession to linguistic insularity to insist on the paradoxes and stumbling blocks of literary language at the level of the line. To the contrary, it is only by cleaving to those phenomena that a true understanding of literary reference—nonmimetic, historical but not historicist—may come to light.

A mode of totality that presupposes the possibility of an absolute whole, or in the terms worked out here a process of formalization that takes no account of its necessary internal limits, of those points in a literary structure where an initial ambition to capture the real fails, is for Livingston "onto-theological"; it is, that is to say, essentially theological in its provenance. To hold to such a vision of totality, one complete in and of itself, has political effects. As Livingston writes, such a structure when transferred to an analysis of the social projects "an ethical-social communal form of life that, in the limit, ensures the smooth possibility of the mutual recognition of any subject . . . by any other."[28] It is not difficult to see such a notion reproduced even in the cautious accounts of world literature advanced by Damrosch and others, the latter threatening, according to Apter, "the entrepreneurial, bulimic drive to anthologize and curriculize the world's cultural resources."[29]

Such a construction of the world would resemble what Livingston refers to as an easy recognizability between every and any agent, one that would deny the irreducible remainders that refuse to be assimilated to such a picture of totality. In the terms of this book, such a process is akin to the assumption of an easy commutability or translatability between the signs that populate a literary text and the putative objects of that text, one that Ponge tarried with only to reject with particular power. Ponge, recall, sets up an initial, symmetrical commutability between literary language and its objects, only to find in the failure of that connection a different, more dynamic kind of literary reference. To retranslate this insight into the terms proffered by Livingston, it is only through the requisite gaps of incompletion that attend any attempt at totality, any attempt to think the global, or indeed at a more local level to think the conscription by a literary text of its worlds, that the truth of those various forms might be glimpsed. Such a truth would be one cognizant of all those mooted ends to truth, to metanarrative, to metalanguage, while insisting that another kind of truth is possible, one that evades the persistent dichotomy between a thoroughgoing relativism on the one hand, and a smooth and untroubled positivism on the other. Those in literary studies may recognize the latter positivism as at least threatened by aspects of the "digital humanities" explored in detail in chapter 1. The relativism may be located as much in the New Historicist attachment to the particular anecdote as an antidote to what, in the latter critical school, are often thought of as insufficiently historical and generalizing theoretical claims, as much as it could be spotted in those second- and third-generation deconstructive critics who sometimes saw fit to overemphasize a text's dissolution at the expense of its paradoxical persistence.

Where Paul de Man's reading of "Correspondances" as analyzed in chapter 4 finds in contradiction or incompletion the absolute failure of the poem's tropic structure, Livingston's proposition of a "strong critique" would instead find a condition of possibility in such moments of seeming impasse. Strong critique would seek "the structure of limit-paradoxes in order to meet the contradictions characteristic of a situation on the level of their real underlying structure."[30] By pushing processes of formalization to their inner limits—Livingston's examples include Gödel's incompleteness theorems and Russell's paradox—one finds reflexive points that, far from being merely extraneous to the structure in question, are in fact the "truth" of that structure. One may then, at what

Livingston refers to as a "metaformal" level, extract consequences for thinking political novelty. As he affirms, "What is crucial is . . . to allow thought, while maintaining its own specific integrity, the unrecognizable as the site of a life to come."[31] Those reflexive points of impasse within all formal systems, and I would include literary structures among them, can, when viewed in a certain light, point beyond themselves to forms of life otherwise unimaginable when paradox and impasse are consigned merely to the category of error.

I wonder, though, whether the end point of Livingston's analysis—the affirmation of thought as itself able to affirm what initially appear to be unbridgeable gaps in structure—makes too much of a virtue of indeterminacy, to say nothing of cognition, and presumably philosophy itself. While the detail with which Livingston engages the results of mathematics and logic sets his work significantly apart from deconstruction per se, there is nonetheless a little of the late Derrida's insistence on a politics "to come"[32] in the notion of a "site" where a new life is—again—"to come." One impatiently wishes to know what such a life and such a politics might look like. Equally, I would question whether the unrecognizable and unexpected are, always and as such, to be welcomed; as Peter Osborne comments on the contemporary, global "horizon of expectations" in the wake of 9/11, "by rendering the 'form of the world' *less* determinate, it heightened expectations of the unexpected."[33] Such an expected unexpectedness has been on the whole, and needless to say, less than liberatory.

This book, at any rate, has argued, via a comparable attention to gaps and failures across a broad swath of literary sources, that concrete instances of nonmimetic connection between literary language and its objects, between poetic innovation and historical potentiality, are locatable when literary form is recognized as possessing its own speculative capacity to partially bend and refigure its various determinants. Think once more of Wallace Stevens's "metaphysical streets" in his "An Ordinary Evening in New Haven" as discussed in chapter 3, the ordinary and the extraordinary forced to occupy the same plane in a feat of poetic speculation nonetheless grounded by its dissonant formality; or consider anew Ponge's formalization of his orange, the very failure of its initial mimetic capture producing a shared resonance around the act of speaking the object's name, the effort by the body to metabolize that object, and the internal dehiscences of the object itself. These acts of novelty are not idealistically produced in a vacuum—my concern is very far from any romantic investment in literary genius—but are generated, rather, through the ongoing ways in which literature must fold into, and refold anew, its ambiguously posed outsides.

It may well be that Livingston's invigorating emphasis on the necessity of totalization—in my terms, the internal necessity for form to engage in an ongoing formalization of itself and its objects, generating the speculative productivity just mentioned—may be reposed as an alternative figure for the global, one that takes inconsistency and incompletion as its condition. But I would wish to darken the perspective thus obtained by taking heed, too, of Peter Osborne's skepticism about the potential of any global "horizon" to truly offer an alternative to the reifications of the contemporary also discussed above: "We will not reclaim a future qualitatively different from the present by reinvesting in the idea of horizon."[34] At the least, however, a multitiered comparative attention to the formal incommensurabilities produced by capital's relentless drive outward and onward may prove the next step in the development of a speculative formalist approach to literature, the initial outline of which it has been my task to draw in this book.

Notes

Introduction

1. For an accessible account of Gödel's theorems, see the entry in the online Stanford Encyclopedia of Philosophy: http://plato.stanford.edu/entries/goedel-incompleteness/, accessed January 2, 2015; Russell's paradox is explained in equally enlightening terms in the same forum: http://plato.stanford.edu/entries/russell-paradox/, accessed January 2, 2015.

2. F. Jameson, *The Prison-House of Language: A Critical Account of Structuralism and Russian Formalism* (Princeton, N.J.: Princeton University Press, 1972).

3. The best account of Derrida's relations to formal and logical paradoxes is to be found in P. Livingston, "Derrida and Formal Logic: Formalising the Undecidable," *Derrida Today* 3.2 (November 2010), 221–39.

4. J. Lacan, *The Seminar of Jacques Lacan, Book 20: Encore*, trans. Bruce Fink (New York: W. W. Norton, 1999), 93.

5. See I. Kant, *Critique of Pure Reason*, trans. Paul Guyer and Allen W. Wood (Cambridge: Cambridge University Press, 1999), 459–524.

6. A most impressive reading of the productivity of formal impasses, one that is as knowledgeable about formal results in mathematical logic as it is about the comparably formalist strategies of the likes of Derrida and Badiou, can be found in P. Livingston, *The Politics of Logic: Badiou, Wittgenstein and the Consequences of Formalism* (New York: Routledge, 2011). Even as Livingston's work has thus far been silent on the question of literary form, my own understanding of form and formalism more generally has benefited immeasurably from his pioneering work.

7. "What we call ideology is precisely the confusion of linguistic with natural reality, of reference with phenomenalism." P. de Man, *The Resistance to Theory* (Minneapolis: University of Minnesota Press, 1986), 11.

8. One thinks, in particular, of the very different writings of Walter Benn Michaels, Jürgen Habermas, and Christopher Ricks, although numerous lesser opponents of theory, especially in its deconstructive guise, could be mentioned. See W. B. Michaels, *The Shape of the Signifier: 1967 to the End of History* (Princeton, N.J.: Princeton University Press, 2006); J. Habermas, *The Philosophical Discourse of Modernity: Twelve Lectures* (Cambridge, Mass.: MIT Press, 1990); and C. Ricks, "In Theory," *London Review of Books* 3.6 (April 16, 1981), 3–6. A useful compendium of writing skeptical of theory's effect on the humanities is D. Patai and W. Corral,

eds., *Theory's Empire: An Anthology of Dissent* (New York: Columbia University Press, 2005).

9. Tom Cohen has been an especially thoughtful critic of culturalism along these lines: "It at times seems that the (re)turn into *representationalism* has involved a larger form of cultural hegemony, an aesthetic regime based on the prevalence of a certain trope, mimesis, that, when identified with 'the political,' displays an often suspect complicity (and even ahistoricity) of its own" (T. Cohen, *Anti-Mimesis: From Plato to Hitchcock* [Cambridge: Cambridge University Press, 1994], 2–3). Cohen's stringent critique of neo-mimetic understandings of aesthetic form are well taken, although I demur somewhat from his wholesale rejection of the language of culture.

10. One of the most impressive critics of the cultural or "identitarian" turn in literary studies, one who nonetheless unconvincingly expands such a critique to the very different tenets of the "high" theory of structuralism and deconstruction, is Walter Benn Michaels. See in particular Michaels, *The Shape of the Signifier.*

11. A representative example is to be found in A. Bloom, *The Closing of the American Mind: How Higher Education Has Failed Democracy and Impoverished the Souls of Today's Students* (New York: Simon and Schuster, 1987).

12. When insisting on the fidelity of Derrida and deconstruction more generally to a model of truth, albeit one set apart from "correspondence" or bivalent models, I have a formidable comrade in Christopher Norris. More than anyone, Norris has defended the pluralist but nonetheless rational link made in Derrida's texts between the apparent impasses that are found when certain linguistic or logical traits are pushed to their limits, and the truthfulness of such impasses, the necessity of the registration of their import if one is to attain an accurate sense of how language and knowledge work. In some of his more recent books, however, Norris risks rhetorically inflating philosophy itself into a kind of master discourse, one that might correct the idle misapprehension of Derrida's work that plays out in "postmodern" literary or cultural studies. While it's no doubt true that conservative critics of Derrida have lazily painted him into a relativist corner, it is vanishingly rare to encounter such a crude portrayal in literary-theoretical appropriations of Derrida and deconstruction. And philosophy, far from being the site of reason that might deliver Derrida from his misinterpretation, has in fact been the almost exclusive province of his denigration and trashing.

13. R. Wellek and A. Warren, *Theory of Literature* (Orlando: Harcourt, 1956), 28.

14. A special edition of *Representations* titled "Surface Reading," edited by Stephen Best and Sharon Marcus, pursued this line of argument. See *Representations* 108.1 (Fall 2009).

15. Repetition, I would wager, recognized as crucial to literary form especially since the work of Roman Jakobson, is not quite the same thing as "refrain." Refrain in lyric poetry tends to denote a repeated phrase, often at the end of the stanza, one that provides the poem with a semantic and vocal center. The repetition that will concern us is, more often, disruptive of such centers, for all the other positive effects repetition will be shown to produce.

16. D. Tiffany, "Cheap Signaling: Class Conflict and Diction in Avant-Garde Poetry," *Boston Review*, July 15, 2014, http://bostonreview.net/poetry/daniel-tiffany-cheap-signaling-class-conflict-and-diction-avant-garde-poetry.

17. J. Culler, *Theory of the Lyric* (Cambridge, Mass.: Harvard University Press, 2015), 8.

18. A.-L. François, *Open Secrets: The Literature of Uncounted Experience* (Stanford: Stanford University Press, 2008), 143.

19. F. Jameson, *The Antinomies of Realism* (London: Verso, 2013), 292.

20. F. Jameson, *Postmodernism, or, The Cultural Logic of Late Capitalism* (London: Verso, 1992).

21. This argument is made intermittently in the impressive P. E. Wegner, *Periodizing Jameson: Dialectics, the University, and the Desire for Narrative* (Evanston, Ill.: Northwestern University Press, 2014).

22. S. Best and S. Marcus, "Surface Reading: An Introduction," *Representations* 108.1 (Fall 2009), 1–21.

23. The slogan originates, of course, with Paul Ricoeur. See P. Ricoeur, *Freud and Philosophy: An Essay on Interpretation*, trans. Denis Savage (New Haven, Conn.: Yale University Press, 1977).

24. See Sprinker's bracing *Imaginary Relations: Aesthetics and Ideology in the Theory of Historical Materialism* (London: Verso, 1987), and W. Montag, *Louis Althusser* (New York: Palgrave Macmillan, 2003).

25. The best reading of Spinoza's materialist practice of scriptural reading is to be found in W. Montag, *Bodies, Masses, Power: Spinoza and His Contemporaries* (London: Verso, 1999).

26. J. Hillis Miller, *Theory Now and Then* (Durham, N.C.: Duke University Press, 1991), 126.

27. Best and Marcus, "Surface Reading," 5.

28. P. Macherey, *A Theory of Literary Production*, trans. Geoffrey Wall (London: Routledge, 1978), 98.

29. Ibid.

30. Best and Marcus, "Surface Reading," 1.

31. I outline Lacan's opposition to this notion at length in my *Lacan and the Concept of the "Real"* (New York: Palgrave Macmillan, 2012). Lacan is especially insistent on this new formulation of the unconscious as a kind of extended, topologically complex surface in his eleventh seminar: J. Lacan, *The Seminar of Jacques Lacan, Book 11: The Four Fundamental Concepts of Psychoanalysis* (1964–65; reprint, New York: W. W. Norton, 1988).

32. Carlo Ginzburg quoted in Best and Marcus, "Surface Reading," 4. For the original, see C. Ginzburg, "Clues: Roots of an Evidential Paradigm," in *Clues, Myths, and the Historical Method*, trans. John and Anne C. Tedeschi (Baltimore: Johns Hopkins University Press, 1992), 101. On the same page of their article, Best and Marcus mistakenly attribute to Ginzburg what is in fact a quotation from Freud; Ginzburg presses the quote into the service of his broader characterization of psychoanalysis as a depth hermeneutic.

33. C. Schmitt, "Tidal Conrad (Literally)," *Victorian Studies* 55.1 (Autumn 2012), 7–29.

34. Ibid., 9.

35. Ibid., 15.

36. J. Conrad, *Heart of Darkness,* ed. Owen Knowles (London: Penguin, 2007), 3.

37. Schmitt, "Tidal Conrad (Literally)," 22.

38. J. Conrad quoted ibid., 22–23.

39. Ibid., 23.

40. The key exploration of the promise and fragility of the denotation/connotation doublet remains Barthes's *S/Z.* See R. Barthes, *S/Z: An Essay,* trans. Richard Miller (New York: Hill and Wang, 1974).

41. One is reminded here of Susan Howe's pioneering work on the eloquent, constitutive silences in the drafts and manuscripts that make up the archive of Emily Dickinson's work. See S. Howe, *The Birth-mark* (Hanover, N.H.: Wesleyan University Press, 1993). Howe, of course, is also known for her own "language" poetry, a movement considered in depth in the final chapter.

42. S. Mallarmé, "L'après-midi d'un faune," in *Collected Poems and Other Verse,* trans. E. H. and A. M. Blackmore (Oxford: Oxford University Press, 2006), 38–41.

43. S. Mallarmé, "Sur l'évolution littéraire [Enquête de Jules Huret]," in *Œuvres complètes ii,* ed. B. Marchel, Bibliothèque de la Pléiade (Paris: Gallimard, 2003), 698; translation taken from Mallarmé, *Collected Poems and Other Verse,* xiii.

44. In this connection, I am unsure of Jameson's assessment of Mallarmé, as when the former writes: "So strong is the power of the sentence that we fail to notice the heterogeneity of its contents or the arbitrariness with which they are placed in relationship" (F. Jameson, "Mallarmé Materialist," in *The Modernist Papers* [London: Verso, 2007], 327). This reads like a good enough summary of sentences in general, but the paratextual interruptions of Mallarmé's verse that Jameson himself acknowledges are enough to question the very pertinence of a syntactical category such as the "sentence," the latter bespeaking a structural predictability that Mallarmé's tremblingly anxious poetry tends to preclude. One might better identify the sentence as one of those ghosts of convention that haunt Mallarmé's verse as it slowly loosens itself from prior poetical regularities, such ghosts nonetheless being crucial to the sense of creative freedom that his texts evoke.

45. C. Baudelaire, "Intoxication," in *The Poems and Prose Poems of Charles Baudelaire,* ed. James Huneker (New York: Brentano's, 1919), 96.

46. Best and Marcus, "Surface Reading," 9.

47. Macherey, *A Theory of Literary Production,* 99.

48. Ibid., 18.

49. Best and Marcus, "Surface Reading."

50. H. Marcuse, *Eros and Civilization: A Philosophical Inquiry into Freud* (Boston: Beacon, 1974), 180.

51. Jameson, *The Antinomies of Realism,* 176.

52. W. Faulkner, *Collected Stories* (New York: Random House, 1950), 647. And see, again, Jameson's discussion in *The Antinomies of Realism,* 176.

53. Here I should note an echo with Martin Hägglund's exemplary analysis

of the logic of temporality in deconstruction. See his *Radical Atheism: Derrida and the Time of Life* (Stanford: Stanford University Press, 2008).

54. See the useful discussion of Schiller's notion of "presentification" in K. Hamburger, *The Logic of Literature* (Evanston, Ill.: Northwestern University Press, 1979), 97–98. I owe this reference to Fredric Jameson's discussion of Hamburger in his *The Antinomies of Realism*, 166–68. For an indispensable presentation of the relationship between Schiller's aesthetic and moral concerns, see T. Eagleton, "Schiller and Hegemony," in *The Ideology of the Aesthetic* (Oxford: Blackwell, 1990), 102–20.

55. R. Barthes, "The Death of the Author," in *Image-Music-Text*, trans. Stephen Heath (New York: Hill and Wang, 1977), 145.

56. C. Levine, *Forms: Whole, Rhythm, Hierarchy, Network* (Princeton, N.J.: Princeton University Press, 2015), 1.

57. Ibid.

58. Ibid., 2.

59. Ibid.

60. Ibid.

61. Ibid.

62. Ibid., 6.

63. Ibid., 16.

64. B. Latour, "Why Has Critique Run out of Steam? From Matters of Fact to Matters of Concern," *Critical Inquiry* 30 (Winter 2004), 225–48.

65. Best and Marcus, "Surface Reading."

66. Levine, *Forms*, 17.

67. Ibid., 18.

68. See in particular the special edition of *Criticism* devoted to *The Wire*. *Criticism* 52.3–4 (Summer/Fall 2010).

69. Levine, *Forms*, 132.

70. Ibid., 134.

71. Ibid., 137.

72. Ibid., 133.

73. This is partly the argument of Carolyn Lesjak's bracing article "Reading Dialectically," engaging earlier article-length treatments of form by Levine. A more sustained attention to Lesjak's argument in this subsequent book would, I think, have been helpful, although one imagines that the appearance of Lesjak's argument only two years ago set practical limits to Levine's engagement here. Nonetheless, Lesjak does receive passing mention. See C. Lesjak, "Reading Dialectically," *Criticism* 55.2 (2013), Article 3, and Levine, *Forms*, 18.

74. Levine, *Forms*, 114.

75. P. de Man, *Blindness and Insight: Essays in the Rhetoric of Contemporary Criticism* (Minneapolis: University of Minnesota Press, 1983).

76. The most accomplished genre analysis to date, one referenced briefly if largely negatively by Levine, is F. Jameson, "Realism and Utopia in *The Wire*," *Criticism* 52.4 (2010), 359–72.

77. F. Moretti, "The Slaughterhouse of Literature," *Modern Language Quarterly* 61.1 (March 2000), 208.

78. The founding document of this approach is surely S. Greenblatt, "Towards a Poetics of Culture," *Southern Review* 20.1 (March 1987), a text I address in chapter 1.

79. A. Pope, "An Essay on Criticism," in *The Major Works*, ed. Pat Rogers (Oxford: Oxford University Press, 2009), 35.

80. The terms originate in the work of Viktor Shklovsky. See V. Shklovsky, *Theory of Prose*, trans. Benjamin Sher (Normal, Ill.: Dalkey Archive, 1991).

81. S. Critchley, *Things Merely Are: Philosophy in the Poetry of Wallace Stevens* (New York: Routledge, 2005), 5.

82. But for excellent exceptions, see Andrzej Warminski's editor's introduction to de Man's *Aesthetic Ideology* (Minneapolis: University of Minnesota Press, 1996), 1–34, and J. Loesberg, "Materialism and Aesthetics: Paul de Man's Aesthetic Ideology," *Diacritics* 27.4 (Winter 1997), 87–108.

83. Jameson describes storytelling, with striking certitude, as "the supreme function of the human mind" (*The Political Unconscious: Narrative as a Socially Symbolic Act* [Ithaca, N.Y.: Cornell University Press, 1981], 123).

Chapter 1

1. Data taken from the website Sample Reality, available here: http://www.samplereality.com/2012/10/17/digital-humanities-at-mla-2013/, accessed May 17, 2013.

2. Private companies, including Google, are increasingly the source of funding for digital projects. For Google's spin on the digital humanities and their importance, see http://googleblog.blogspot.com/2010/07/our-commitment-to-digital-humanities.html. It is hard to imagine Google funding an inquiry into the politics and anti-aesthetics of the language poets, although stranger things have transpired . . .

3. A characterization parodied by Stanley Fish when he wrote of "[this] new insurgency . . . What rough beast has slouched into the neighborhood threatening to upset everyone's applecart?" ("The Old Order Changeth," *New York Times*, December 26, 2011, http://opinionator.blogs.nytimes.com/2011/12/26/the-old-order-changeth/).

4. The previously cited website Sample Reality has a useful list of topics and paper titles given at Digital Humanities–related panels at the MLA convention in the last few years, available at the URL in note 1. For a useful glossary of the often intimidating jargon used in digital humanities circles (jargon no less recondite than that associated with prior movements in critical theory), put together by THATcamp of New England, see https://docs.google.com/document/d/129_260mbp6C6JaqmylmhMTXA1sv7YYQ0OLsAOAOoCJE/edit?pli=1.

5. S. Zeki, "Art and the Brain," *Daedalus* 127.2 (1998), 71.

6. See http://www.crassh.cam.ac.uk/page/276/digital-humanities.htm.

7. J. Gottschall, *Literature, Science, and a New Humanities* (New York: Palgrave Macmillan, 2008). Gottschall's book outlines an extreme defense of the

new literary positivism, advocating for literary studies to adopt wholesale a deductive empiricism conditioned exclusively by the experimental sciences.

8. See L. Althusser, "On the Materialist Dialectic," in *For Marx*, trans. Ben Brewster (1965; reprint, London: Verso, 2010), 161–219.

9. Stephen Marche neatly summarizes this take, writing, "Literature cannot meaningfully be treated as data. The problem is essential rather than superficial: literature is not data. Literature is the opposite of data." S. Marche, "Literature Is Not Data: Against the Digital Humanities," *Los Angeles Review of Books*, October 28, 2012, http://lareviewofbooks.org/article.php?id=1040. Representative of this general retrenchment of literary humanism, albeit without a focus on the digital humanities, is C. White, *The Science Delusion: Asking the Big Questions in a Culture of Easy Answers* (New York: Melville House, 2013).

10. Chun's contribution to the panel "The Dark Side of the Digital Humanities," conducted at the 2013 MLA convention in Boston, is available in text form here: http://www.c21uwm.com/2013/01/09/the-dark-side-of-the-digital-humanities-part-1/.

11. S. Ramsay, *Reading Machines: Toward an Algorithmic Criticism* (Champaign: University of Illinois Press, 2011). Ramsay's excellent book will serve as my foil in the latter third of this chapter.

12. There are numerous such careless if eminently marketable polemics, but for a representative example see A. Sokal, *Beyond the Hoax: Science, Philosophy and Culture* (New York: Oxford University Press, 2010); D. Lehman, *Signs of the Times: Deconstruction and the Fall of Paul de Man* (New York: Poseidon, 1991).

13. For all the institutional and political problems that its subjects faced, Rolf Wiggershaus's comprehensive and transcontinental history of the Frankfurt School could serve as an example here. See R. Wiggershaus, *The Frankfurt School: Its History, Theories, and Political Significance*, trans. Michael Robertson (Cambridge, Mass.: MIT Press, 1995). More recently, one might consult Benoit Peeters's biography of Jacques Derrida, where even the objectionable insiderism and elitism of postwar French academia wasn't enough to stop the emergence of a truly distinctive and radical theory with genuine interdisciplinary power. See B. Peeters, *Derrida: A Biography*, trans. Andrew Brown (Cambridge: Polity, 2012). The contemporary university seems increasingly hostile to such speculative and ambitious thinking.

14. For the contemporary U.K. context, see the superb A. McGettigan, *The Great University Gamble: Money, Markets and the Future of Higher Education* (London: Pluto, 2013). For the United States, see, among a slew of excellent articles and books, S. Slaughter and G. Rhoades, *Academic Capitalism and the New Economy: Markets, State, and Higher Education* (Baltimore: Johns Hopkins University Press, 2009); D. Bok, *Universities in the Marketplace: The Commercialization of Higher Education* (Princeton, N.J.: Princeton University Press, 2004); B. Ginsberg, *The Fall of the Faculty: The Rise of the All-Administrative University and Why It Matters* (New York: Oxford University Press, 2011); M. Miyoshi, "Ivory Tower in Escrow," *boundary 2*, 2.27 (Spring 2000). Miyoshi is especially caustic about the silence of critical theorists in the face of the corporatization of the university.

15. F. Moretti, *Signs Taken for Wonders* (London: Verso, 1988).

16. For a good cross-section of responses, the more critical of which often come close to Prendergast's analysis, see J. Goodwin and J. Holbo, eds., *Reading Graphs, Maps, and Trees: Responses to Franco Moretti* (Anderson, S.C.: Parlor, 2011).

17. C. Prendergast, "Evolution and Literary History: A Response to Franco Moretti," *New Left Review* 34 (July/August 2005), 49. Prendergast has recently resumed his critical analysis of Moretti in the form of a review essay on the latter's recent books *The Bourgeois* and *Distant Reading*. See C. Prendergast, "Across the Between," *New Left Review* 86 (March/April 2014), 151–58.

18. F. Moretti, "Graphs, Maps, Trees: Abstract Models for Literary History 3," *New Left Review* 28 (July/August 2004), 48, hereafter shortened to "GMT3." The first essay was published in *New Left Review* 24 (November/December 2003), 67–93 (hereafter "GMT1"); the second is to be found in *New Left Review* 26 (March/April 2004), 79–103 (hereafter "GMT2").

19. GMT3, 48.

20. F. Moretti, "The End of the Beginning: A Reply to Christopher Prendergast," *New Left Review* 41 (September/October 2006), 75.

21. GMT3, 62.

22. A more consequential reframing of the problem of "World Literature" is to be found in E. Apter, *Against World Literature: On the Politics of Untranslatability* (New York: Verso, 2013). I'll discuss Apter's arguments further in the conclusion.

23. GMT3, 60.

24. GMT3, 59–60.

25. GMT3, 62.

26. For an excellent account of the kinds of singularity that literary language can generate, see D. Attridge, *The Singularity of Literature* (New York: Routledge, 2004).

27. GMT3, 62.

28. F. Moretti, "The Slaughterhouse of Literature," *Modern Language Quarterly* 61.1 (March 2000), 208.

29. F. Moretti, "More Conjectures," *New Left Review* 20 (March/April 2003), 81.

30. There are some pungent remarks on the links between formalism, organicism, and the *politesse* of antitheoretical literary-critical eclecticism in T. Eagleton, "Liberality and Order: The Criticism of John Bayley," *New Left Review* 1.110 (July/August 1978), 29–40.

31. This is, by necessity, one of the moments in this chapter where I will be unable to account for the internal heterogeneity of what comes under an indifferently general theoretical label, if "theoretical" is even the right term. On the latter score, Jameson is right, I think, when he calls New Historicism less a theory or set of theories and more a "shared writing practice" (F. Jameson, *Postmodernism, or, The Cultural Logic of Late Capitalism* [London: Verso, 1992], 184). For an insightful essay on the movement that usefully distinguishes between American and British instantiations, see C. Prendergast, "Circulating Representations: New Historicism and the Poetics of Culture," *SubStance* 28.1 (1999), 90–104.

32. Greenblatt, "Towards a Poetics of Culture," 3.

33. Ibid., 5.

34. See, especially, F. Jameson, *The Political Unconscious: Narrative as a Socially Symbolic Act* (Ithaca, N.Y.: Cornell University Press, 1981).

35. Jameson, *Postmodernism,* 188.

36. LaCapra quoted in M. Jay, "Historical Explanation and the Event: Reflections on the Limits of Contextualization," *New Literary History* 42.4 (Autumn 2011), 560.

37. GMT2, 94.

38. F. Moretti, "'Operationalizing': or, The Function of Measurement in Modern Literary Theory," *New Left Review* 84 (November/December 2013), 108.

39. Ibid., 107.

40. Ibid., 108.

41. See especially H. White, *Metahistory: The Historical Imagination in Nineteenth Century Europe* (Baltimore: Johns Hopkins University Press, 1975). More recently, see H. White, *The Practical Past,* ed. Ed Dimendberg (Evanston, Ill.: Northwestern University Press, 2014).

42. An especially sophisticated example of this trend can be found in J.-M. Rabaté, *1913: The Cradle of Modernism* (Oxford: Wiley-Blackwell, 2007).

43. GMT3, 56.

44. GMT1, 82.

45. F. Moretti, *Graphs, Maps, Trees: Abstract Models for Literary History* (London: Verso, 2005), 2.

46. GMT3, 50.

47. GMT1, 76.

48. M. Cooke, "Mediterranean Thinking: From Netizen to Medizen," *Geographical Review* 89.2 (April 1999), 292.

49. Jacques Rancière, in a recent interview, has argued that one is more likely to access the multiple scales and temporalities that Moretti seeks in his broad-scale quantitative approach through the rigorous close-reading of a short passage of text; while a defense of close-reading per se isn't my intention here, Rancière's comments are worth quoting at some length: "I like the method that first shows the thing and ask what constitutes its specificity and what makes that specificity possible and thinkable. This is a way of foiling the opposition . . . between the 'close reading' of the 'canonical' text, qua practice of the aesthete, and the politically correct view that privileges the circulation of themes in the multiplicity of works addressed to the multitude. I continue to think that the attentive reading of a page of a Balzac—but also of a letter by the joiner Gauny—can tell us more about society and the relations of the novel with society than Franco Moretti's maps" (J. Rancière and Oliver Davis, "On *Aisthesis*—An Interview," in *Rancière Now,* ed. Oliver Davis [Cambridge: Polity, 2013], 204–5). This may be the place to comment on the glaring irony that, in the current critical climate, it is precisely those most associated with "high theory"—Rancière, after all, being an ex-collaborator with Louis Althusser and an extraordinarily ambitious theorist in his own right—that are "conservatively" defending close reading. We're bearing witness to a strange changing of the guard, where the digital practitioners are, in their very adherence to pretheoretical tenets, somehow

positioned as the avant-garde ranged against the theory holdouts (this author included), whose apparent commitment to a close literary analysis risks seeming old hat, at least so long as the claims of novelty from the New Positivists are taken at face value.

50. GMT1, 16.

51. Prendergast, "Evolution and Literary History."

52. Prendergast, "Circulating Representations," 94.

53. E. Apter, "Global *Translatio*: The 'Invention' of Comparative Literature," *Critical Inquiry* 29.2 (Winter 2003), 256.

54. Gottschall, *Literature, Science, and a New Humanities*, 12.

55. L. Althusser and É. Balibar, *Reading Capital*, trans. Ben Brewster (London: New Left Books, 1970), 43.

56. Ibid.

57. G. Bachelard quoted in D. Lecourt, *Marxism and Epistemology: Bachelard, Canguilhem and Foucault*, trans. Ben Brewster (London: New Left Books, 1975), 52.

58. See my *Post-Rationalism: Psychoanalysis, Epistemology and Marxism in Post-war France* (London: Bloomsbury, 2013).

59. C. Colebrook, introduction to C. Colebrook, T. Cohen, and J. Hillis-Miller, *Theory and the Disappearing Future: On de Man, on Benjamin* (New York: Routledge, 2012), 16.

60. S. Greenblatt, "Towards a Poetics of Culture," *Southern Review* 20.1 (March 1987), 7.

61. G. Bachelard, *Le rationalisme appliqué* (Paris: PUF, 2004), 56; translation taken from P. Maniglier, "What Is a Problematic?," *Radical Philosophy* 173 (May/June 2012), 22.

62. J. Ramazani, *Transnational Poetics* (Chicago: University of Chicago Press, 2009).

63. Ramsay, *Reading Machines.*

64. L. Samuels and J. McGann, "Deformance and Interpretation," *New Literary History* 30.1 (Winter 1999), 37.

65. Ramsay, *Reading Machines*, 16.

66. Ibid., 2.

67. Ibid., 10.

68. Ibid.

69. Ibid., 16.

70. Ibid.

71. Ibid., 3.

72. Ibid., 16.

73. Ibid.

74. G. Bachelard, *Earth and Reveries of Will*, trans. K. Haltman (Dallas: Dallas Institute, 2002), 39.

75. For an insightful feminist analysis of the novel, one among many, see J. Goldman, *The Feminist Aesthetics of Virginia Woolf: Modernism, Post-Impressionism, and the Politics of the Visual* (Cambridge: Cambridge University Press, 1998), 186–207. See also N. Black, *Virginia Woolf as Feminist* (Ithaca, N.Y.: Cornell University Press, 2003).

76. S. Ramsay, *Reading Machines*, 13.

77. See Rapaport's comments on the eclipse of theory here: http://users.wfu.edu/rapapoh/TheoryBlog-2.html.

78. V. Shklovsky, *Theory of Prose*, trans. Benjamin Sher (Normal, Ill.: Dalkey Archive, 1991), 22.

79. Ibid.

80. P. Osborne, *Anywhere or Not at All: Philosophy of Contemporary Art* (London: Verso, 2013), 34.

81. Ibid., 35.

Chapter 2

1. See G. Harman, *Towards Speculative Realism: Essays and Lectures* (London: Zero Books, 2010). Object-oriented ontology is one branch of so-called "speculative realism," a variant that places particular emphasis on the autonomy of objects from human apprehension or capture.

2. P. Hallward, "Anything Is Possible: A Reading of Quentin Meillassoux's 'After Finitude,'" in *The Speculative Turn: Continental Materialism and Realism*, ed. L. Bryant, N. Srnicek, and G. Harman (Victoria: Re.press, 2011), 130–42.

3. Bryant works out many of his ideas on his dynamic blog; see http://larvalsubjects.wordpress.com. See also his *Democracy of Objects* (Ann Arbor: Open Humanities, 2011).

4. Badiou tempts such a criticism, most recently in his self-consciously Platonic reconstruction of communism as an invariant Idea; see his *The Communist Hypothesis* (London: Verso, 2010). The most perspicacious criticism along these lines has come from Peter Hallward. See P. Hallward, "Order and Event," *New Left Review* 53 (September–October 2008), 97–122.

5. A. Badiou, *Theory of the Subject*, trans. Bruno Bosteels (London: Continuum, 2010), 188.

6. J. D. Lyons and S. G. Nichols Jr., eds., *Mimesis: From Mirror to Method, Augustine to Descartes* (Hanover, N.H.: University Press of New England, 1982), 1. See also the discussion in S. Derwin, *The Ambivalence of Form: Lukács, Freud, and the Novel* (Baltimore: Johns Hopkins University Press, 1992), 4, 7–34.

7. The notion of a "flat ontology," where every ontological actor is granted the same agental capacity as any other, comes to Bryant from the French anthropologist Bruno Latour, whose work always threatens to lapse into a kind of sophisticated descriptionism, the tracing of networks between "actants" whose equality and access to power is assumed in advance. For a convincing critique of Latour's flat ontology along these lines, see B. Noys, *The Persistence of the Negative: A Critique of Contemporary Continental Theory* (Edinburgh: Edinburgh University Press, 2010), 80–106.

8. J. Lacan, "Overture to This Collection," in *Écrits*, trans. Bruce Fink (New York: W. W. Norton, 2006), 4. Dany Nobus's discussion of this quote from Lacan is unequaled in its clarity. See D. Nobus, "That Obscure Object of Psychoanalysis," *Continental Philosophy Review* 46.2 (August 2013), 183–84.

9. At the time of the completion of this book, the beginnings of a renaissance of interest in Cavaillès's crucial writings could be detected, heralded in particular by the publication of Knox Peden's book *Spinoza contra Phenomenology: French Rationalism from Cavaillès to Deleuze* (Stanford: Stanford University Press, 2014). See, in particular, "From Consciousness to the Concept: The Spinozism of Jean Cavaillès" (pp. 17–65).

10. See P. Sollers and F. Ponge, *Entretiens de Francis Ponge avec Philippe Sollers* (Paris: Éditions du Seuil, 1970). See also Barbara Johnson's discussion in *Persons and Things* (Cambridge, Mass.: Harvard University Press, 2008), 32; the translation used here is taken from Johnson's extraordinary book.

11. F. Ponge, "The Oyster," translation taken from Johnson, *Persons and Things*, 31.

12. Ibid., 27–34.

13. P. de Man, *Allegories of Reading* (New Haven, Conn.: Yale University Press, 1979), 178.

14. G. Lukács, *The Theory of the Novel*, trans. Anna Bostock (Boston: MIT Press, 1971), 112.

15. See, in particular, Benjamin's powerful essay "On Language as Such and on the Languages of Man," in *Selected Writings Volume 1, 1913–1926*, ed. Marcus Bullock and Michael W. Jennings (Cambridge, Mass.: Belknap Press, 1996), 62–74.

16. H. Crane, "A Name for All," in *The Complete Poems of Hart Crane*, ed. Marc Simon (New York: Liveright, 2010), 119.

17. Ibid.

18. Ibid.

19. Ibid.

20. De Man, *Allegories of Reading*, 178.

21. Crane, "A Name for All," 119.

22. In J. Derrida, *Signéponge-Signsponge*, trans. Richard Rand (New York: Columbia University Press, 1984); I'll have cause to discuss Derrida's reading of Ponge later in the chapter.

23. For a recent take that reads the proliferation of smiles in Crane's verse through a queer optic, see M. Snediker, "Hart Crane's Smile," *Modernism/modernity* 12.4 (November 2005), 629–58. The argument is developed in Snediker's *Queer Optimism: Lyric Personhood and Other Felicitous Persuasions* (Minneapolis: University of Minnesota Press, 2008).

24. Ponge, "The Oyster," 31.

25. See the discussion in my *Post-Rationalism: Psychoanalysis, Epistemology and Marxism in Postwar France* (London: Bloomsbury, 2013), 49–81.

26. Derrida, *Signéponge-Signsponge*, 118.

27. W. Benjamin, *The Origin of German Tragic Drama*, trans. J. Osborne (London: Verso, 2003; reprint), 162.

28. See Johnson, *Persons and Things*, 32.

29. I should mention here my debt to Tracy McNulty, who engaged me in a lengthy discussion of Ponge during the drafting of this chapter and whose insights have helped to shape my own reflections.

30. See G. Harman, *Tool Being: Heidegger and the Metaphysics of Objects* (Chicago: Open Court, 2002).

31. J. Rancière, *Mallarmé: The Politics of the Siren*, trans. Steven Corcoran (London: Continuum, 2011).

32. Ibid., 31.

33. S. Mallarmé, *Divagations*, trans. Barbara Johnson (Cambridge, Mass.: Harvard University Press, 2007), 204.

34. B. Johnson, "Poetry and Syntax: What the Gypsy Knew," in *The Barbara Johnson Reader: The Surprise of Otherness*, ed. M. Feuerstein, B. J. González, L. Porten, and K. Valens (Durham, N.C.: Duke University Press, 2014), 30.

35. Q. Meillassoux, *The Number and the Siren: A Decipherment of Mallarmé's "Coup de Des,"* trans. Robin Mackay (Falmouth: Urbanomic, 2012), 41.

36. C. P. Snow, *The Two Cultures and the Scientific Revolution* (Cambridge: Cambridge University Press, 1960); for a highly suggestive analysis of the links and divergences between poetic "intuition" and scientific formalism, the divide that this chapter is, nonetheless, moving to at least partially overcome, see J. Hyppolite, *Logic and Existence*, trans. Leonard Lawlor and Amit Sen (1953; reprint, Albany: SUNY Press, 1997).

37. Recent work by Catherine Malabou and Adrian Johnston goes some way to redress this lack, but they also seem wary of jumping fully into the tangle of epistemological problems that would, for instance, face anyone who would wish to find a neurochemical correlate for the unconscious; the unconscious, far from being a physical entity, is understood by Freud and psychoanalysis more generally as a process, caught between and productive of the unity and separation of language and body, desire and drive. Johnston, it should be noted, is especially alert to the dangers of such reductive temptations. See A. Johnston and C. Malabou, *Self and Emotional Life: Philosophy, Psychoanalysis, and Neuroscience* (New York: Columbia University Press, 2013).

38. For an incomplete but useful reminder of the necessary difficulties, political and otherwise, of international literary translation and dissemination, see E. Apter, *Against World Literature: On the Politics of Untranslatability* (New York: Verso, 2013). I'll discuss Apter's reflections further in the conclusion. For a theoretical reflection on translation that bears new fruit on each subsequent reading, see W. Benjamin, "The Task of the Translator," in *Illuminations*, ed. Hannah Arendt (New York: Harcourt, 1968), 69–83. Finally, for a superbly ambitious attempt to simultaneously stage the problem and propose something of a solution, see B. Cassin, E. Apter, J. Lezra, and M. Wood, eds., *Dictionary of Untranslatables: A Philosophical Lexicon* (Princeton, N.J.: Princeton University Press, 2014).

39. E. Minkowski, "Prose and Poetry (Astronomy and Cosmology)," trans. J. J. Kockelmans, in *Phenomenology and the Natural Sciences: Essays and Translations*, edited by J. J. Kockelmans and T. J. Kisiel (Evanston, Ill.: Northwestern University Press, 1970), 240, 246; originally published in E. Minkowski, *Vers une cosmologie* (Paris: Aubier, 1936), 163–72.

40. J. Cavaillès, *On Logic and the Theory of Science*, trans. T. J. Kisiel, in Kockelmans and Kisiel, *Phenomenology and the Natural Sciences*, 358; originally published

as J. Cavaillès, *Sur la logique et la théorie de la science*, 2nd ed. (Paris: Presses Universitaires de France, 1960).

41. Ibid., 376.

42. Ibid.

43. L. Montrose, "Professing the Renaissance: The Poetics and Politics of Culture," in *The New Historicism*, ed. H. Aram Veeser (New York: Routledge, 1989), 20.

44. S. Felman, "On Reading Poetry," in *The Literary Freud: Mechanisms of Defense and the Poetic Will*, ed. J. Smith (New Haven, Conn.: Yale University Press, 1980), 141.

45. For my own take on Lacan's crucial theories of language, of non-sense and the Real, see my "The 'Signifier-in-Relation,' the 'Signifier-in-Isolation,' and the Concept of the 'Real,'" in "Lacan," special issue, *Parrhesia* 14 (2012), 56–70, http://www.parrhesiajournal.org/parrhesia14/parrhesia14_eyers.pdf.

46. Cavaillès, *On Logic and the Theory of Science*, 374.

47. Ibid., 376.

48. Ibid., 374.

49. W. Stevens, *The Collected Poems* (New York: Alfred A. Knopf, 1971), 76.

50. A. Kojève, *Introduction to the Reading of Hegel: Lectures on the "Phenomenology of Spirit,"* trans. J. H. Nichols, ed. Allan Bloom (Ithaca, N.Y.: Cornell University Press, 1980). For illuminating discussions of Kojève's exponential influence on subsequent currents in French thought, see J. Butler, *Subjects of Desire: Hegelian Reflections in Twentieth Century France* (New York: Columbia University Press, 1999), and M. Poster, *Existential Marxism in Postwar France: From Sartre to Althusser* (Princeton, N.J.: Princeton University Press, 1975).

51. F. Jameson, *The Political Unconscious: Narrative as a Socially Symbolic Act* (Ithaca, N.Y.: Cornell University Press, 1981), 81; see also the discussion in T. Eagleton, *The Event of Literature* (New Haven, Conn.: Yale University Press, 2012), 170–71.

52. Stevens, *The Collected Poems*, 76.

53. F. Lentricchia, *Ariel and the Police: Michel Foucault, William James, and Wallace Stevens* (Madison: University of Wisconsin Press, 1988), 10–11.

54. T. Hughes and Drue Heinz, "The Art of Poetry," *Paris Review* (Spring 1995), http://www.theparisreview.org/interviews/1669/the-art-of-poetry-no-71-ted-hughes.

55. J. Ladrière, "Mathematics in a Philosophy of Science" (1959), trans. T. J. Kisiel, in Kockelmans and Kisiel, *Phenomenology and the Natural Sciences*, 449–50.

56. Ibid., 453.

57. But there is, of course, much more to Heidegger's reading of poetry than merely this. For an exemplary account, see D. N. Smith, *Sounding/Silence: Martin Heidegger at the Limits of Poetics* (New York: Fordham University Press, 2013).

58. Cavaillès, *On Logic and the Theory of Science*, 408.

59. I have taken this translation from an invaluable online repository of translations by Seamus Cooney of Western Michigan University. I prefer Cooney's rendering of the poem to that found in the English print editions available to

date. Cooney's translation is available along with the original French at http://unix.cc.wmich.edu/~cooneys/poems/fr/ponge.orange.html. Further references to "L'orange" in the text above are taken from Cooney's online translation.

60. This being, at least, the reading of Jason R. Rudy, for whom the bodily irruptions of Victorian poetry should be understood as a political symptom as much as an aesthetic contrivance; see his *Electric Meters: Victorian Physiological Poetics* (Athens: Ohio University Press, 2009). I owe this reference to Barbara Barrow.

61. F. Jameson, *The Antinomies of Realism* (London: Verso, 2013), 54.

62. E. Zola, *The Belly of Paris*, trans. Brian Nelson (Oxford: Oxford University Press, 2007), 91; quoted in Jameson, *The Antinomies of Realism*, 54.

63. Jameson, *The Antinomies of Realism*, 54.

64. Ibid.

65. Ibid.

66. N. Royle, *Veering: A Theory of Literature* (Edinburgh: Edinburgh University Press, 2011), 156.

67. Ibid., 154.

68. Eyers, *Post-Rationalism.*

69. F. Jameson, *The Prison-House of Language: A Critical Account of Structuralism and Russian Formalism* (Princeton, N.J.: Princeton University Press, 1972).

70. M. Heidegger, *Being and Time*, trans. John Macquarrie and Edward Robinson (1927; reprint, New York: Harper, 2008).

71. Jameson, *The Prison-House of Language*, 70.

72. Ibid.

73. V. Shklovsky, *Theory of Prose*, trans. Benjamin Sher (Normal, Ill.: Dalkey Archive, 1991), 22.

74. Ibid.

75. Ibid.

76. Ibid.

77. Meillassoux, *The Number and the Siren*, 42.

78. P. de Man, *Aesthetic Ideology*, ed. A. Warminski (Minneapolis: University of Minnesota, 1996), 83.

79. M. Sprinker, *Imaginary Relations: Aesthetics and Ideology in the Theory of Historical Materialism* (London: Verso, 1987), 14.

80. K. Marx, *Grundrisse*, trans. Martin Nicolaus (New York: Penguin, 1973), 111; Sprinker discusses Marx's comments at some length in his *Imaginary Relations*, 12–15, 273–76.

Chapter 3

1. The best introduction to Badiou's imposing philosophy, a philosophy that includes not just political theory but also a root-and-branch ontology, remains P. Hallward, *A Subject to Truth: Badiou* (Minneapolis: University of Minnesota Press, 2003). See also E. Pluth, *Badiou: A Philosophy of the New* (Cambridge: Polity, 2010); C. Norris, *Badiou's "Being and Event": A Reader's Guide* (London: Continuum, 2009).

2. Systematic accounts of Badiou's thinking on art and literature are rather thin on the ground. A comparative study is to be found in J.-J. Lecercle, *Badiou and Deleuze Read Literature* (Edinburgh: Edinburgh University Press, 2010). Many of the most important of Badiou's writings on poetry have recently been collected in A. Badiou, *The Age of the Poets: And Other Writings on Twentieth-Century Poetry and Prose,* ed. Bruno Bosteels (London: Verso, 2014). I have written a long review essay on the latter volume for the journal *boundary 2,* forthcoming.

3. W. Stevens, *The Collected Poems* (New York: Alfred A. Knopf, 1971), 129.

4. Ibid., 128.

5. S. Critchley, *Things Merely Are: Philosophy in the Poetry of Wallace Stevens* (New York: Routledge, 2005), 21.

6. Ibid., 75.

7. Ibid., 21.

8. Robert Pogue Harrison, "Not Ideas about the Thing but the Thing Itself," *New Literary History* 30.3 (Summer 1999), 661–73.

9. Ibid., 661.

10. Stevens, *The Collected Poems,* 343.

11. Ibid., 343–44.

12. For just one index of this, see the rapidly growing popularity of Bruno Latour's actor-network theory in literary studies. A philosophical outgrowth of the latter, "object-oriented ontology," was recently featured in a special edition of *New Literary History.* See *New Literary History* 43.2 (Spring 2012), 183–281.

13. C. Levine, "Strategic Formalism: Toward a New Method in Cultural Studies," *Victorian Studies* 48.4 (Summer 2006), 625–57.

14. A. Badiou, "'Say Yes to Love, or Else Be Lonely': *Magnolia*" in *Cinema,* trans. Susan Spitzer (Cambridge: Polity, 2013), 192.

15. B. Noys, *The Persistence of the Negative: A Critique of Contemporary Continental Theory* (Edinburgh: Edinburgh University Press, 2010).

16. A. Badiou, *L'être et l'événement 2: Logiques des mondes* (Paris: Seuil, 2006); A. Badiou, *Logics of Worlds: Being and Event 2,* trans. Alberto Toscano (London: Continuum, 2009).

17. Bloom explicitly situates Stevens in the romantic lineage of Wordsworth, Shelley, and Keats in his now-canonical *Wallace Stevens: The Poems of Our Climate* (Ithaca, N.Y.: Cornell University Press, 1977).

18. A. Badiou, *Handbook of Inaesthetics,* trans. Alberto Toscano (Stanford: Stanford University Press, 2005), xiv.

19. Bloom uses this phrase in his review of Helen Vendler's *On Extended Wings: Wallace Stevens' Longer Poems, New York Times,* October 5, 1969.

20. Badiou, *Handbook of Inaesthetics,* 55.

21. Ibid., 25.

22. F. Nietzsche, *The Birth of Tragedy and The Genealogy of Morals,* trans. Francis Golffing (1872; reprint, New York: Doubleday Anchor Books, 1956), 20.

23. Ibid.

24. J. Lacan, "Psychoanalysis and Its Teaching," in *Écrits,* trans. Bruce Fink (New York: W. W. Norton, 2006), 376.

25. Stevens, *The Collected Poems,* 396.

26. Coleridge quoted in M. H. Abrams, *The Mirror and the Lamp: Romantic Theory and the Critical Tradition* (Ithaca, N.Y.: Cornell University Press, 1971), 116.

27. W. Stevens, *The Palm at the End of the Mind: Selected Poems and a Play*, ed. Holly Stevens (1971; reprint, New York: Vintage, 1990), 364.

28. Stevens, *The Collected Poems*, 525.

29. Ibid., 526–27.

30. Perhaps the most poetically accomplished of contemporary songwriters, Bill Callahan, images the unexpected austerity of spring as follows: "The wind is pushing the clouds along / Out of sight / A power is putting them away / A power that moves things neurotically // Like a widow with a rosary / And everything is aweing and tired of praise / And mountains don't need my accolades / And spring looks bad lately anyways / Like death warmed over . . . We call it spring though things are dying." B. Callahan, "Spring," *Dream River*, Drag City, 2013.

31. Stevens, *The Collected Poems*, 528.

32. I should note here the implicit echo with Martin Hägglund's arguments about deconstruction, mortality, and the desire for mortal survival. It would be interesting to test his highly suggestive theses against Stevens's poetic vision of nature qua materiality, and its conditioning and disfiguring of our projects of representation. See M. Hägglund, *Radical Atheism: Derrida and the Time of Life* (Stanford: Stanford University Press, 2008).

33. A. Badiou, *Philosophy for Militants*, trans. Bruno Bosteels (New York: Verso, 2012), 45.

34. Ibid., 46.

35. Ibid., 54.

36. Ibid.

37. Bloom, *Wallace Stevens*, 226.

38. Stevens, *The Collected Poems*, 318–19.

39. Badiou, *Philosophy for Militants*, 56.

40. This is, to be sure, a rather more brutal form of irony than is to be found in what Marjorie Perloff refers to as Stevens's general "ironic modes." For Perloff, the late poetry is too often treated with a philosophical solemnity that its sense of irony, its aloofness and ambiguity, eludes. As she writes, "The speaker in these poems is less a philosopher than a sophisticated, aloof spectator, whose attitude to the various 'isms' he reflects upon is highly ambivalent." Perloff is right, I think, to highlight the contradiction between Stevens's philosophical ambition and his frequent rhetorical levity, but the consequence of the irony I discuss here is less the effect of a distance from things, and more of a direct, even violent intervention in them, the better to disbar the sense of sentimentality that the figures used may otherwise produce. M. Perloff, "Irony in Wallace Stevens's 'The Rock,'" *American Literature* 36.3 (November 1964), 328.

41. Stevens, *The Palm at the End of the Mind*, 256.

42. Badiou, *Philosophy for Militants*, 58.

43. Ibid., 55; Stevens, *The Collected Poems*, 319.

44. Stevens, *The Collected Poems*, 318.

45. Badiou, *Philosophy for Militants*, 53.

46. Stevens, *The Collected Poems*, 318.

47. Badiou, *Handbook of Inaesthetics*, 25.

48. Stevens, *The Collected Poems*, 319.

49. Ibid.

50. Ibid.

51. Stevens, *The Collected Poems*, 396.

52. See C. Brooks, *The Well Wrought Urn: Studies in the Structure of Poetry* (New York: Harvester, 1956), 178–92; F. Kermode, *Romantic Image* (New York: Routledge, 1957), 59–111.

53. W. Empson, *Seven Types of Ambiguity* (1930; reprint, New York: New Directions, 1947), 190.

54. Stevens, *The Collected Poems*, 325.

55. Ibid., 325–26.

56. Stevens, *The Collected Poems*, 315.

57. Critchley, *Things Merely Are*, 34.

58. J. Hillis Miller, "Wallace Stevens's Poetry of Being," in *The J. Hillis Miller Reader*, ed. J. Wolfreys (Stanford: Stanford University Press, 2005), 199.

59. Ibid.

60. Ibid., 207.

61. Novalis quoted in W. O'Brien, *Novalis: Signs of Revolution* (Durham, N.C.: Duke University Press, 1995), 270.

62. Stevens, *The Collected Poems*, 339.

63. A. Badiou, "Drawing," *The Symptom* 12 (Fall 2011), http://lacan.com/symptom12/?p=65.

64. Ibid.

65. A. Badiou, *Being and Event*, trans. Oliver Feltham (London: Continuum, 2005), 191.

66. Badiou provides an especially poignant reflection on his debt to Sartre in his *Pocket Pantheon*, trans. David Macey (London: Verso, 2009), 14–36.

67. Badiou, "Drawing."

68. Stevens, *The Collected Poems*, 344.

69. Ibid., 176.

70. Ibid.

71. Ibid., 177.

72. Ibid.

73. Ibid., 465.

74. Ibid., 243.

75. J. Wiskus, *The Rhythm of Thought: Art, Literature, and Music after Merleau-Ponty* (Chicago: University of Chicago Press, 2013), 7.

76. Stevens, *The Collected Poems*, 177.

77. H. Bloom, *Wallace Stevens: The Poems of Our Climate* (Ithaca, N.Y.: Cornell University Press, 1977), 305.

78. Stevens, *The Collected Poems*, 129.

79. Ibid., 471.

80. Ibid., 472.

81. Ibid., 473.

82. See A. Goldstone, *Fictions of Autonomy: Modernism from Wilde to de Man* (Oxford: Oxford University Press, 2013), 149–86.

83. Ibid., 375.

84. P. de Man, *Allegories of Reading: Figural Language in Rousseau, Nietzsche, Rilke, and Proust* (New Haven, Conn.: Yale University Press, 1979), 106; also see L. M. Jenkins, *Wallace Stevens: Rage for Order* (Brighton: Sussex Academic Press, 2000), 158 n. 63.

85. Goethe quoted in W. Breckman, *Adventures of the Symbolic: Post-Marxism and Radical Democracy* (New York: Columbia University Press, 2013), 31.

86. See de Man, *Allegories of Reading*.

Chapter 4

1. For representative examples, see Q. Meillassoux, *After Finitude: An Essay on the Necessity of Contingency*, trans. R. Brassier (London: Continuum, 2010); G. Harman, *Towards Speculative Realism: Essays and Lectures* (London: Zero Books, 2010).

2. See B. Latour, *Reassembling the Social: An Introduction to Actor-Network Theory* (Oxford: Oxford University Press, 2007), among a myriad of other texts by Latour and others.

3. See note 1 above.

4. The New Critics were a loosely associated group of literary critics, influential in the middle decades of the twentieth century, who emphasized close reading, disregard for the question of authorial intention and historical "context" (if not history per se), and the idea that each text had components that would allow it to be seen as an organic whole. Famous names associated with the "movement" include Cleanth Brooks, I. A. Richards, William K. Wimsatt, and Monroe Beardsley.

5. P. de Man, *Aesthetic Ideology*, ed. A. Warminski (Minneapolis: University of Minnesota Press, 1996).

6. The claim is made with eager vehemence, albeit with precious little corresponding rigor, in D. Lehman, *Signs of the Times: Deconstruction and the Fall of Paul de Man* (New York: Poseidon, 1991). For a spirited defense of de Man, see J. Culler, "Paul de Man's War and the Aesthetic Ideology," *Critical Inquiry* 15.4 (Summer 1989), 777–83. For the infamous war writings themselves, see P. de Man, *War Journalism, 1939–1943*, ed. W. Hamacher, N. Hertz, and T. Keenan (Lincoln: University of Nebraska Press, 1988).

7. A. Warminski, "Introduction: Allegories of Reference," in P. de Man, *Aesthetic Ideology*, ed. A. Warminski (Minneapolis: University of Minnesota Press, 1996), 7.

8. P. de Man, "Phenomenality and Materiality in Kant," in *Aesthetic Ideology*, 70–91.

9. T. Cohen, "Reflections on Post 'Post-mortem de Man,'" in *Ideology and Inscription: "Cultural Studies" after Benjamin, de Man and Bakhtin* (Cambridge: Cambridge University Press, 1998), 49.

10. P. de Man, *The Resistance to Theory* (Minneapolis: University of Minnesota Press, 1986), 11.

11. De Man, "Phenomenality and Materiality in Kant," 71.

12. Ibid., 72.

13. L. Althusser, "Ideology and Ideological State Apparatuses," in *Lenin and Philosophy and Other Essays*, trans. Ben Brewster (London: New Left Books, 1971), 127–88.

14. De Man, "Phenomenality and Materiality in Kant," 73.

15. See P. de Man, *The Rhetoric of Romanticism* (New York: Columbia University Press, 1984).

16. De Man, "Phenomenality and Materiality in Kant," 77.

17. Ibid., 78.

18. R. Jakobson and M. Halle, *Fundamentals of Language* (Berlin: Mouton de Gruyter, 1956).

19. Wordsworth quoted in de Man, "Phenomenality and Materiality in Kant," 82.

20. Ibid.

21. Kant quoted ibid., 80.

22. Ibid., 81.

23. Ibid., 87.

24. Ibid., 88.

25. Ibid., my emphasis.

26. Ibid.

27. Ibid., 89.

28. P. de Man, "Sign and Symbol in Hegel's *Aesthetics*," in *Aesthetic Ideology*, 104.

29. P. de Man, "Anthropomorphism and Trope in the Lyric," in *The Rhetoric of Romanticism* (New York: Columbia University Press, 1984), 239–62.

30. Ibid., 257.

31. Ibid.

32. B. Johnson, "Anthropomorphism in Lyric and Law," *Yale Journal of Law and Humanities* 10.2 (1998), 555. See also Johnson's important reflections on the figure of the "correspondence" as crucial more generally to mid-nineteenth-century French literary culture in her "Poetry and Its Double: Two *Invitations au Voyage*," in *The Critical Difference* (Baltimore: Johns Hopkins University Press, 1980), 31 and *passim*.

33. The original French versions of Baudelaire's poems are now out of copyright. Versions taken from the "definitive" edition of 1868 are available at the following website, from which I have transcribed "Correspondances": http://fleursdumal.org/poem/103.

34. Translation taken from C. Baudelaire, *Les fleurs du mal*, trans. Richard Howard (Boston: David R. Godine, 1983), 15.

35. De Man, "Anthropomorphism and Trope in the Lyric," 250.

36. Ibid.

37. Ibid.

38. P. de Man, "Kant's Materialism," in *Aesthetic Ideology*, ed. A. Warminski (Minneapolis: University of Minnesota Press, 1996), 128.

39. E. Wilson, *Axel's Castle: A Study in the Imaginative Literature of 1870–1930* (New York: Scribner, 1931), 10.

40. See R. Williams, *The Country and the City* (Oxford: Oxford University Press, 1973) and *The Politics of Modernism: Against the New Conformists* (New York: Verso, 2007).

41. W. Benjamin, *Charles Baudelaire: A Lyric Poet in the Era of High Capitalism* (London: New Left Books, 1973). See also C. Prendergast, "Representation or Embodiment? Walter Benjamin and the Politics of *Correspondances*," in *The Triangle of Representation* (New York: Columbia University Press, 2000), 101–17.

42. The central reading remains Benjamin's (see note 35 above). See also C. Prendergast, *Paris and the Nineteenth Century* (Oxford: Blackwell, 1995).

43. Transcribed from http://fleursdumal.org/poem/214.

44. I have preferred to adopt the translation of "Obsession" from http://fleursdumal.org/poem/214, which is superior, on my reckoning, to that found in the previously referenced translation of *Les fleurs du mal* by Richard Howard.

45. De Man, "Anthropomorphism and Trope in the Lyric," 255.

46. Ibid., 262.

47. G. W. F. Hegel, *Phenomenology of Spirit*, trans. A. V. Miller (Oxford: Oxford University Press, 1977), 111–19.

Chapter 5

1. For the romantics, see, among a slew of other candidates, J. J. McGann, *The Romantic Ideology* (Chicago: University of Chicago Press, 1985). For the lesser-known spasmodic poets, a term initially applied by William Edmonstoune Aytoun to Victorian poetry by the likes of George Gilfillan, Alexander Smith, and Gerald Massey, see J. Rudy, *Electric Meters: Victorian Physiological Poetics* (Athens: Ohio University Press, 2009). For the moderns, see, among many others, M. Levenson, *A Genealogy of Modernism: A Study of English Literary Doctrine, 1908–1922* (Cambridge: Cambridge University Press, 1984).

2. The definitive analysis remains F. Jameson, "Postmodernism, or, The Cultural Logic of Late Capitalism," *New Left Review* 146 (July/August 1984), 53–92. For a recent and persuasive critique of the pertinence of "postmodernism" as a periodizing term, if not as a mere means of accessing the self-reflexivity of the contemporary novel, see P. Osborne, "The Postconceptual Condition, or, The Cultural Logic of High Capitalism Today," *Radical Philosophy* 184 (March/April 2014), 19–27. To the extent that the ironizing tone of much "postmodern" fiction (itself a category surely consigned now to the 1990s) may also be associated with a resolute depthlessness, Jameson remains of use, but for a useful critique of the link so often made between the postmodern and the foregrounding of surfaces, see P. Duncan, "Taking the Smooth with the Rough: Texture, Emotion, and the Other Postmodern," *PMLA* 192.2 (March 2014), 204–23.

3. Richard Seymour captures this broad Cold War consensus well: "In the United States of the early Cold War . . . the objective of defeating Communism domestically and abroad won the support of a broad class alliance. This objective unified an otherwise fractious ruling class for a period of time, helped suppress and marginalise their domestic enemies, and won consent from workers who were promised free unionism and rising wages in contrast to the Soviet system of low wages and industrial tyranny" (R. Seymour, *Against Austerity* [London: Pluto, 2014], 38–39).

4. The most influential statement from the Right was F. Fukuyama, *The End of History and the Last Man* (New York: Free Press, 1992). Policy wonks of the Center-Left, ostensibly in power on the rise of the Clintons (whose policies, nonetheless, shifted the political gravity firmly to the Right), reached comparable conclusions, a phenomenon recently surveyed with precision by Perry Anderson through the lens of American foreign policy of the last fifty years or so. See P. Anderson, "American Foreign Policy and Its Thinkers," special issue, *New Left Review* (September/October 2013).

5. B. Andrews and C. Bernstein, eds., *The L-A-N-G-U-A-G-E Book* (Carbondale and Edwardsville: Southern Illinois University Press, 1984), ix.

6. H. Sussman, "Prolegomena to Any Present and Future Language Poetry," in *The Task of the Critic: Poetics, Philosophy, Religion* (New York: Fordham University Press, 2005), 39. Sussman's essay is notable, nonetheless, for the comprehensiveness with which it situates its close readings, all centered on works by Charles Bernstein, within the history of language poetry, early and late. While this chapter addresses multiple poets associated with the movement and neglected by Sussman, its theoretical task, related as much to the broader claims of the book as a whole, precludes a thoroughgoing contexualization of language poetry as a movement.

7. See, especially, S. Freud, "Three Essays on the Theory of Sexuality," in *Standard Edition of the Complete Psychological Works of Sigmund Freud*, vol. 7, trans. James Strachey (1905; reprint, New York: Vintage, 2000). For a compelling Lacanian reading of the relationship between the erogenous zones and the Symbolic, see S. Leclaire, *Psychoanalyzing: On the Order of the Unconscious and the Practice of the Letter*, trans. Peggy Kamuf (Stanford: Stanford University Press, 1998). I discuss the latter text in detail in my *Lacan and the Concept of the "Real"* (New York: Palgrave Macmillan, 2012), 121–59.

8. Sussman, "Prolegomena to Any Present and Future Language Poetry," 48.

9. R. Silliman, *ABC* (San Francisco: Tuumba Press, 1983). Tuumba was a small press crucial to the distribution of language writing, and I have benefited from the thoughtful history of the imprint recounted by Ann Vickery in her important *Leaving Lines of Gender: A Feminist Genealogy of Language Writing* (Hanover, N.H.: Wesleyan University Press, 2000), 63–77.

10. R. Silliman, *The New Sentence* (New York: Roof Books, 1987).

11. M. Perloff, "Language Poetry and the Lyric Subject: Ron Silliman's Albany, Susan Howe's Buffalo," *Critical Inquiry* 25.3 (Spring 1999), 416.

12. R. Silliman, "Albany," in *ABC*, n.p.

13. L. Eigner, "Approaching Things," in Andrews and Bernstein, *The L-A-N-G-U-A-G-E Book*, 3.

14. Perloff, "Language Poetry and the Lyric Subject," 416.

15. G. Deleuze, "Postscript on the Societies of Control," *October* 59 (Winter 1992), 3–7.

16. R. Creeley, "Photo" (1975), in *The Collected Poems of Robert Creeley 1945–1975* (Berkeley: University of California Press, 2006), 553.

17. F. Jameson, *The Political Unconscious: Narrative as a Socially Symbolic Act* (Ithaca, N.Y.: Cornell University Press, 1981).

18. See P. Renshaw, *The Wobblies: The Story of the IWW and Syndicalism in the United States* (Lanham, Md.: Ivan R. Dee, 1999).

19. See 2nd Avenue Poetry, "Blue Horizon," http://www.2ndavepoetry.com/andrewsbv1.html.

20. Ibid.

21. S. Mallarmé, *Divagations*, trans. Barbara Johnson (Cambridge, Mass.: Harvard University Press, 2007), 204.

22. Coleridge quoted in G. H. Hartman, *Saving the Text: Literature/Derrida/Philosophy* (Baltimore: Johns Hopkins University Press, 1981), 1.

23. R. Barthes, "The Death of the Author," in *Image-Music-Text*, trans. Stephen Heath (New York: Hill and Wang, 1977), 145.

24. Peter Osborne has recommended the replacement of the wishful phrase "late capitalism" with "high capitalism" as a more adequate means of capturing the often-baleful truths of our current political predicament. I will engage with Osborne's recent diagnoses of capitalism and culture in the conclusion. See Osborne, "The Postconceptual Condition," 19–27, and P. Osborne, *Anywhere or Not at All: Philosophy of Contemporary Art* (London: Verso, 2013).

25. Silliman, *The New Sentence*, 20.

26. See, for instance, J. Christensen, *Romanticism at the End of History* (Baltimore: Johns Hopkins University Press, 2004).

27. Ibid., 31.

28. Freud's most accessible discussion of the phenomenon of resistance, including this tendency of resistance to conjure fantasmatic enemies, can be found in S. Freud, *A General Introduction to Psychoanalysis*, trans. Joan Riviere (1920; reprint, New York: Pocket Books, 1975).

29. J. Culler, "Lyric, History, and Genre" (2007), in *The Lyric Theory Reader: A Critical Anthology*, ed. V. Jackson and Y. Prins (Baltimore: Johns Hopkins University Press, 2014), 68.

30. Ibid., 91.

31. Ibid., 89.

32. Ibid., 91.

33. W. B. Yeats, *The Collected Poems of W. B. Yeats*, ed. Richard. J. Finneran (New York: Scribner, 1996), 335.

34. L. Hejinian, *The Guard* (San Francisco: Tuumba, 1984), n.p. Marjorie Perloff selected the same excerpt for discussion in her "Can(n)on to the Right of Us, Can(n)on to the Left of Us: A Plea for Difference" (1987), now anthologized in the superb *Lyric Theory Reader*. See Jackson and Prins, *The Lyric Theory Reader*, 460–77.

35. Henry Sussman has equally noted how the appearance of more

traditional verse forms within language poetry may produce an even more radical effect than if fragmentation and innovation were to reign unchecked. Referring to the use of lyric conventions in Charles Bernstein's "Amblyopia," Sussman writes: "This field of poetry's most devastating theorizing, its most explosive undermining of conceptual and formal expectations, may well take place in its most conventional-seeming lyrics" (Sussman, "Prolegomena to Any Present and Future Language Poetry," 54). I have referred to this effect in previous chapters as the productivity of constriction, as the potentiality unleashed by the disciplining of verse by meter and other formal strategies. One awaits with considerable excitement a book by Tracy McNulty that promises to explore this effect with specific reference to the Lacanian concept of the Symbolic: T. McNulty, *Wrestling with the Angel: Experiments in Symbolic Life* (New York: Columbia University Press, 2014).

36. L. Hejinian, "The Rejection of Closure," in *The Language of Inquiry* (Berkeley: University of California Press, 2000), 43.

37. Jameson, *The Political Unconscious*, 42.

38. Barthes's position did not remain the same, but became, by the time of *S/Z*, a kind of deconstruction *avant la lettre*, or, better, a formalism that insisted nonetheless on the dissolutive *telos* of all forms, a position partially reproduced, despite its more explicitly Derridean heritage, in the recent work of Catherine Malabou on the question of neurological damage. See C. Malabou, *The New Wounded: From Neurosis to Brain Damage*, trans. Steven Miller (New York: Fordham University Press, 2012), and R. Barthes, *S/Z: An Essay*, trans. Richard Miller (New York: Hill and Wang, 1974). My position, as I've distinguished it also from the likes of de Man, places an unapologetic emphasis on the *constructive* effects of dissolution, of the ways in which a seeming de-formation may well lay the ground for construction to come. Malabou, to her credit, sounds this more affirmative note in earlier works. See, for example, C. Malabou, *The Future of Hegel: Plasticity, Temporality and Dialectic*, trans. Lisabeth During (London: Routledge, 2004); C. Malabou, *What Should We Do with Our Brains?*, trans. Sebastian Rand (New York: Fordham University Press, 2008).

39. For an excellent obituary of Laplanche that covers both the biographical and intellectual, see Nicholas Ray, "Jean Laplanche, 1924–2012: Forming New Knots," *Radical Philosophy* 174 (July/August 2012).

40. J. Laplanche, "Time and the Other," in *Essays on Otherness*, ed. John Fletcher (London: Routledge, 1999), 241–42.

41. Ibid., 245.

42. Ibid, 247.

43. Ibid.

44. Ibid., 248.

45. S. Mallarmé quoted in E. Wilson, *Axel's Castle: A Study in the Imaginative Literature of 1870–1930* (New York: Scribner, 1931), 20.

46. Ibid., 248.

47. Ibid.

48. J. Laplanche, "The Drive and Its Source-Object," in *Essays on Otherness*, ed. John Fletcher (London: Routledge, 1999), 129.

49. Ibid., 130.

50. J. Laplanche, "Implantation, Intromission," in Fletcher, *Essays on Otherness*, 139.

51. J. Kucich, "The Unfinished Historicist Project: In Praise of Suspicion," *Victoriographies* 1.1 (2011), 67.

52. I have much to say about the specifically psychoanalytic manifestations of these logics in my book *Lacan and the Concept of the "Real."*

53. H. Bloom, "The Breaking of Form," in H. Bloom, P. de Man, J. Derrida, G. Hartman, and J. Hillis Miller, *Deconstruction and Criticism* (London: Continuum, 2004), 9; see also H. Bloom, *The Anxiety of Influence: A Theory of Poetic Form* (1973; reprint, Oxford: Oxford University Press, 1997); H. Bloom, *A Map of Misreading* (1975; reprint, Oxford: Oxford University Press, 2003).

54. Laplanche, "Time and the Other," 248.

Conclusion

1. S. Coleridge and W. Wordsworth, *Lyrical Ballads*, ed. M. Gamer and D. Porter (Plymouth: Broadview, 2008), 172–73. See Barbara Johnson's exemplary discussion of this passage in her "Strange Fits: Poe and Wordsworth on the Nature of Poetic Language," in B. Johnson, *The Barbara Johnson Reader: The Surprise of Otherness*, ed. M. Feuerstein, B. Johnson Gonzáles, L. Porten, and K. Valens (Durham, N.C.: Duke University Press, 2014), 44–57.

2. For a stimulating account of English romanticism in its conflicted relations with the contracts and compromises of commodity culture, see G. Batten, *The Orphaned Imagination: Melancholy and Commodity Culture in English Romanticism* (Durham, N.C.: Duke University Press, 1998).

3. The limitations of broadly Foucauldian readings of literature that employ power as a primary motif are explored in A. Anderson, *The Way We Argue Now: A Study in the Cultures of Theory* (Princeton, N.J.: Princeton University Press, 2006). I confess to finding Anderson's attempt to reinvigorate a version of communicative Enlightenment largely unconvincing, but the argument is gaining ground. Affect theory of a kind gained a boost with the publication of Sianne Ngai's innovative *Our Aesthetic Categories: Zany, Cute, Interesting* (Cambridge, Mass.: Harvard University Press, 2012).

4. R. Barthes, *S/Z: An Essay*, trans. Richard Miller (New York: Hill and Wang, 1974), 82–83; quoted in F. Jameson, *Brecht and Method* (New York: Verso, 1999), 63.

5. A. de Campos, "Concrete Poetry: A Manifesto," in *Contemporary Poetics*, ed. L. Armand (Evanston, Ill.: Northwestern University Press, 2007), 213.

6. Jameson, *Brecht and Method*, 59.

7. He does so in the article "How Do We Recognize Strong Critique?," to be discussed presently. See P. Livingston, "How Do We Recognize Strong Critique?," *Crisis and Critique* 3 (2014), 85–115.

8. G. Lukács, "The Ideology of Modernism," in *The Meaning of Contemporary Realism*, trans. John and Necke Mander (London: Merlin, 1963), 17–46.

9. P. Osborne, *Anywhere or Not at All: Philosophy of Contemporary Art* (London: Verso, 2013), 35.

10. Ibid.

11. For an up-to-date anthology of the crucial essays published on the topic in recent decades, see D. Damrosch, ed., *World Literature in Theory* (New York: Wiley-Blackwell, 2014). Much more critical resources may be found in, for example, the dossier published in *Comparative Literature* 62.4 (Fall 2010). See especially R. Weninger, "Lost in Lit-Terra, or, What Is and to What End Do We Study World Literature?," *Comparative Literature* 62.4 (Fall 2010), 315–35.

12. E. Apter, *Against World Literature: On the Politics of Untranslatability* (New York: Verso, 2013), 2.

13. The latter criticism is made with particular force in P. Hitchcock, *The Long Space: Transnationalism and Postcolonial Form* (Stanford: Stanford University Press, 2005).

14. D. Damrosch, *What Is World Literature?* (Princeton, N.J.: Princeton University Press, 2003), 5.

15. F. Moretti, "Conjectures on World Literature," *New Left Review* 1 (January–February 2000), 54–68.

16. Ibid., 57

17. B. Brecht, *Brecht on Theater*, ed. and trans. John Willett (New York: Hill and Wang, 1957), 37–38; quoted in F. Jameson, *Brecht and Method* (New York: Verso, 1999), 90.

18. Ibid., 37–38, 90.

19. Osborne, *Anywhere or Not at All*, 34.

20. Damrosch, *What Is World Literature?*, 4.

21. Osborne, *Anywhere or Not at All*, 25.

22. Ibid., 34.

23. Ibid., 34–35.

24. R. Silliman, "Albany," in *ABC* (San Francisco: Tuumba, 1983), n.p.

25. Livingston, "How Do We Recognize Strong Critique?"

26. See, for instance, A. Badiou, *Being and Event*, trans. Oliver Feltham (London: Continuum, 2005).

27. Livingston, "How Do We Recognize Strong Critique?," 87.

28. Ibid., 91.

29. Apter, *Against World Literature*, 3.

30. Livingston, "How Do We Recognize Strong Critique?," 97.

31. Ibid., 113.

32. See, for instance, the analysis developed at length in J. Derrida, *Rogues: Two Essays on Reason*, trans. Pascale-Anne Brault (Stanford: Stanford University Press, 2005).

33. Osborne, *Anywhere or Not at All*, 210.

34. Ibid., 211.

Bibliography

Abrams, M. H. *The Mirror and the Lamp: Romantic Theory and the Critical Tradition.* Ithaca, N.Y.: Cornell University Press, 1971.

Althusser, Louis. "Ideology and Ideological State Apparatuses." In *Lenin and Philosophy and Other Essays,* translated by Ben Brewster. London: New Left Books, 1971.

———. "On the Materialist Dialectic." In *For Marx,* translated by Ben Brewster. London: Verso, 2010.

Althusser, Louis, and Étienne Balibar. *Reading Capital.* Translated by Ben Brewster. London: New Left Books, 1970.

Anderson, Amanda. *The Way We Argue Now: A Study in the Cultures of Theory.* Princeton, N.J.: Princeton University Press, 2006.

Anderson, Perry, ed. "American Foreign Policy and Its Thinkers." Special issue, *New Left Review* 83 (September/October 2013).

Andrews, Bruce, and Charles Bernstein, eds. *The L-A-N-G-U-A-G-E Book.* Carbondale and Edwardsville: Southern Illinois University Press, 1984.

Apter, Emily. *Against World Literature: On the Politics of Untranslatability.* New York: Verso, 2013.

———. "Global *Translatio*: The 'Invention' of Comparative Literature." *Critical Inquiry* 29.2 (Winter 2003).

Attridge, Derek. *The Singularity of Literature.* New York: Routledge, 2004.

Bachelard, Gaston. *Earth and Reveries of Will.* Translated by K. Haltman. Dallas: Dallas Institute, 2002.

———. *Le rationalisme appliqué.* Paris: PUF, 2004.

Badiou, Alain. *The Age of the Poets: And Other Writings on Twentieth-Century Poetry and Prose.* Edited by Bruno Bosteels. New York: Verso, 2014.

———. *Being and Event.* Translated by Oliver Feltham. London: Continuum, 2005.

———. *The Communist Hypothesis.* London: Verso, 2010.

———. "Drawing." *The Symptom* 12 (Fall 2011).

———. *Handbook of Inaesthetics.* Translated by Alberto Toscano. Stanford: Stanford University Press, 2005.

———. *L'être et l'événement 2: Logiques des mondes.* Paris: Seuil, 2006.

———. *Logics of Worlds: Being and Event 2.* Translated by Alberto Toscano. London: Continuum, 2009.

———. *Philosophy for Militants.* Translated by Bruno Bosteels. New York: Verso, 2012.

———. *Pocket Pantheon.* Translated by David Macey. London: Verso, 2009.

———. "'Say Yes to Love, or Else Be Lonely': *Magnolia*." In *Cinema*, translated by Susan Spitzer. Cambridge: Polity, 2013.

———. *Theory of the Subject*. Translated by Bruno Bosteels. London: Continuum, 2010.

Barthes, Roland. "The Death of the Author." In *Image-Music-Text*, translated by Stephen Heath. New York: Hill and Wang, 1977.

———. *S/Z: An Essay*. Translated by Richard Miller. New York: Hill and Wang, 1974.

Batten, Guinn. *The Orphaned Imagination: Melancholy and Commodity Culture in English Romanticism*. Durham, N.C.: Duke University Press, 1998.

Baudelaire, Charles. "Correspondances" (French). http://fleursdumal.org/poem/103.

———. "Intoxication." In *The Poems and Prose Poems of Charles Baudelaire*, edited by James Huneker. New York: Brentano's, 1919.

———. *Les fleurs du mal*. Translated by Richard Howard. Boston: David R. Godine, 1983.

———. "Obsession" (French and English translation). http://fleursdumal.org/poem/214.

Benjamin, Walter. *Charles Baudelaire: A Lyric Poet in the Era of High Capitalism*. London: New Left Books, 1973.

———. "On Language as Such and on the Languages of Man." In *Selected Writings Volume 1, 1913–1926*, edited by Marcus Bullock and Michael W. Jennings. Cambridge, Mass.: Belknap, 1996.

———. *The Origin of German Tragic Drama*. Translated by J. Osborne. London: Verso, 2003.

———. "The Task of the Translator." In *Illuminations*, edited by Hannah Arendt. New York: Harcourt, 1968.

Best, Stephen, and Sharon Marcus. "Surface Reading: An Introduction." *Representations* 108.1 (Fall 2009), 1–21.

Black, Naomi. *Virginia Woolf as Feminist*. Ithaca, N.Y.: Cornell University Press, 2003.

Bloom, Allan. *The Closing of the American Mind: How Higher Education Has Failed Democracy and Impoverished the Souls of Today's Students*. New York: Simon and Schuster, 1987.

Bloom, Harold. *The Anxiety of Influence: A Theory of Poetic Form*. 1973; reprint, Oxford: Oxford University Press, 1997.

———. "The Breaking of Form." In Harold Bloom, Paul de Man, Jacques Derrida, Geoffrey Hartman, and J. Hillis Miller, *Deconstruction and Criticism*. London: Continuum, 2004.

———. *A Map of Misreading*. 1975; reprint, Oxford: Oxford University Press, 2003.

———. Review of Helen Vendler's *On Extended Wings: Wallace Stevens' Longer Poems*. *New York Times*, October 5, 1969.

———. *Wallace Stevens: The Poems of Our Climate*. Ithaca, N.Y.: Cornell University Press, 1977.

Bok, Derek. *Universities in the Marketplace: The Commercialization of Higher Education.* Princeton, N.J.: Princeton University Press, 2004.

Brecht, Bertolt. *Brecht on Theater.* Edited and translated by John Willett. New York: Hill and Wang, 1957.

Breckman, Warren. *Adventures of the Symbolic: Post-Marxism and Radical Democracy.* New York: Columbia University Press, 2013.

Brooks, Cleanth. *The Well Wrought Urn: Studies in the Structure of Poetry.* New York: Harvester, 1956.

Bryant, Levi. *Democracy of Objects.* Ann Arbor: Open Humanities, 2011.

Butler, Judith. *Subjects of Desire: Hegelian Reflections in Twentieth Century France.* New York: Columbia University Press, 1999.

Cassin, Barbara, Emily Apter, Jacques Lezra, and Michael Wood, eds. *Dictionary of Untranslatables: A Philosophical Lexicon.* Princeton, N.J.: Princeton University Press, 2014.

Cavaillès, Jean. *On Logic and the Theory of Science.* Translated by T. J. Kisiel. In *Phenomenology and the Natural Sciences: Essays and Translations,* edited by J. J. Kockelmans and T. J. Kisiel. Evanston, Ill.: Northwestern University Press, 1970.

———. *Sur la logique et la théorie de la science.* 2nd ed. Paris: Presses Universitaires de France, 1960.

Christensen, Jerome. *Romanticism at the End of History.* Baltimore: Johns Hopkins University Press, 2004.

Chun, Wendy. "The Dark Side of the Digital Humanities." *Thinking C21,* September 1, 2013, http://www.c21uwm.com/2013/01/09/the-dark-side-of-the-digital-humanities-part-1/.

Cohen, Tom. *Anti-Mimesis: From Plato to Hitchcock.* Cambridge: Cambridge University Press, 1994.

———. "Reflections on Post 'Post-mortem de Man.'" In *Ideology and Inscription: "Cultural Studies" after Benjamin, de Man and Bakhtin.* Cambridge: Cambridge University Press, 1998.

Colebrook, Claire. Introduction to C. Colebrook, T. Cohen, and J. Hillis-Miller, *Theory and the Disappearing Future: On de Man, on Benjamin.* New York: Routledge, 2012.

Coleridge, Samuel, and William Wordsworth. *Lyrical Ballads.* Edited by M. Gamer and D. Porter. Plymouth: Broadview, 2008.

Conrad, Joseph. *Heart of Darkness.* Edited by Owen Knowles. London: Penguin, 2007.

Cooke, Miriam. "Mediterranean Thinking: From Netizen to Medizen." *Geographical Review* 89.2 (April 1999).

Creeley, Robert. "Photo" (1975). In *The Collected Poems of Robert Creeley 1945–1975.* Berkeley: University of California Press, 2006.

Crane, Hart. "A Name for All." In *The Complete Poems of Hart Crane,* edited by Marc Simon. New York: Liveright, 2010.

Critchley, Simon. *Things Merely Are: Philosophy in the Poetry of Wallace Stevens.* New York: Routledge, 2005.

Culler, Jonathan. "Lyric, History, and Genre" (2007). In *The Lyric Theory Reader: A Critical Anthology*, edited by V. Jackson and Y. Prins. Baltimore: Johns Hopkins University Press, 2014.

———. "Paul de Man's War and the Aesthetic Ideology." *Critical Inquiry* 15.4 (Summer 1989), 777–83.

———. *Theory of the Lyric.* Cambridge, Mass.: Harvard University Press, 2015.

Damrosch, David. *What Is World Literature?* Princeton, N.J.: Princeton University Press, 2003.

———, ed. *World Literature in Theory.* New York: Wiley-Blackwell, 2014.

De Campos, Augusto. "Concrete Poetry: A Manifesto." In *Contemporary Poetics,* edited by L. Armand. Evanston, Ill.: Northwestern University Press, 2007.

De Man, Paul. *Aesthetic Ideology.* Edited by A. Warminski. Minneapolis: University of Minnesota Press, 1996.

———. *Allegories of Reading: Figural Language in Rousseau, Nietzsche, Rilke, and Proust.* New Haven, Conn.: Yale University Press, 1979.

———. *Blindness and Insight: Essays in the Rhetoric of Contemporary Criticism.* Minneapolis: University of Minnesota Press, 1983.

———. "Kant's Materialism." In *Aesthetic Ideology,* edited by Andrzej Warminski. Minneapolis: University of Minnesota Press, 1996.

———. "Phenomenality and Materiality in Kant." In *Aesthetic Ideology,* edited by A. Warminski. Minneapolis: University of Minnesota Press, 1996.

———. *The Resistance to Theory.* Minneapolis: University of Minnesota Press, 1986.

———. *The Rhetoric of Romanticism.* New York: Columbia University Press, 1984.

———. "Sign and Symbol in Hegel's *Aesthetics.*" In *Aesthetic Ideology,* edited by A. Warminski. Minneapolis: University of Minnesota Press, 1996.

———. *War Journalism, 1939–1943.* Edited by W. Hamacher, N. Hertz, and T. Keenan. Lincoln: University of Nebraska Press, 1988.

Deleuze, Gilles. "Postscript on the Societies of Control." *October* 59 (Winter 1992).

Derrida, Jacques. *Rogues: Two Essays on Reason.* Translated by Pascale-Anne Brault. Stanford: Stanford University Press, 2005.

———. *Signéponge-Signsponge.* Translated by Richard Rand. New York: Columbia University Press, 1984.

Derwin, Susan. *The Ambivalence of Form: Lukács, Freud, and the Novel.* Baltimore: Johns Hopkins University Press, 1992.

Duncan, Pansy. "Taking the Smooth with the Rough: Texture, Emotion, and the Other Postmodern." *PMLA* 192.2 (March 2014).

Eagleton, Terry. *The Event of Literature.* New Haven, Conn.: Yale University Press, 2012.

———. "Liberality and Order: The Criticism of John Bayley." *New Left Review* 1.110 (July/August 1978).

———. "Schiller and Hegemony." In *The Ideology of the Aesthetic.* Oxford: Blackwell, 1990.

Empson, William. *Seven Types of Ambiguity.* New York: New Directions, 1947.

Eyers, Tom. *Lacan and the Concept of the "Real."* New York: Palgrave Macmillan, 2012.

———. *Post-Rationalism: Psychoanalysis, Epistemology and Marxism in Postwar France.* London: Bloomsbury, 2013.

———. "The 'Signifier-in-Relation,' the 'Signifier-in-Isolation,' and the Concept of the 'Real.'" In "Lacan," special issue, *Parrhesia* 14 (2012).

Faulkner, William. *Collected Stories.* New York: Random House, 1950.

Felman, Shoshana. "On Reading Poetry." In *The Literary Freud: Mechanisms of Defense and the Poetic Will,* edited by J. Smith. New Haven, Conn.: Yale University Press, 1980.

Ferris, David. *Theory and the Evasion of History.* Baltimore: Johns Hopkins University Press, 1993.

Fish, Stanley. "The Old Order Changeth." *New York Times,* December 26, 2011, http://opinionator.blogs.nytimes.com/2011/12/26/the-old-order-changeth/.

François, Anne-Lise. *Open Secrets: The Literature of Uncounted Experience.* Stanford: Stanford University Press, 2008.

Freud, Sigmund. *A General Introduction to Psychoanalysis.* Translated by Joan Riviere. 1920; reprint, New York: Pocket Books, 1975.

———. "Three Essays on the Theory of Sexuality." In *Standard Edition of the Complete Psychological Works of Sigmund Freud,* vol. 7, translated by James Strachey. 1905; reprint, New York: Vintage, 2000.

Fukuyama, Francis. *The End of History and the Last Man.* New York: Free Press, 1992.

Geras, Norman. "Post-Marxism?" *New Left Review* 1.163 (May/June 1987).

Ginsberg, Benjamin. *The Fall of the Faculty: The Rise of the All-Administrative University and Why It Matters.* New York: Oxford University Press, 2011.

Ginzburg, Carlo. "Clues: Roots of an Evidential Paradigm." In *Clues, Myths, and the Historical Method,* translated by John and Anne C. Tedeschi. Baltimore: Johns Hopkins University Press, 1992.

Goldman, Jane. *The Feminist Aesthetics of Virginia Woolf: Modernism, Post-Impressionism, and the Politics of the Visual.* Cambridge: Cambridge University Press, 1998.

Goldstone, Andrew. *Fictions of Autonomy: Modernism from Wilde to de Man.* Oxford: Oxford University Press, 2013.

Goodwin, Jonathan, and John Holbo, eds. *Reading Graphs, Maps, and Trees: Responses to Franco Moretti.* Anderson, S.C.: Parlor, 2011.

Gottschall, Jonathan. *Literature, Science, and a New Humanities.* New York: Palgrave Macmillan, 2008.

Greenblatt, Stephen. "Towards a Poetics of Culture." *Southern Review* 20.1 (March 1987).

Habermas, Jürgen. *The Philosophical Discourse of Modernity: Twelve Lectures.* Cambridge, Mass.: MIT Press, 1990.

Hägglund, Martin. *Radical Atheism: Derrida and the Time of Life.* Stanford: Stanford University Press, 2008.

Hallward, Peter. "Anything Is Possible: A Reading of Quentin Meillassoux's 'After Finitude.'" In *The Speculative Turn: Continental Materialism and Realism,* edited by L. Bryant, N. Srnicek, and G. Harman. Victoria: Re.press, 2011.

———. "Order and Event." *New Left Review* 53 (September/October 2008).

———. *A Subject to Truth: Badiou.* Minneapolis: University of Minnesota Press, 2003.

Hamburger, Käte. *The Logic of Literature.* Evanston, Ill.: Northwestern University Press, 1979.

Harman, Graham. *Tool Being: Heidegger and the Metaphysics of Objects.* Chicago: Open Court, 2002.

———. *Towards Speculative Realism: Essays and Lectures.* London: Zero Books, 2010.

Harrison, Robert Pogue. "Not Ideas about the Thing but the Thing Itself." *New Literary History* 30.3 (Summer 1999), 661–73.

Hartman, Geoffrey. *Saving the Text: Literature/Derrida/Philosophy.* Baltimore: Johns Hopkins University Press, 1981.

Hegel, Georg W. F. *Phenomenology of Spirit.* Translated by A. V. Miller. Oxford: Oxford University Press, 1977.

Heidegger, Martin. *Being and Time.* Translated by John Macquarrie and Edward Robinson. 1927; reprint, New York: Harper, 2008.

Hejinian, Lyn. *The Guard.* San Francisco: Tuumba, 1984.

———. "The Rejection of Closure." In *The Language of Inquiry.* Berkeley: University of California Press, 2000.

Hitchcock, Peter. *The Long Space: Transnationalism and Postcolonial Form.* Stanford: Stanford University Press, 2005.

Howe, Susan. *The Birth-mark.* Hanover, N.H.: Wesleyan University Press, 1993.

Hughes, Ted, and Drue Heinz. "The Art of Poetry." *Paris Review* (Spring 1995).

Hyppolite, Jean. *Logic and Existence.* Translated by Leonard Lawlor and Amit Sen. 1953; reprint, Albany: SUNY Press, 1997.

Jackson, V., and Y. Prins, eds. *The Lyric Theory Reader: A Critical Anthology.* Baltimore: Johns Hopkins University Press, 2014.

Jakobson, Roman, and Morris Halle. *Fundamentals of Language.* Berlin: Mouton de Gruyter, 1956.

Jameson, Fredric. *The Antinomies of Realism.* London: Verso, 2013.

———. *Brecht and Method.* New York: Verso, 1999.

———. *The Modernist Papers.* London: Verso, 2007.

———. *The Political Unconscious: Narrative as a Socially Symbolic Act.* Ithaca, N.Y.: Cornell University Press, 1981.

———. "Postmodernism, or, The Cultural Logic of Late Capitalism." *New Left Review* 1.146 (July/August 1984).

———. *Postmodernism, or, The Cultural Logic of Late Capitalism.* London: Verso, 1992.

———. *The Prison-House of Language: A Critical Account of Structuralism and Russian Formalism.* Princeton, N.J.: Princeton University Press, 1972.

———. "Realism and Utopia in *The Wire.*" *Criticism* 52.4 (2010), 359–72.

Jay, Martin. "Historical Explanation and the Event: Reflections on the Limits of Contextualization." *New Literary History* 42.4 (Autumn 2011).

Jenkins, Lee M. *Wallace Stevens: Rage for Order.* Brighton: Sussex Academic Press, 2000.

Johnson, Barbara. "Anthropomorphism in Lyric and Law." *Yale Journal of Law and Humanities* 10.2 (1998).

———. *Persons and Things.* Cambridge, Mass.: Harvard University Press, 2008.

———. "Poetry and Its Double: Two *Invitations au Voyage.*" In *The Critical Difference.* Baltimore: Johns Hopkins University Press, 1980.

———. "Poetry and Syntax: What the Gypsy Knew." In *The Barbara Johnson Reader: The Surprise of Otherness,* edited by M. Feuerstein, B. J. González, L. Porten, and K. Valens. Durham, N.C.: Duke University Press, 2014.

———. "Strange Fits: Poe and Wordsworth on the Nature of Poetic Language." In *The Barbara Johnson Reader: The Surprise of Otherness,* edited by Melissa Feuerstein, Bill Johnson Gonzáles, Lili Porten, and Keja Valens. Durham, N.C.: Duke University Press, 2014.

Johnston, Adrian, and Catherine Malabou. *Self and Emotional Life: Philosophy, Psychoanalysis, and Neuroscience.* New York: Columbia University Press, 2013.

Kant, Immanuel. *Critique of Pure Reason.* Translated by Paul Guyer and Allen W. Wood. Cambridge: Cambridge University Press, 1999.

Kermode, Frank. *Romantic Image.* New York: Routledge, 1957.

Kojève, Alexandre. *Introduction to the Reading of Hegel: Lectures on the "Phenomenology of Spirit."* Translated by J. H. Nichols, edited by Allan Bloom. Ithaca, N.Y.: Cornell University Press, 1980.

Kucich, John. "The Unfinished Historicist Project: In Praise of Suspicion." *Victoriographies* 1.1 (2011).

Lacan, Jacques. "Overture to This Collection." In *Écrits,* translated by Bruce Fink. New York: W. W. Norton, 2006.

———. "Psychoanalysis and Its Teaching." In *Écrits,* translated by Bruce Fink. New York: W. W. Norton, 2006.

———. *The Seminar of Jacques Lacan, Book 11: The Four Fundamental Concepts of Psychoanalysis.* 1964–65; reprint, New York: W. W. Norton, 1988.

———. *The Seminar of Jacques Lacan, Book 20: Encore.* Translated by Bruce Fink. New York: W. W. Norton, 1999.

Laclau, Ernesto, and Chantal Mouffe. *Hegemony and Socialist Strategy: Towards a Radical Democratic Politics.* 2nd ed. London: Verso, 2001.

Ladrière, Jean. "Mathematics in a Philosophy of Science" (1959). Translated by T. J. Kisiel. In *Phenomenology and the Natural Sciences: Essays and Translations,* edited by J. J. Kockelmans and T. J. Kisiel. Evanston, Ill.: Northwestern University Press, 1970.

Laplanche, Jean. "The Drive and Its Source-Object." In *Essays on Otherness,* edited by John Fletcher. London: Routledge, 1999.

———. "Implantation, Intromission." In *Essays on Otherness,* edited by John Fletcher. London: Routledge, 1999.

———. "Time and the Other." In *Essays on Otherness,* edited by John Fletcher. London: Routledge, 1999.

Latour, Bruno. *Reassembling the Social: An Introduction to Actor-Network Theory.* Oxford: Oxford University Press, 2007.

Lecercle, J.-J. *Badiou and Deleuze Read Literature*. Edinburgh: Edinburgh University Press, 2010.

Leclaire, Serge. *Psychoanalyzing: On the Order of the Unconscious and the Practice of the Letter*. Translated by Peggy Kamuf. Stanford: Stanford University Press, 1998.

Lecourt, Dominique. *Marxism and Epistemology: Bachelard, Canguilhem and Foucault*. Translated by Ben Brewster. London: New Left Books, 1975.

Lehman, David. *Signs of the Times: Deconstruction and the Fall of Paul de Man*. New York: Poseidon, 1991.

Leighton, Angela. *On Form: Poetry, Aestheticism, and the Legacy of a Word*. Oxford: Oxford University Press, 2007.

Lentricchia, Frank. *Ariel and the Police: Michel Foucault, William James, and Wallace Stevens*. Madison: University of Wisconsin Press, 1988.

Lesjak, C. "Reading Dialectically." *Criticism* 55.2 (2013).

Levenson, Michael. *A Genealogy of Modernism: A Study of English Literary Doctrine, 1908–1922*. Cambridge: Cambridge University Press, 1984.

Levine, Caroline. *Forms: Whole, Rhythm, Hierarchy, Network*. Princeton, N.J.: Princeton University Press, 2015.

———. "Strategic Formalism: Toward a New Method in Cultural Studies." *Victorian Studies* 48.4 (Summer 2006), 625–57.

Levinson, Marjorie. "What Is New Formalism?" *PMLA* 122.2 (March 2007), 558–69.

Livingston, Paul. "Derrida and Formal Logic: Formalising the Undecidable." *Derrida Today* 3.2 (November 2010), 221–39.

———. "How Do We Recognize Strong Critique?" *Crisis and Critique* 3 (2014), 85–115.

———. *The Politics of Logic: Badiou, Wittgenstein and the Consequences of Formalism*. New York: Routledge, 2011.

Loesberg, Jonathan. "Materialism and Aesthetics: Paul de Man's Aesthetic Ideology." *Diacritics* 27.4 (Winter 1997), 87–108.

Lukács, Georg. "The Ideology of Modernism." In *The Meaning of Contemporary Realism*, translated by John and Necke Mander. London: Merlin, 1963.

———. *The Theory of the Novel*. Translated by Anna Bostock. Boston: MIT Press, 1971.

Lyons, John D., and Stephen G. Nichols Jr., eds. *Mimesis: From Mirror to Method, Augustine to Descartes*. Hanover, N.H.: University Press of New England, 1982.

Macherey, Pierre. *A Theory of Literary Production*. Translated by Geoffrey Wall. London: Routledge, 1978.

Malabou, Catherine. *The Future of Hegel: Plasticity, Temporality and Dialectic*. Translated by Lisabeth During. London: Routledge, 2004.

———. *The New Wounded: From Neurosis to Brain Damage*. Translated by Steven Miller. New York: Fordham University Press, 2012.

———. *What Should We Do with Our Brains?* Translated by Sebastian Rand. New York: Fordham University Press, 2008.

Mallarmé, Stephane. *Collected Poems and Other Verse*. Translated by E. H. and A. M. Blackmore. Oxford: Oxford University Press, 2006.

———. *Divagations*. Translated by Barbara Johnson. Cambridge, Mass.: Harvard University Press, 2007.

———. "L'après-midi d'un faune." In *Collected Poems and Other Verse*, translated by E. H. and A. M. Blackmore. Oxford: Oxford University Press, 2006.

———. *Mallarmé: The Politics of the Siren*. Translated by Steven Corcoran. London: Continuum, 2011.

———. "Sur l'évolution littéraire [Enquête de Jules Huret]." In *Œuvres complètes ii*, edited by B. Marchel. Bibliothèque de la Pléiade. Paris: Gallimard, 2003.

Maniglier, Patrice. "What Is a Problematic?" *Radical Philosophy* 173 (May/June 2012).

Marche, Stephen. "Literature Is Not Data: Against the Digital Humanities." *Los Angeles Review of Books*, October 28, 2012, http://lareviewofbooks.org/article.php?id=1040.

Marcuse, Herbert. *Eros and Civilization: A Philosophical Inquiry into Freud*. Boston: Beacon, 1974.

Marx, Karl. *Grundrisse*. Translated by Martin Nicolaus. New York: Penguin, 1973.

McGann, Jerome J. *The Romantic Ideology*. Chicago: University of Chicago Press, 1985.

McGettigan, Andrew. *The Great University Gamble: Money, Markets and the Future of Higher Education*. London: Pluto, 2013.

McNulty, Tracy. *Wrestling with the Angel: Experiments in Symbolic Life*. New York: Columbia University Press, 2014.

Meillassoux, Quentin. *After Finitude: An Essay on the Necessity of Contingency*. Translated by R. Brassier. London: Continuum, 2010.

———. *The Number and the Siren: A Decipherment of Mallarmé's "Coup de Des."* Translated by Robin Mackay. Falmouth: Urbanomic, 2012.

Michaels, Walter Benn. *The Shape of the Signifier: 1967 to the End of History*. Princeton, N.J.: Princeton University Press, 2006.

Miller, J. Hillis. *Theory Now and Then*. Durham, N.C.: Duke University Press, 1991.

———. "Wallace Stevens's Poetry of Being." In *The J. Hillis Miller Reader*, edited by J. Wolfreys. Stanford: Stanford University Press, 2005.

Minkowski, Eugene. "Prose and Poetry (Astronomy and Cosmology)." Translated by J. J. Kockelmans. In *Phenomenology and the Natural Sciences: Essays and Translations*, edited by J. J. Kockelmans and T. J. Kisiel. Evanston, Ill.: Northwestern University Press, 1970.

———. *Vers une cosmologie*. Paris: Aubier, 1936.

Miyoshi, Masao. "Ivory Tower in Escrow." *boundary 2* 2.27 (Spring 2000).

Montag, Warren. *Bodies, Masses, Power: Spinoza and His Contemporaries*. London: Verso, 1999.

———. *Louis Althusser*. New York: Palgrave Macmillan, 2003.

Montrose, Louis. "Professing the Renaissance: The Poetics and Politics of Culture." In *The New Historicism*, edited by H. Aram Veeser. New York: Routledge, 1989.

Moretti, Franco. "Conjectures on World Literature." *New Left Review* 1 (January–February 2000), 54–68.

———. "The End of the Beginning: A Reply to Christopher Prendergast." *New Left Review* 41 (September/October 2006).
———. "Graphs, Maps, Trees: Abstract Models for Literary History 1." *New Left Review* 24 (November/December 2003).
———. "Graphs, Maps, Trees: Abstract Models for Literary History 2." *New Left Review* 26 (March/April 2004).
———. "Graphs, Maps, Trees: Abstract Models for Literary History 3." *New Left Review* 28 (July/August 2004).
———. *Graphs, Maps, Trees: Abstract Models for Literary History*. London: Verso, 2005.
———. "More Conjectures." *New Left Review* 20 (March/April 2003).
———. "'Operationalizing': or, The Function of Measurement in Modern Literary Theory." *New Left Review* 84 (November/December 2013).
———. *Signs Taken for Wonders*. London: Verso, 1988.
———. "The Slaughterhouse of Literature." *Modern Language Quarterly* 61.1 (March 2000).
Ngai, Sianne. *Our Aesthetic Categories: Zany, Cute, Interesting*. Cambridge, Mass.: Harvard University Press, 2012.
Nietzsche, Friedrich. *The Birth of Tragedy and The Genealogy of Morals*. Translated by Francis Golffing. New York: Doubleday Anchor, 1956.
Nobus, Danny. "That Obscure Object of Psychoanalysis." *Continental Philosophy Review* 46.2 (August 2013).
Norris, Christopher. *Badiou's "Being and Event": A Reader's Guide*. London: Continuum, 2009.
Noys, Benjamin. *The Persistence of the Negative: A Critique of Contemporary Continental Theory*. Edinburgh: Edinburgh University Press, 2010.
O'Brien, William. *Novalis: Signs of Revolution*. Durham, N.C.: Duke University Press, 1995.
Osborne, Peter. *Anywhere or Not at All: Philosophy of Contemporary Art*. London: Verso, 2013.
———. "The Postconceptual Condition, or, The Cultural Logic of High Capitalism Today." *Radical Philosophy* 184 (March/April 2014), 19–27.
Patai, Daphne, and Wilfrido Corral, eds. *Theory's Empire: An Anthology of Dissent*. New York: Columbia University Press, 2005.
Peden, Knox. "From Consciousness to the Concept: The Spinozism of Jean Cavaillès." In *Spinoza Contra Phenomenology: French Rationalism from Cavaillès to Deleuze*. Stanford: Stanford University Press, 2014.
Peeters, Benoît. *Derrida: A Biography*. Translated by Andrew Brown. Cambridge: Polity, 2012.
Perloff, Marjorie. "Can(n)on to the Right of Us, Can(n)on to the Left of Us: A Plea for Difference" (1987). In *The Lyric Theory Reader: A Critical Anthology*, edited by V. Jackson and Y. Prins. Baltimore: Johns Hopkins University Press, 2014.
———. "Irony in Wallace Stevens's 'The Rock.'" *American Literature* 36.3 (November 1964).

———. "Language Poetry and the Lyric Subject: Ron Silliman's Albany, Susan Howe's Buffalo." *Critical Inquiry* 25.3 (Spring 1999).

Pluth, Ed. *Badiou: A Philosophy of the New.* Cambridge: Polity, 2010.

Ponge, Francis. "L'orange." French transcription and English translation by Seamus Cooney. http://unix.cc.wmich.edu/~cooneys/poems/fr/ponge.orange.html, accessed February 13, 2013.

———. "The Oyster." Translation taken from B. Johnson, *Persons and Things.* Cambridge, Mass.: Harvard University Press, 2008.

Pope, Alexander. "An Essay on Criticism." In *The Major Works,* edited by Pat Rogers. Oxford: Oxford University Press, 2009.

Poster, Mark. *Existential Marxism in Postwar France: From Sartre to Althusser.* Princeton, N.J.: Princeton University Press, 1975.

Prendergast, Christopher. "Across the Between." *New Left Review* 86 (March/April 2014), 151–58.

———. "Circulating Representations: New Historicism and the Poetics of Culture." *SubStance* 28.1 (1999), 90–104.

———. "Evolution and Literary History: A Response to Franco Moretti." *New Left Review* 34 (July/August 2005).

———. *Paris and the Nineteenth Century.* Oxford: Blackwell, 1995.

———. "Representation or Embodiment? Walter Benjamin and the Politics of *Correspondances.*" In *The Triangle of Representation.* New York: Columbia University Press, 2000.

Rabaté, Jean-Michel. *1913: The Cradle of Modernism.* Oxford: Wiley-Blackwell, 2007.

Ramazani, Jahan. *Transnational Poetics.* Chicago: University of Chicago Press, 2009.

Ramsay, Stephen. *Reading Machines: Toward an Algorithmic Criticism.* Champaign: University of Illinois Press, 2011.

Rancière, Jacques. *Mallarmé: The Politics of the Siren.* Translated by Steven Corcoran. London: Continuum, 2011.

Rancière, Jacques, and Oliver Davis. "On *Aisthesis*—An Interview." In *Rancière Now,* edited by Oliver Davis. Cambridge: Polity, 2013.

Rapaport, Herman. *Theory Blog.* http://users.wfu.edu/rapapoh/TheoryBlog-2.html.

Ray, Nicholas. "Jean Laplanche, 1924–2012: Forming New Knots." *Radical Philosophy* 174 (July/August 2012).

Renshaw, Patrick. *The Wobblies: The Story of the IWW and Syndicalism in the United States.* Lanham, Md.: Ivan R. Dee, 1999.

Ricks, Christopher. "In Theory." *London Review of Books* 3.6 (April 16, 1981).

Ricoeur, Paul. *Freud and Philosophy: An Essay on Interpretation.* Translated by Denis Savage. New Haven, Conn.: Yale University Press, 1977.

Royle, Nicholas. *Veering: A Theory of Literature.* Edinburgh: Edinburgh University Press, 2011.

Rudy, Jason. *Electric Meters: Victorian Physiological Poetics.* Athens: Ohio University Press, 2009.

Samuels, Lisa, and Jerome McGann. "Deformance and Interpretation." *New Literary History* 30.1 (Winter 1999).

Schmitt, Cannon. "Tidal Conrad Literally." *Victorian Studies* 55.1 (Autumn 2012), 7–29.

Seymour, Richard. *Against Austerity*. London: Pluto, 2014.

Shklovsky, Viktor. *Theory of Prose*. Translated by Benjamin Sher. Normal, Ill.: Dalkey Archive, 1991.

Silliman, Ron. *ABC*. San Francisco: Tuumba, 1983.

———. "Albany." In *ABC*. San Francisco: Tuumba, 1983.

———. *The New Sentence*. New York: Roof Books, 1977.

Slaughter, Sheila, and Gary Rhoades. *Academic Capitalism and the New Economy: Markets, State, and Higher Education*. Baltimore: Johns Hopkins University Press, 2009.

Smith, David Nowell. *Sounding/Silence: Martin Heidegger at the Limits of Poetics*. New York: Fordham University Press, 2013.

Snediker, Michael. "Hart Crane's Smile." *Modernism/modernity* 12.4 (November 2005), 629–58.

———. *Queer Optimism: Lyric Personhood and Other Felicitous Persuasions*. Minneapolis: University of Minnesota Press, 2008.

Snow, C. P. *The Two Cultures and the Scientific Revolution*. Cambridge: Cambridge University Press, 1960.

Sokal, Alan. *Beyond the Hoax: Science, Philosophy and Culture*. New York: Oxford University Press, 2010.

Sollers, Philippe, and Francis Ponge. *Entretiens de Francis Ponge avec Philippe Sollers*. Paris: Éditions du Seuil, 1970.

Sprinker, Michael. *Imaginary Relations: Aesthetics and Ideology in the Theory of Historical Materialism*. London: Verso, 1987.

Stevens, Wallace. *The Collected Poems*. New York: Alfred A. Knopf, 1971.

———. *The Palm at the End of the Mind: Selected Poems and a Play*. Edited by Holly Stevens. 1971; reprint, New York: Vintage, 1990.

Sussman, Henry. "Prolegomena to Any Present and Future Language Poetry." In *The Task of the Critic: Poetics, Philosophy, Religion*. New York: Fordham University Press, 2005.

Tiffany, Daniel. "Cheap Signaling: Class Conflict and Diction in Avant-Garde Poetry." *Boston Review*, July 15, 2014, http://bostonreview.net/poetry/daniel-tiffany-cheap-signaling-class-conflict-and-diction-avant-garde-poetry.

Vickery, Anne. *Leaving Lines of Gender: A Feminist Genealogy of Language Writing*. Hanover, N.H.: Wesleyan University Press, 2000.

Warminski, Andre. "Introduction: Allegories of Reference." In P. de Man, *Aesthetic Ideology*, edited by A. Warminski. Minneapolis: University of Minnesota Press, 1996.

Wegner, Phillip E. *Periodizing Jameson: Dialectics, the University, and the Desire for Narrative*. Evanston, Ill.: Northwestern University Press, 2014.

Weninger, Robert. "Lost in Lit-Terra, or, What Is and to What End Do We Study World Literature?" *Comparative Literature* 62.4 (Fall 2010), 315–35.

White, Curtis. *The Science Delusion: Asking the Big Questions in a Culture of Easy Answers.* New York: Melville House, 2013.

White, Hayden. *Metahistory: The Historical Imagination in Nineteenth Century Europe.* Baltimore: Johns Hopkins University Press, 1975.

———. *The Practical Past.* Edited by Ed Dimendberg. Evanston, Ill.: Northwestern University Press, 2014.

Wiggershaus, Rolf. *The Frankfurt School: Its History, Theories, and Political Significance.* Translated by Michael Robertson. Cambridge, Mass.: MIT Press, 1995.

Williams, Raymond. *The Country and the City.* Oxford: Oxford University Press, 1973.

———. *The Politics of Modernism: Against the New Conformists.* New York: Verso, 2007.

Wilson, Edmund. *Axel's Castle: A Study in the Imaginative Literature of 1870–1930.* New York: Scribner, 1931.

Wiskus, Jessica. *The Rhythm of Thought: Art, Literature and Music after Merleau-Ponty.* Chicago: University of Chicago Press, 2013.

Wordsworth, William. *The Prelude 1799, 1805, 1850.* Edited by J. Wordsworth, M. H. Abrams, and S. Gill. New York: Norton, 1979.

Yeats, William Butler. *The Collected Poems of W. B. Yeats.* Edited by Richard J. Finneran. New York: Scribner, 1996.

Zeki, Semir. "Art and the Brain." *Daedalus* 127.2 (1998).

Zola, Emile. *The Belly of Paris.* Translated by Brian Nelson. Oxford: Oxford University Press, 2007.

Index